THE ROMANTICS

THE
ROMANTICS

AN ANTHOLOGY CHOSEN BY

GEOFFREY GRIGSON

To
JOHN PIPER
Bupton, Clevancy, Hafod,
Fawley & Snowhill

This edition first published in 2008
by Faber and Faber Ltd
3 Queen Square, London WC1N 3AU

Printed by Books on Demand GmbH, Norderstedt

All rights reserved
© The Estate of Geoffrey Grigson, 1942

The right of Geoffrey Grigson to be identified as author of this work has been asserted in accordance with Section 77 of the Copyright, Designs and Patents Act 1988

This book is sold subject to the condition that it shall not, by way of trade or otherwise, be lent, resold, hired out or otherwise circulated without the publisher's prior consent in any form of binding or cover other than that in which it is published and without a similar condition including this condition being imposed on the subsequent purchaser

A CIP record for this book is available from the British Library

ISBN 978–0–571–24285–6

PREFACE

Life is a most disorderly river, sometimes in flood, sometimes low; always threatening; the beginning, the end and the further bank out of view, like one of the big rivers so wide, that, when you stand and watch them, you think they ought to turn into a lake, keep still, and not flow with such a deep, pointless, muddy resolve. Gerard Hopkins tried to draw the exact swirl of broken and moving water. But you cannot draw exactly the Romantic swirl—or any other section of the river. You can draw two lines across the map of the river—the map of as much as can be seen. You can plot the turns, the banks, the pools, and so on. But the lines—well, the lines are chosen; only there because you put them there. They cannot distinguish a beginning or an end. So this book is not answering any exam question about Romantic poetry or painting. It is a blended drink—what I like by feeling, so much per cent, what I like by judgement, so much, and what I believe represents a few of the few miles of the great historical river of feeling. I cannot say that the blend is perfect, that the two likings coincide, that the charting is correct. But please remember ingredients one, two, and three of the blend, when you ask, why is this odd thing in the book? You must take your choice, each time, out of the trio.

The charting: it begins with Jakob Boehme. Boehme, more than anyone else, made the eighteenth century believe that the world was the image of Paradise; it was the type of the heavenly pomp. And man had a spark of the divine essence. Very well: things, therefore, were partly good; and were to be trusted. Angels were likened to children picking flowers in the May meadows. Men were told to present themselves each as a "naked spirit before God in simplicity and purity." Here was a world view; and the things made good were the things also which scientists, in the tradition of Bacon ("Those who determine not to conjecture and guess, but to find out and know; not to invent fables and romances of worlds, but to look into and dissect the nature of this real world, must consult only things themselves"), were anxious to investigate. To begin with, the philosopher or man of science, could also be the man of God. The Reverend William Stukeley, for instance, picked flowers in the angelic semblance with the Reverend Stephen Hales, one of the great experimenters of the time; and Stukeley observed eclipses for Halley, the astronomer, but he did so in view of Stonehenge, which he measured scientifically, and treated religiously as the temple of the Druids. Who were the Druids? Of course, men with religion in a primitive, but pure stage. But the link between innocent Boehme and the subtle Bacon begins to break after fifty years or so. The heart of Coleridge goes dry. The morning redness alters into a black evening of great storms. Beddoes, the next generation to Coleridge, finds the May meadow no longer innocent. Bees frequent flowers, earwigs, too, and the flowers may also be poisonous. The Fiends of Commerce show their teeth in a smile, "an age of economic revolution and anarchy" in which "the complications of industrial phenomena were such as to bewilder the strongest mind." The followers of Boehme and of Law, his interpreter—"The Son of flame; enthusiastic Law," Chatterton called him—dwindle into eccentrics; and a new era of compromise, individualism, and self-satisfaction, or else of madness, defeat, and the defiance of Father Mapple's sermon in Moby Dick, creeps in. Too simple a charting. But Coleridge, the friend of Sir Humphry Davy, the reader of all scientific transactions; the swallower of laughing gas, the intense searcher after the Why, can be quoted to show it has some truth. "The writings of these mystics (Fox, Boehme and Law) acted in no slight degree to prevent my mind from being imprisoned within the outline of any simple dogmatic system. They contributed to keep alive the heart in the head,"—but the heart withered and died —"gave me an indistinct, yet stirring and working presentiment, that all the products of the merely reflective faculty partook of death, and were as the rattling twigs and sprays in winter, into which a sap was yet to be propelled, from some root to which I had not penetrated, if they were to afford any sort of food or shelter. If they were too often a moving cloud of smoke to me by day, yet they were always a pillar of fire throughout the night, during my wanderings through the wilderness of doubt, and enabled me to skirt, without crossing, the sandy deserts of utter unbelief."

And what I like by feeling. The vigour and curiosity of the Englishmen of the eighteenth century. The glitter and sparkle, the fire and the vegetable gold. Blake. The sequaceous notes of the harp of Æolus playing the music of Heaven. The colours in a Reynolds or a Gainsborough dress. The flowers in a woman's hand in a picture by Stubbs whose own hand smelt of dissecting embryos, tygers, and hens, and horses). The gleaming ivy on the ruined arch of a Gothick Abbey. Then, underneath that arch, the entry of the snake, which Chatterton saw glittering in the jungles of an African eclogue or on the hills of Bristol. The Sarsar, or the icy wind of death. The devastated area of the Upas Tree; and the little, stoat-eyed, vigorous demon, or troll, from the Swiss mountains, Fuseli, sowing pride (how excellent) and death—Fuseli R. A. on a high rock in Pembrokeshire, over the Bay of Bristol, crying "Grand, grand, Jesu Christ, how grand," and Lawrence seeing him, and sketching him there as Milton's devil gazing into the abyss. The crash of the tower at Fonthill. Then Thomas Hood, stretching the neck of the Last Man, and stepping himself into the haunted house:

> Huge drops roll'd down the walls, as if they wept;
> And where the cricket used to chirp so shrilly,
> The toad was squatting and the lizard crept
> On that damp hearth and chilly.

In the May meadow of the garden the pink was now choked by the burdock, and the marigold grew among the nettles:

> If but a rat had linger'd in the house,
> To lure the thought into a social channel!

But the fire never does go out in a total compromise; and I like, with judgement, Clare among the lunatics, in his asylum window "snatching the sun's eternal ray" and keeping his spirit with the free; Hölderlin also proclaiming love in Germany; old Landor watching the Dirce flow under the pink and white oleanders; old Dorset Barnes still loving "the blue-hill 'd worold's flow' ry ground"; Dana watching the iceberg moving against the stars; Ruskin watching the light on the glaciers; Melville hearing the hollow despair under his boots across the Babylonian eating-house in London, and then crying "O Father!—chiefly known to me by Thy rod—mortal or immortal, here I die. I have striven to be Thine, more than to be this world's. Yet this is nothing; I leave eternity to Thee: for what is man that he should live out the lifetime of his God?"

You may call it a false charting—certainly it is incomplete—or a one-sided feeling. But neither would have been to human discredit. The Romantics are not to be sneered at; though I do not believe the absolute end, that "man must live, as he dreams, alone." The thing to do about the Romantics is to read them and look—if you can find them—at their pictures; not only that, but to forget some of the abstract theorizing of the school-books, and to follow them in their actuality. Precisely, in their images, their words and their paint and their buildings and their music. The May meadows, the harp of Æolus, the Anaconda, the Heliotrope, the glowworm in its own light, the flower in its own perfume ("every tiring you love is the centre of a paradise"), the moon in the blue sky, the glittering ice, the fire-screen, the lion, the tyger, the cry of the jackal under the ruins, the chemical discovery, Ozymandias, the after-image, the Glory, the Shining of Jupiter, the roots in the sunken road, the Wandering Jew, the vampyre, the worms in the mouth, the eyes where the nipples of life ought to protrude. And the thing I should like to do, bit by bit, is a vast following out of The Road To Xanadu, reading not only the poems, seeing not only the pictures, but going back over the Klondike of Milton, inch by inch, reading the philosophers, the mystics, the theologians, the travellers, the plant-physiologists, the chemists, the antiquaries, the anatomists, the speculators, the transactions of all the societies, looking at the buildings, the gardens, the curved mahogany doors and the ivory door plates; the auriculas and the pinks, the carved flowers on the pillar (as on the reredos of Christ Church, Bristol), the fabrics; listening to the harp of Æolus clamped into the window, the songs and the music; and piecing together the chryselephantine image of the Romantics, trying on a big scale to catch and Analyse the whole passage of the flooded intimidating river between my arbitrary lines.

I shall not, by the way, apologize for some things left out, or defend their omission;— the philosophers and the politicians, but *everything canndt be here, and I wanted the images; the natural philosophers or scientists and the theologians— bits are here, perhaps not enough; Scott ("not twenty lines of Scott's poetry will ever reach posterity, it has relation to nothing"), Hazlitt, Carlyle; and much more. Also there is good reason not to reset all the crown jewels of Romanticism,* Kubla Khan, *Keats's* Nightingale, *Wordsworth's* Intimations, *and so on— even though my setting would not, here, have been absolutely the usual one.*

CONTENTS

	PAGE
PART ONE. THE MORNING REDNESS: Nos. 1-147	1
PART TWO. THE PEAK: Nos. 148-246	119
PART THREE. THE SENSUAL VALLEY: Nos. 247-297	201
PART FOUR. THE FINISH: Nos. 298-387	245
NOTES	333
LIST OF AUTHORS	355

Where only part of a poem has been used, this is always made clear by dots at the beginning, or at the end, or in the body of the extract. Dots are also used to mark something left out in prose extracts.

PART I: THE MORNING REDNESS

View this world diligently and consider what manner of fruit, sprouts, and branches grow out of the Salitter *of the earth, from trees, plants, herbs, roots, flowers, oil, wine, corn, and whatever else there is that thy heart can find out; all is a type of the heavenly pomp.*

Jakob Boehme.

1. HOPE

My banks they are furnish'd with bees,
    Whose murmur invites one to sleep;
My grottos are shaded with trees,
    And my hills are white-over with sheep.
I seldom have met with a loss,
    Such health do my fountains bestow;
My fountains all border'd with moss,
    Where the harebells and violets grow.

Not a pine in my grove is there seen,
    But with tendrils of woodbine is bound:
Not a beech's more beautiful green,
    But a sweet-briar entwines it around.
Not my fields in the prime of the year,
    More charms, than my cattle unfold:
Not a brook that is limpid and clear,
    But it glitters with fishes of gold.

One would think she might like to retire
    To the bow'r I have labour'd to rear;
Not a shrub that I heard her admire,
    But I hasted and planted it there.
Oh how sudden the jessamine strove
    With the lilac to render it gay!
Already it calls for my love,
    To prune the wild branches away.

From the plains, from the woodlands and groves,
    What strains of wild melody flow?
How the nightingales warble their loves
    From thickets of roses that blow!
And when her bright form shall appear,
    Each bird shall harmoniously join
In a concert so soft and so clear,
    As—she may not be fond to resign.

I have found out a gift for my fair;
   I have found where the wood-pigeons breed:
But let me that plunder forbear,
   She will say' twas a barbarous deed.
For he ne'er could be true, she aver'd,
   Who could rob a poor bird of its young:
And I lov'd her the more, when I heard
   Such tenderness fall from her tongue.

I have heard her with sweetness unfold
   How that pity was due to a dove:
That it ever attended the bold,
   And she call'd it the sister of love.
But her words such a pleasure convey,
   So much I her accents adore,
Let her speak, and whatever she say,
   Methinks I should love her the more.

Can a bosom so gentle remain
   Unmov'd, when her Corydon sighs!
Will a nymph that is fond of the plain,
   These plains and this valley despise?
Dear regions of silence and shade!
   Soft scenes of contentment and ease!
Where I could have pleasingly stray'd,
   If aught, in her absence, could please.

But where does my Phyllida stray!
   And where are her grots and her bow'rs?
Are the groves and the valleys as gay,
   And the shepherds as gentle as ours?
The groves may perhaps be as fair,
   And the face of the valleys as fine;
The swains may in manners compare,
   But their love is not equal to mine.

William Shenstone.

2. THE COUNTRY LIFE

Now whilst you are canvassing matters of politique, and disposing of Empires, and the like, if any care of your old friend remains I will let you know what I am about. I am fallen into a very pretty mixture of business and amusement, wherein happiness of life consists. Last summer I spent in fitting up part of my house, and levelling my ground for gardening, in which I am at this time very intent. I am planting greens, flowers, alcoves, herbs, fruit trees, and what not? I am laying out the stations of dyals, urns, and statues, inoculating mistletoe, and trying vegetable experiments. Within doors I am fitting up my study, which has a most charming prospect over my garden and adjacent valley, pretty much like that at Amesbury, and just within hearing of a great cascade of the river, which is very noble and solemn; that by day raises the mind to a pitch fit for study, by night lulls one asleep with a most grateful noise. . . .

I have worked so hard in my garden as to sweat out all the London fog, am become vastly athletic, and can eat almost a whole fillet of veal without orange. . . . My ancient country complexion is returned to my cheeks, the blood flows brisk through every anastomosis, my lips recover their pristin red, and my own locks, moderately curled, resemble the Egyptian picture of Orus Apollo, or the emblem of rejuveniscence. It would ravish you to think with what pleasure I take a book in my hand and walk about my garden, my own territorys, mea regna, as Virgil calls it, surrounded with the whole complication of natures charms. *William Stukeley.*

3. FLOWERS TO GOD

SURELY nature is a book, and every page rich with sacred hints. To an attentive mind the garden turns preacher, and its blooming tenants are so many lively sermons. What an engaging pattern, and what an excellent lesson, have we here! —So, let the redeemed of the Lord look unto JESUS, and be conformed to their beloved. Let us all be heliotropes (if I may use the expression) to the Sun of Righteousness.

James Hervey.

4. CELINDA AND THE HARP OF ÆOLUS

SOME years ago, a twelve-stringed instrument was contrived by a very ingenious musician, by whom it was aptly called the harp of Æolus, because, being properly applied to a stream of air, it produces a wild irregular variety of harmonious sounds, that seem to be the effect of enchantment, and wonderfully dispose the mind for the most romantic situations. Fathom, who was really a virtuoso in music, had brought one of those new-fashioned guitars into the country, and as the effect of it was still unknown in the family, he that night converted it to the purposes of his amour, by fixing it in the casement of a window belonging to the gallery, exposed to the west wind, which then blew in a gentle breeze. The strings no sooner felt the impression of the balmy zephyr, than they began to pour forth a stream of melody more ravishingly delightful than the song of Philomel, the warbling brook, and all the concert of the wood. The soft and tender notes of peace and love were swelled up, with the most delicate and insensible transition, into a loud hymn of triumph and exultation, joined by the deep-toned organ, and a full choir of voices which gradually decayed upon the air, until it died away in distant sound, as if a flight of angels had raised the song in their ascent to heaven. Yet the chords hardly ceased to vibrate after the expiration of this overture, which ushered in a composition in the same pathetic style; and this again was succeeded by a third, almost without pause or intermission, as if the artist's hand had become indefatigable, and the theme never to be exhausted.

His heart must be quite callous, and his ear lost to all distinction, who could hear such a harmony without emotion; how deeply then must it have affected the delicate Celinda . . . [whom Ferdinand Fathom thereupon seduced].

Tobias Smollett.

5. THE TEMPLE OF AVEBURY

i

WHEN we contemplate the elegance of this country of *Wiltshire*, and the great works of antiquity therein, we may be persuaded that the two atlantic islands, and the islands of the blessed, which *Plato* plato and other anciebt wirters mention were those in reality of *Britain* and *Ireland*. They who first took possession of this country, thought it worthy of their care, and built those noble works therein, which have been the admiration of all ages. *Stonehenge* we have endeavoured to describe; and we are not more surpris'd at the extraordinary magnitude of the work of *Abury*, than that it should have escap'd the observation of the curious: a place in the direct *Bath*-road from *London*. Passing from *Marlborough* hither, 'tis the common topic of amusement for travellers to observe the grey weathers on *Marlborough* downs, which are the same kind of stones as this of our antiquity, lying dispers'd on the surface of the ground, as nature originally laid them. When we come to this village we see the largest of those stones in great numbers, set upright in the earth, in circles, in parallel lines, and other regular figures, and a great part inclos'd in a vast circular ditch, of above 1000 foot diameter. And what will further excite one's curiosity, the *vallum* or earth, which is of solid chalk, dug out of that ditch, thrown on the outside; quite contrary to the nature of castles and fortifications. The ditch alone, which is wide and deep, is a very great labour, and the rampart very high, and makes the appearance of a huge amphitheatre, for an innumerable company of spectators; but cannot possibly be design'd for offence or defence. This is twice passed by all the travellers: and its oddness will arrest one's attention, if the stones escap'd it. The mighty carcase of *Stonehenge* draws great numbers of people out of their way every day, as to see a sight: and it has exercised the pens of the learned to account for it. But *Abury*, a much greater work and more extensive design, by I know not what unkind fate, was altogether overlooked, and in the utmost danger of perishing. . . .

Just before I visited the place to endeavour at preserving the memory of it, the inhabitants were fallen into the custom of demolishing the stones, chiefly out of covetousness of the little area of ground each stood on. First they dug great pits in the earth and buried them. The expence of digging the grave was more than 30 years purchase of the spot they possess'd when standing. After this they found the knack of burning them; which has made most miserable havock of this famous temple. One *Tom Robinson*, the *Herostratus* of *Abury*, is particularly eminent for this kind of execution, and he very much glories in it. The method is to dig a pit by the side of the stone, till it falls down, then to burn many loads of straw under it. They draw lines of water along it when heated, and then with smart strokes of a great sledge hammer, its prodigious bulk is divided into many lesser parts. But this *Atto de Se* commonly costs thirty shillings in fire and labour, sometimes twice as much. . . .

They have sometimes used of these stones for building houses; but say, they may have them cheaper, in more manageable places, from the grey weathers. One of these stones will build an ordinary house; yet the stone being a kind of marble, or rather granite, is always moist and dewy in winter, which proves damp and unwholesome, and rots the furniture. The custom of thus destroying them is so late, that I could easily trace the *obit* of every stone; who did it, for what purpose, and when, and by what method, what house or wall was built out of it, and the like. Every year that I frequented this country I found several of them wanting; but the places very apparent whence they were taken. So that I was well able, as then, to make a perfect ground plot of the whole, and all its parts. This is now twenty years ago. 'Tis to be fear'd, that had it been deferr'd till this time, it would have been impossible. And this stupendous fabric, which for some thousands of years had braved the continual assaults of weather, and by the nature of it, when left to itself, like the pyramids of *Egypt*, would have lasted as long as the globe, must have fallen a sacrifice to the wretched ignorance and avarice of a little village unluckily placed within it; and the curiosity of the thing would have been irretrievable.

ii

As you are a Druid and fellow labourer at Abury, I shall open to you part of the secrett of it, desiring you not to communicate it to any but Druids. The form of that stupendous work is the picture of the Deity, more particularly of the Trinity, but most particularly what they called the Father and the Word, who created all things; this figure you find on the tops of all the obelisks, etc., being equivalent to the Hebrew Tetragrammaton. A snake proceeding from a circle is the eternal procession of the Son, from the first cause. The Ægyptians frequently added wings to it, then it was the Trinity properly, but our ancestors judged, I suppose, that they could not well represent the wings in stone-work, so omitted them. The Ægyptians call this figure Hemptha; the Greeks, in abbrevated writing, used it for Daimon, or the good genius; the Brachmans, in the East Indias, use it; the Chinese; the ancient Persians, with whom it still remains at Persepolis; the Americans; our Britons. This shows it was extremely ancient. But of all nations our ancestors have had the greatest veneration for it, that have expanded it in so laborious a picture, above 3 miles long. Now the ancients did not onely intend by it to picture out the infinite power, wisdom, the inexhaustible fund of ideas, and the like, in the Divine mind; but they actually meant by it the three essences or existences of the Supreme, which we call the Trinity: 3 personalitys, two derivative from the first, and self-originated, but all eternal, infinite, etc., consequently God. . . . My main motive in pursuing this subject is to combat the deists from an unexpected quarter, and to preserve so noble a monument of our ancestors' piety, I may add, orthodoxy. *William Stukeley.*

6. THE RAPE OF HELEN

> . . . Dispel, my fair, with smiles, the tim'rous cloud
> That hangs on thy clear brow. So Helen look'd,
> So her white neck reclin'd, so was she borne
> By the young Trojan to his gilded bark
> With fond reluctance, yielding modesty,
> And oft reverted eye, as if she knew not
> Whether she fear'd, or wish'd to be pursued.
> *Thomas Gray.*

7. MISTLETOE, FOXGLOVES, AND DRUIDS

THERE are many reasons why the Druids were so fond of mistletoe. One was that it was a most beautiful plant, flourishing in winter time. 2, that it was produc'd in an uncommon manner: not by the ordinary proceedure of nature, and indeed by a secret and unknown manner. 3, that it came to its high maturity at mid winter when all nature lyes dormant. 4, that it was upon many of these accounts a type of the expected Messiah.

3 reasons why the Druids were fond of foxgloves. 1, the purple flower is in color and shape like the patriarchal priestly miter. 2, the plant flowers at the time of midsummer sacrifice. 3, for its great medicinal virtues. *William Stukeley.*

8. THE GLACIERS OF CHAMONIX: ENGLISHMEN DISCOVER THE ALPS

WE set out about noon, the 22nd of June, and crossed the Arve over a wooden bridge. Most maps place the *glacieres* on the same side with Chamoigny, but this is a mistake. We were quickly at the foot of the mountain, and began to ascend by a very steep path through a wood of fir and larche trees. We made many halts to refresh ourselves, and take breath, but we kept on at a good rate. After we had passed the wood, we came to a kind of meadow, full of large stones, and pieces of rock, that were broke off, and fallen down from the mountain; the ascent was so steep that we were obliged sometimes to cling to them with our hands, and make use of sticks, with sharp irons at the end, to support ourselves. Our road lay slant ways, and we had several places to cross where the *avalanches* of snow were fallen, and had made terrible havock; there was nothing to be seen but trees torn up by the roots, and large stones, which seemed to lie without any support; every step we set, the ground gave way, and had it not been for our staffs and our hands, we must many times have gone down the precipice. We had an uninterrupted view quite to the bottom of the mountain, and the steepness of the descent, join'd to the height where we were, made a view terrible enough to make most people's heads turn. In short, after climbing with great labour for four hours and three quarters, we got to the top of the mountain; from whence we had the pleasure of beholding objects of an extraordinary nature. We were on the top of a mountain, which, as well as we could judge, was least twice as high as Mount Saleve, from thence we had a full view of the *glacieres*. I own to you that I am extremely at a loss how to give a right idea of it; as I know no one thing which I have ever seen that has the least resemblance to it.

The description which travellers give of the seas of Greenland seems to come the nearest to it. You must imagine your lake put in agitation by a strong wind, and frozen all at once, perhaps even that would not produce the same appearance.

The *gladeres* consist of three large valleys, that form a kind of Y, the tail reaches into the Val d'Aoste, and the two horns into the valley of Chamoigny, the place where we ascended was between them, from whence we plainly saw the valley, which forms one of these horns. . . .

These valleys, although at the top of a high mountain, are surrounded by other mountains; the tops of which being naked and craggy rocks, shoot up immensely high; something resembling old *Gothic* buildings or mines, nothing grows upon them, they are all the year round covered with snow; and our guides assured us, that neither the *chamois*, nor any birds, ever went so high as the top of them.

Those who search after crystal, go in the month of August to the foot of these rocks, and strike against them with pickaxes; if they hear them resound as if they were hollow, they work there, and opening the rock, they find caverns full of crystalizations. . . . Our curiosity did not stop there, we were resolved to go down upon the ice; we had about four hundred yards to go down, the descent was excessively steep, and all of a dry crumbling earth, mixt with gravel, and little loose stones, which afforded us no firm footing, so that we went down partly falling, and partly sliding on our hands and knees. At length we got upon the ice, where our difficulty ceased, for that was extremely rough and afforded us good footing; we found in it an infinite number of cracks, some we could step over, others were several feet wide. These cracks were so deep, that we could not even see to the bottom; those who go in search of crystal are often lost in them, but their bodies are generally found again after some days, perfectly well preserved. Our guides assured us, that these cracks change continually, and that the whole *glaciere* has a kind of motion. In going up the mountain we often heard something like a clap of thunder, which, as we were informed by our guides, was caused by fresh cracks then making; but as there were none made while we were upon the ice, we could not determine whether it was that, or *avalanches* of snow, or perhaps rocks falling; though since travellers observe, that in Greenland the ice cracks with a noise resembling thunder, it might very well be what our guides told us. As in all countries of ignorance people are extremely superstitious, they told us many strange stories of witches, etc., who come to play their pranks upon the *glacieres*, and dance to the sound of instruments. *William Windham.*

9. THE KITCHEN GARDEN

WHAT a fund of choice accommodations is here! what a source of wholesome dainties! and all for the enjoyment of man. Why does the parsley, with her frizzled locks, shag the border; or why the celery, with her whitening arms, perforate the mould; but to render his soups savoury? The asparagus shoots its tapering stems, to offer him the first fruits of the season; and the artichoke spreads its turgid top, to give him a treat of vegetable marrow. The tendrils of the cucumber creep into the sun; and, though basking in its hottest rays, they secrete for their master, and barrel up for his use, the most cooling juices of the soil. The beans stand firm like files of embattled troops; the pease rest upon their props, like so many companies of invalids; while both replenish their pods with the fatness of the earth, on purpose to pour it on their owner's table. *James Hervey.*

10. A PRIVATE STONEHENGE

I SPENT Saturday morning last with Ivo Talbois, King of the Girvii. His garden is very curious and entertaining. The greens are exceeding fine and stately, and his collection, and exotic plants, flowers, shrubs, etc., is highly delightful. He loaded me home with roots and seeds of pomegranat, balm of gilead, etc., for my garden. He has a nice closet of pictures; his library, medals, and the like, I need not tell you are very valuable. I had like to have forgot his collection of children, being No. X boys and girls, aequâ proportione. My wife miscarried 3 days after your letter to me, the second time. The embrio, about as big as a filberd, I buryd under the high altar in the chappel of my hermitage vineyard; for there I built a niche in a ragged wall oregrown with ivy, in which I placed my roman altar, a brick from Verulam, and a waterpipe lately sent me by my Lord Colrain from Marshland. Underneath is a camomile bed for greater ease of the bended knee, and there we enterred it, present my wives mother, and aunt, with ceremonys proper to the occasion. If you enquire what I am about: I am making a temple of the druids, as I call it, 'tis thus; there is a circle of tall filberd trees in the nature of a hedg, which is 70 foot diameter, round it is a walk 15 foot broad, circular too, so that the whole is 100 foot diameter. This walk from one high point slopes each way so gradually, till you come to the lowest which is the opposite point, and there is the entrance to the temple, to which the walk may be esteemed as the portico. When you enter the innermost circle or temple, you see in the center an antient appletree oregrown with sacred mistletoe; round it is another concentric circle of 50 foot diameter made of pyramidal greens, at equal intervals, that may appear verdant, when the fruit trees have dropt their leaves. These pyramidals are in imitation of the inner circles at Stonehenge. The whole is included within a square wall on all sides, except that where is the grand avenue to the porticoe, which is a broad walk of old apple trees. The angles are filled up with fruit trees, plumbs, pears, walnuts, apple trees, and such are likewise interspersed in the filberd hedg and borders, with some sort of irregularity to prevent a stiffness in the appearance, and make it look more easy and natural. But in that point where is the entrance from the portico into the temple is a tumulus, which was denominated snowdrop hill, being in Christmas time covered ore with that pretty, and early, flower, but I must take it for a cairn or Celtic barrow. I have sketched you out the whole thing on the other page; it was formed out of an old ortchard.

These are some of the amusements of us country folk. Insted of the pleasures of London conversation, we are content with natures converse, where we meet with no envy, slander, or uneasyness, whatever. If yours be more poignant, ours are more serene, more certain, more lasting; but I need not preach up rural delights to you. *William Stukdey.*

11. MOISTURE OF THE EARTH AND AIR

THE moisture of the earth, and of the circumambient air, passed through proper strainers, and disposed in a range of pellucid tubes; this performs all the wonders and produces all the beauties of vegetation. This creeps along the fibres of the low spreading moss, and climbs to the very tops of the lofty waving cedars. This attracted by the root, and circulating through invisible canals, this bursts into gems, expands itself into leaves, and clothes the forest with all its verdant honours.— This one, plain and simple cause gives birth to all the charms which deck the youth and maturity of the year. This blushes in the early hepatica, and flames in the late advancing poppy. This reddens into blood in the veins of the mulberry; and attenuates itself into leafen gold, to create a covering for the quince. This breathes in all the fragrant gales of our garden, and weeps odorous gums in the groves of Arabia.—So wonderful is our Creator in counsel, and so excellent in working!
James Hervey.

12. HE COMPLAINS HOW SOON THE PLEASING NOVELTY OF LIFE IS OVER

AH me, my friend! it will not, will not last!
   This fairy-scene, that cheats our youthful eyes!
The charm dissolves; th' aerial music's past;
   The banquet ceases, and the vision flies.

Where are the splendid forms, the rich perfumes,
    Where the gay tapers, where the spacious dome?
Vanish'd the costly pearls, the crimson plumes,
    And we delightless, left to wander home!

Vain now are books, the sage's wisdom vain!
    What has the world to bribe our steps astray?
Ere reason learns by study'd laws to reign,
    The weaken'd passions, self-subdued, obey.

Scarce has the sun sev'n annual courses roll'd,
    Scarce shewn the whole that fortune can supply;
Since, not the miser so caress'd his gold,
    As I, for what it gave, was heard to sigh.

On the world's stage I waiv'd some sprightly part;
    To deck my native fleece with tawdry lace;
'Twas life,' 'twas taste, and—oh my foolish heart!
    Substantial joy was fix'd in pow'r and place.

And you, ye works of art! allur'd mine eye,
    The breathing picture, and the living stone:
"Tho' gold, tho' splendour, heav'n and fate deny,
    Yet might I call one Titian stroke my own!"

Smit with the charms of fame, whose lovely spoil,
    The wreathe, the garland, fire the poet's pride,
I trim'd my lamp, consum'd the midnight oil—
    But soon the paths of health and fame divide!

Oft too I pray'd, 'twas nature, form'd the pray'r,
    To grace my native scenes, my rural home;
To see my trees express their planter's care,
    And gay, on Attic models, raise my dome.

But now 'tis o'er, the dear delusion's o'er!
    A stagnant breezeless air becalms my soul:
A fond aspiring candidate no more,
    I scorn the palm before I reach the goal.

O youth! enchanting stage, profusely blest!
  Bliss ev'n obtrusive courts the frolic mind;
Of health neglectful, yet by health carest;
  Careless of favour, yet secure to find.

Then glows the breast, as op'ning roses fair;
  More free, more vivid than the linnet's wing;
Honest as light, transparent ev'n as air,
  Tender as buds, and lavish as the spring.

Not all the force of manhood's active might,
  Not all the craft to subtle age assign'd,
Not science shall extort that dear delight,
  Which gay delusion gave the tender mind.

Adieu soft raptures! transports void of care!
  Parent of raptures, dear deceit, adieu!
And you, her daughters, pining with despair,
  Why, why, so soon her fleeting steps pursue!

Tedious again to curse the drizzling day!
  Again to trace the wintry tracts of snow!
Or, sooth'd by vernal airs, again survey
  The self-same hawthorns bud, and cowslips blow!

O life! how soon of ev'ry bliss forlorn!
  We start false joys, and urge the devious race:
A tender prey; that cheats our youthful morn,
  Then sinks untimely, and defrauds the chace.
                                        William Shenstone.

13. SWEET THINGS OF NATURE

I SPEND at present, or rather live twice over, a good deal of time in my garden. You can't but imagine that traversing a little spot of one's own is vastly more delightful than even the mall, or the heath of Hampstead, or the ring, and the like, where we have nothing proper but the common air, and scarcely that without the sophistication, and corruption, necessary to the neighbourhood of you Capnopolitans. This morning I set with my own hands two or three yards of ocymum, majorana, melissa, and some more herbs of that sort, sweeter than the names themselves, under the windows of my dining room parlor, over which is my bedchamber and study. These have a south-east aspect, and with the rising beams of the sun exhale their odiferous steams with great profusion. My whole garden near the house is planted with all the sweet things of nature. At this time my circus, or amphitheatre of 100 foot diameter, full of fruit trees, is as white as a sheet with flowers and that color lying as it were upon the deep green of the opposite declivity beyond the river, makes an appearance to me, in my hall, surprizingly beautiful, especially toward morning or evening, when the sun shines aslaunt the hill sides, and *shadowy sets off the face of things* as Milton expresseś it.

William Stukeley.

14. THE NIGHTINGALE

... But hark; I hear her liquid tone.
    Now, Hesper, guide my feet
Down the red marle with moss o'ergrown,
Through yon wild thicket next the plain,
Whose hawthorns choke the winding lane
    Which leads to her retreat.

See the green space: on either hand
    Inlarg'd it spreads around:
See, in the midst she takes her stand,
Where one old oak his awful shade
Extends o'er half the level mead
    Inclos'd in woods profound.

Hark, how through many a melting note
    She now prolongs her lays:
How sweetly down the void they float!
The breeze their magic path attends:
The stars shine out: the forest bends:
    The wakeful heifers gaze. . . .

Mark Akenside

15. THE GOD OF LOVE

NEVER think of God but as an infinity of overflowing love, who wills nothing by the creation, but to be the comfort, the blessing, and joy of every life according to its capacity. And let this idea, which is the truth of truths, animate and govern all that you think, or say, or do, either towards God, or man.

William Law.

16. THE KRAKEN, KRAXEN, OR KRABBEN

I AM now come to the third and incontestibly the largest Sea-monster in the world; it is called Kraken, Kraxen, or as some name it, Krabben, that word being applied by way of eminence to this creature. This last name seems indeed best to agree with the description of this creature, which is round, flat, and full of arms, or branches. Others call it also Horven, or Soe-Horven, and some Anker-trold . . . Our fishermen unanimously affirm, and without the least variation in their accounts, that when they row out several miles to sea, particularly in the hot Summer days, and by their situation (which they know by taking a view of certain points of land) expect to find 80 or 100 fathoms of water, it often happens that they do not find above 20 or 30, and sometimes less. At these places they generally find the greatest plenty of Fish, especially Cod and Ling. Their lines, they say, are no sooner out than they may draw them up with the hooks all full of Fish; by this they judge that the Kraken is at the bottom. They say this creature causes those unnatural shallows mentioned above, and prevents their sounding. These the fishermen are always glad to find, looking upon them as a means of their taking an abundance of Fish. There are sometimes twenty boats or more got together, and throwing out their lines at a moderate distance from each other; and the only thing they have to observe is, whether the depth continues the same, which they know by their lines, or whether it grows shallower by their seeming to have less water. If this last be the case, they find that the Kraken is raising himself nearer the surface, and then it is not time for them to stay any longer; they immediately leave off fishing, take to their oars, and in a few minutes after they see this enormous monster come up to the surface of the water; he there shows himself sufficiently, though his whole body does not appear, which in all likelihood no human eye ever beheld . . . its back or upper part, which seems to be in appearance about an English mile in circumference, (some say more, but I chuse the least for greater certainty) looks at first like a number of small islands, surrounded with something that floats and fluctuates like sea-weeds. Here and there a large rising is observed like sandbanks, on which various kinds of small Fishes are seen continually leaping about till they roll off into the water from the sides of it; at last several bright points or horns appear, which grow thicker and thicker the higher they rise above the surface of the water, and sometimes they stand up as high and as large as the masts of middle-siz'd vessels. It seems that these are the creature's arms, and, it is said, if they were to lay hold of the largest man of war, they would pull it down to the bottom. After this monster has been on the surface of the water a short time, it begins slowly to sink again, and then the danger is as great as before; because the motion of his sinking causes such a swell in the sea, and such an eddy or whirlpool, that it draws everything down with it, like the current of the river Male. . . . As this enormous Sea-animal in all probability may be reckon'd of the Polype, or of the Star-fish kind, as shall hereafter be more fully proved, it seems that the parts which are seen rising at its pleasure, and are called arms, are properly the tentacula, or feeling instruments, called horns as well as arms. With these they move themselves, and likewise gather in their food.

   Besides these, for this last purpose the great Creator has also given this creature a strong and peculiar scent, which it can emit at certain times, and by means of which it beguiles and draws other Fish to come in heaps about it. This animal has another strange property, known by the experience of a great many old fishermen. They observe that for some months the Kraken or the Krabben is continually eating, and in other months he always voids his excrements. During this evacuation the surface of the water is coloured with the excrement, and appears quite thick and turbid. This muddiness is said to be so very agreeable to the smell or taste of other Fishes, or to both, that they gather together from all parts to it, and keep for that purpose directly over the Kraken: he then opens his arms or horns, seizes or swallows his welcome guests, and converts them, after the due time, by digestion, into a bait for other Fish of the same kind. I relate what is affirmed by many; but I cannot give so certain assurances of this particular, as I can of the existence of this surprizing creature; though I do not find anything in it absolutely contrary to nature. *Rev. Erich Pontoppidan.*

17. THE OUTBIRTH OF ETERNITY

TEMPORAL nature, opened to us by the Spirit of God, becomes a *volume* of holy instruction to us, and leads us into all the mysteries and secrets of eternity. For as everything in temporal nature is *descended* out of that which is eternal, and stands as a *palpable visible outbirth* of it, so when we know how to separate the *grossness, death, and darkness* of time from it, we find what it is in its eternal state. Fire, and light, and air in this world are not only a true resemblance of the Holy Trinity in Unity, but are the Trinity itself in its most *outward lowest* kind of existence or manifestation; for there could be no fire, fire could not *generate* light, air could not proceed from both, these three could not thus be united, and thus divided, but because they have their *root* and *original* in the tri-unity of the Deity. *william Law.*

18. INSCRIPTION FOR A GROTTO

> To me, whom in their lays the shepherds call
> Actaea, daughter of the neighbouring stream,
> This cave belongs. The fig tree and the vine,
> Which o'er the rocky entrance downward shoot,
> Were plac'd by Glycon. He with cowslips pale,
> Primrose, and purple lychnis, deck'd the green
> Before my threshold, and my shelving walls
> With honeysuckle cover'd. Here at noon,
> Lull'd by the murmur of my rising fount,

I slumber: here my clustering fruits I tend;
Or from the humid flowers, at break of day,
Fresh garlands weave, and chace from all my bounds
Each thing, impure or noxious. Enter-in,
O stranger, undismay'd. Nor bat, nor toad
Here lurks: and if thy breast of blameless thoughts
Approve thee, not unwelcome shalt thou tread
My quiet mansion: chiefly, if thy name
Wise Pallas and the immortal muses own.
                                        Mark Akenside.

19. ORIGINALS

An *Original* may be said to be of a *vegetable* nature; it rises spontaneously from the vital root of genius; it *grows*, it is not made: *Imitations* are often a sort of *manufacture* wrought up by those *mechanics, art,* and *labour,* out of pre-existent materials not their own.

Again: We read *Imitation* with somewhat of his languor, who listens to a twice-told tale: Our spirits rouze at an *Original*; that is a perfect stranger, and all throng to learn news from a foreign land: and tho' it comes, like an *Indian* prince, adorned with feathers only, having little of weight; yet of our attention it will rob the more solid, if not equally new. Thus every telescope is lifted at a new-discovered star; it makes a hundred astronomers in a moment, and denies equal notice to the sun.
                                        Edward Young.

20. GLASS-CASE No. VI

1. The bohea tree.
2. The Bible in shorthand.
3. A book wrote in the Malabar Language on the leaves of the plant papyrus, or paper weed, and which first gave the name to the paper now wrote on.
4. Priapus, the god of gardens, formerly worshipped by the Egyptians.
5. A snakes egg,
6. A piece of nun's skin.
7. A set of beads made of the bones of St. Anthony of Padua, and consecrated by Pope Clement.

8. A butterfly from Portmahon.
9. A curious horse shoe fish.
10. A necklace made of Job's egg tears.
11. The reverse of the broad seal of the commonwealth of England, 1651.
12. The owl moth.
13. Pads of Tamarinds.
14. An alligator's egg.

Exhibit in Don Saltero's Coffee-house of Rarities.

21. HIS BEDCHAMBER

WHERE the Red Lion, flaring o'er the way,
Invites each passing stranger that can pay;
Where Calvert's butt, and Parson's black champagne,
Regale the drabs and bloods of Drury-lane;
There in a lonely room, from bailiffs snug,
The Muse found Scroggen stretch'd beneath a rug;
A window, patch'd with paper, lent a ray,
That dimly show'd the state in which he lay;
The sanded floor that grits beneath the tread;
The humid wall with paltry pictures spread:
The royal game of goose was there in view,
And the twelve rules the royal martyr drew;
The seasons, fram'd with listing, found a place,
And brave prince William show'd his lamp-black face:
The morn was cold, he views with keen desire
The rusty grate unconscious of a fire;
With beer and milk arrears the frieze was scor'd,
And five crack'd teacups dress'd the chimney board;
A nightcap deck'd his brows instead of bay,
A cap by night—a stocking all the day!

Oliver Goldsmith.

22. THE FATAL SISTERS: AN ODE

In the eleventh century Sigurd, Earl of the Orkney-Islands, went with a fleet of ships and a considerable body of troops into Ireland, to the assistance of *Sictryg with the silken beard*, who was then making war on his father-in-law *Brian*, King of Dublin: the Earl and all his forces were cut to pieces, and *Sictryg* was in danger of a total defeat; but the enemy had a greater loss by the death of *Brian*, their King, who fell in the action. On Christmas-day, (the day of the battle) a Native of *Caithness* in Scotland saw at a distance a number of persons on horseback riding at full speed towards a hill, and seeming to enter into it. Curiosity led him to follow them, till looking through an opening in the rocks he saw twelve gigantic figures resembling women: they were all employed about a loom; and as they wove they sung the following dreadful song; which when they had finished, they tore the web into twelve pieces, and (each taking her portion) galloped Six to the North and as many to the South.

> Now the storm begins to lower,
> (Haste, the loom of Hell prepare,)
> Iron-sleet of arrowy shower
> Hurtles in the darken'd air.
>
> Glitt'ring lances are the loom,
> Where the dusky harp we strain,
> Weaving many a Soldier's doom,
> *Orkney's* woe, and *Randver's* bane.
>
> See the griesly texture grow,
> ('Tis of human entrails made,)
> And the weights, that play below,
> Each a gasping Warrior's head.
>
> Shafts for shuttles, dipt in gore,
> Shoot the trembling cords along.
> Sword, that once a Monarch bore,
> Keep the tissue close and strong.
>
> *Mista* black, terrific Maid,
> *Sangrida*, and *Hilda* see,
> Join the wayward work to aid:
> 'Tis the woof of victory.
>
> Ere the ruddy sun be set,
> Pikes must shiver, javelins sing,
> Blade with clattering buckler meet,
> Hauberk crash, and helmet ring.
>
> (Weave the crimson web of war)
> Let us go, and let us fly,
> Where our Friends the conflict share,
> Where they triumph, where they die.

As the paths of fate we tread,
Wading thro' th' ensanguin'd field:
Gonduta, and *Geira*, spread
O'er the youthful King your shield.

We the reins to slaughter give,
Ours to kill, and ours to spare:
Spite of danger he shall live.
(Weave the crimson web of war)

They, whom once the desart-beach
Pent within its bleak domain,
Soon their ample sway shall stretch
O'er the plenty of the plain.

Low the dauntless Earl is laid,
Gor'd with many a gaping wound:
Fate demands a nobler head;
Soon a King shall bite the ground.

Long his loss shall Eirin weep,
Ne'er again his likeness see;
Long her strains in sorrow steep,
Strains of Immortality!

Horror cover all the heath,
Clouds of carnage blot the sun.
Sisters, weave the web of death;
Sisters, cease, the work is done.

Hail the task, and hail the hands!
Songs of joy and triumph sing!
Joy to the victorious bands;
Triumph to the younger King.

Mortal, thou that hear'st the tale.
Learn the tenour of our song.
Scotland, thro' each winding vale
Far and wide the notes prolong.

Sisters, hence with spurs of speed:
Each her thundering faulchion wield;
Each bestride her sable steed.
Hurry, hurry to the field.

Thomas Gray.

23. ADAM AND EVE EXPELLED

I NOW began to construct our habitation under the shade of the spreading cedar. I fix'd in the earth a circle of strong stakes, and interwove them with flexible twigs. While I was thus employ'd EVE was conveying the stream among the flowers; gathering ripe fruits, supporting, with small sticks, the bending stalks of the variegated shrubs, and pruning their luxuriant branches. Then it was that we began to eat our bread by the sweat of our brows.

I went to the river to fetch reeds to cover our cottage: there I saw five ewes, white as the southern clouds, and with them a young ram, feeding by the side of the water. I approach'd them without noise, fearing they would fly me, like the tyger and the lion, who, before our fatal transgression, us'd to play with the kid or the lamb at our feet. But, instead of endeavouring to escape me, they suffer'd me to stroke their fleeces, and I drove them before me with a reed to our hill, where I intended that they should for the future feed. EVE was busy'd in erecting a bower, and did not, immediately on my return, observe my little flock; but they soon discover'd themselves by their bleating. She started at the sound, and dropp'd the boughs from her hand thro' fear; but soon recovering, she cry'd, with joy in her countenance, O Adam! they are gentle and fond as in Paradise. Welcome, pretty animals! ye shall live with us. All ye want is here. Ye need not stray; for here are flowery pastures, fragrant herbage, and a clear spring. Your innocent sporting will give us delight, while we attend our trees and flowers.

Solomon Gessner.

24. A TALE OF THE TIMES OF OLD

A TALE of the times of old! The deeds of days of other years l The murmur of thy streams, O Lora! brings back the memory of the past. The sound of thy woods, Garmallar, is lovely in mine ear. Dost thou not behold, Malvina, a rock with its head of heath? Three aged pines bend from its face; green is the narrow plain at its feet; there the flower of the mountain grows, and shakes its white head in the breeze. The thistle is there above shedding its aged beard. Two stones, half sunk in the ground, show their heads of moss. The deer of the mountain avoids the place, for he beholds a dim ghost standing there. The mighty lie, O Malvina! in the narrow plain of the rock.

A tale of the times of old! The deeds of days of other years! *James Macpherson.*

25. MELANCHOLY, ENTHUSIASM, SUPERSTITION

RELIGIOUS MELANCHOLY was the daughter of ENTHUSIASM and SUPERSTITION; she was nursed, by her mother, in the cell of a DOMINICAN convent; and her only food was bread and water. As the parents had no other view for their daughter, than the inheritance of immortality, she was never instructed in human learning; for it was a maxim with them, that Ignorance is the mother of Devotion, and that enlightened reason serves only to cavil against the impulses of Heaven. From her mother, MELANCHOLY inherited gloominess and fear; and from her father, disordered and unequal passions, flights, raptures, and reveries—she spent her days in mortification and her nights in terror; for she was taught to believe, that her Devotion would be acceptable to her God, in proportion as it was distressful to herself. From that perswasion she passed the greatest part of her life in penal austerities: but, as she was the child of ENTHUSIASM, she was sometimes visited with a gleam of fanatic joy, which shone through the gloom of her cell; and, during those intervals, she asserted that she was in Heaven. Those intervals, however, as they were too powerful for a mortal mind, were very short and very rare: her exhausted spirits were afterwards reduced to the lowest languor; and she, who, the last moment, was exulting in the ecstasies of Heaven, was now aghast on the brink of Hell.

Such was the life of Religious MELANCHOLY; till the benevolent Father of Nature, pitying her undeserved miseries, and weary of her preposterous devotion, delivered the innocent wretch from that being she had received in vain.

John Langhorne.

26. THE FADING FLOWER

BEND thy blue course, O stream! round the narrow plain of Lutha. Let the green woods hang over it, from their hills: the sun looks on it at noon. The thistle is there on its rock and shakes its beard to the wind. The flower hangs its heavy head, waving, at times, to the gale. "Why dost thou awake me, O gale!" it seems to say, "I am covered with the drops of heaven. The time of my fading is near, the blast that shall scatter my leaves. To-morrow shall the traveller come; he that saw me in my beauty shall come. His eyes will search the field, but they will not find me."

James Macpherson.

27. THE LASS WITH THE GOLDEN LOCKS

No more of my Harriot, of Polly no more,
Nor all the bright beauties that charm'd me before;
My heart for a slave to gay Venus I've sold,
And barter'd my freedom for ringlets of gold:
I'll throw down my pipe, and neglect all my flocks,
And will sing to my lass with the golden locks.

Though o'er her white forehead the gilt tresses flow,
Like the rays of the Sun on a hillock of snow;
Such painters of old drew the queen of the fair,
'Tis the taste of the ancients, 'tis classical hair,
And though witlings may scoff, and though raillery mocks,
Yet I'll sing to my lass with the golden locks.

To live and to love, to converse and be free,
Is loving, my charmer, and living with thee:
Away go the hours in kisses and rhyme,
Spite of all the grave lectures of old father Time;
A fig for his dials, his watches and clocks,
He's best spent with the lass of the golden locks.

Than the swan in the brook she's more dear to my sight,
Her mien is more stately, her breast is more white,
Her sweet lips are rubies, all rubies above,
They are fit for the language or labour of love;
At the Park, in the Mall, at the play in the box,
My lass bears the bell with her golden locks.

Her beautiful eyes, as they roll or they flow,
Shall be glad for my joy, or shall weep for my woe;
She shall ease my fond heart, and shall sooth my soft pain,
While thousands of rivals are sighing in vain;
Let them rail at the fruit they can't reach, like the fox,
While I have the lass with the golden locks.

Christopher Smart.

28. THE SEASONS

... Glist'ning with dew the green-hair'd Spring
Walks through the woods, and smiling in her train,
   Youth flutters gay on cherub wing,
And Me exulting lifts the eye to Heaven.
     And crown'd with bearded grain,
   And hay-grass breathing odours bland,
Bold Summer comes in manhood's lusty prime.
     Anon his place is given
   To veteran Autumn: yellow glows
His waving robe: with conscious mien sublime
   He proudly lifts his sun-brown'd brows
     High o'er the loaded clime.
For him the full-orb'd Moon with orange rays
Gilds the mild night; for him her course delays;

>   And jolly wealth lies wide beneath his hand,
>   But soon decrepit age he shows,
>   And all his golden honours past,
>   Naked before October's blast
>   He flies the plunder'd lands. . . .
>   W. J. Mickle.

29. GOD THE EVERLASTING LIGHT OF THE SAINTS ABOVE

> Ye golden Lamps of Heav'n, farewel,
>   With all your feeble Light:
> Farewel, thou ever-changing Moon,
>   Pale Empress of the night!
>
> And thou refulgent Orb of Day
>   In brighter flames array'd,
> My Soul, that springs beyond thy Sphere,
>   No more demands thine Aid.
>
> Ye Stars are but the shining Dust
>   Of my divine Abode,
> The Pavement of those heav'nly Courts,
>   Where I shall reign with God. . . .
>   *Philip Doddridge.*

30. EVENING AT THE ABBEY

> . . . The river murmurs, and the breathing gale
>   Whispers the gently-waving boughs among;
> The star of ev'ning glimmers o'er the dale,
>   And leads the silent host of Heaven along.
>
> How bright, emerging o'er yon brown-clad height,
>   The silver empress of the night appears!
> Yon limpid pool reflects a stream of light,
>   And faintly in its breast the woodland bears.

The waters, tumbling o'er their rocky bed,
   Solemn and constant, from yon dell resound;
The lonely hearths blaze o'er the distant glebe,
   The bat, low-wheeling, skims the dusky ground.

August and hoary, o'er the sloping dale,
   The gothic abbey rears its sculptur'd towers;
Dull through the roofs resounds the whistling gale;
   Dark solitude among the pillars low'rs. . . .
                          W. J. Mickle.

31. THE MOWERS

. . . Their scythes upon the adverse bank
      Glitter 'mongst th' entangled trees,
   Where the hazels form a rank
      And curtsey to the courting breeze. . . .
                          Christopher Smart.

32. THE SUN

O THOU that rollest above, round as the shield of my fathers I whence are thy beams, O sun!—thy everlasting light? Thou comest forth in thy awful beauty, the stars hide themselves in thy sky: the moon cold and pale sinks in the western wave. But thou thyself movest alone: who can be a companion of thy course? The oaks of the mountains fall; the mountains themselves decay with years; the ocean shrinks and grows again; the moon herself is lost in heaven; but thou art for ever the same, rejoicing in the brightness of thy course. When the world is dark with tempests, when thunder rolls and lightning flies, thou lookest in thy beauty from the clouds, and laughest at the storm. But to Ossian, thou lookest in vain; for he beholds thy beams no more, whether thy yellow hair flows on the eastern clouds, or thou tremblest at the gates of the west. But thou art perhaps, like me, for a season, and thy years will have an end. Thou shalt sleep in thy clouds, careless of the voice of the morning. Exult then, O sun, in the strength of thy youth! age is dark and unlovely; it is like the glimmering light of the moon, when it shines through broken clouds and the mist is on the hills: the blast of the north is on the plain—the traveller shrinks in the midst of his journey.

James Macpherson.

33. THE JOY OF GRIEF

SON of Alpin, strike the string. Is there aught of joy in the harp? Pour it then on the soul of Ossian: It is folded in mist. I hear thee, O bard! in my night. But cease the lightly trembling sound. The joy of Grief belongs to Ossian, amidst his dark-brown years.

Green thorn of the hill of ghosts, that shakest thy head to nightly winds! I hear no sound in thee; is there no spirit's windy skirt now rustling in thy leaves? Often are the steps of the dead in the dark-eddying blasts; when the moon, a dun shield from the east, is rolled along the sky.

Ullin, Carril, and Ryno, voices of the days of old I Let me hear you, while yet it is dark, to please and awake my soul. I hear you not, ye sons of song; in what hall of clouds is your rest? Do you touch the shadowy harp, robed with morning mist, where the rustling sun comes forth from his green-headed waves? *James Macplierson.*

34. PSALM CXL VIII

> HOSANNA to the King
>   On his eternal throne,
> Let heaven's high convex ring
>   With pray'r and praise alone!
> Praise him which treads th' etherial vault,
> And with the theme your strains exalt.
>
> Praise him, cherubic flights,
>   And ye seraphic fires,
> Angelical delights
>   With voices, lutes and lyres;
> And vie who shall extol him most,
> Ye blest innumerable host I

Praise him, thou source of heat,
    Great ruler of the day,
And thou serenely sweet,
    O moon, his praise display;
Praise him ye glorious lights that are,
The planet and the sparkling star.

Praise him, ye heav'n above,
    The highest heav'n sublime,
Where tun'd to truth and love
    The spheres symphonious chime;
Praise him where holy spirits lave,
Ye waters of eternal wave.

Let them to praise his name
    With choral musick flow;
For from his sword they came,
    He spake and it was so;
His are the glorious, great and fair,
For he commanded, and they were

—For he hath made them fast
    For ever and again;
For ever they shall last,
    And in their spheres remain;
In all their movements seek or shun,
The law that he commands is done.

Praise ye the Lord of earth,
    All ye that dwell therein,
And leap with active mirth,
    Ye fish of ev'ry fin;
Praise ye, that hide where ocean sleeps,
Ye dragons of unfathom'd deeps.

Ye meteors, fire and hail,
    With ev'ry cloud that snows
As o'er the land they sail,
    And various wind that blows
The rapid terror of the storm,
At once his mandate to perform.

Ye mountains of the air,
   And hills of less degree,
And you ye groves that bear
   On ev'ry goodly tree
The summer fruits, and vernal bloom,
And lofty cedars of perfume!

Ye beasts that haunt the wild,
   From servile bondage loose,
Ye cattle tame and mild
   For man's domestic use,
Ye reptiles of the ground adore,
Ye birds sing praises, as ye soar.

Praise him, each scepter'd seer
   Advanc'd to hold the helm,
And to his praise appear,
   Ye people of the realm;
Ye princes of the world renown'd,
And judges, that the laws expound

Ye youths the maids engage
   In melody divine,
Let infancy with age
   To praise the Lord combine,
Whose name, whose merits have no end,
But measure and immense transcend.

He shall exalt the crest
   Of his peculiar fold,
And all the wise and blest
   This festival shall hold,
Ev'n Jacob's sons and Judah's bands,
Whose faith, whose firm allegiance stands.
                Christopher Smart.

35. A LANDSCAPE

Now that Summer's ripen'd bloom
Frolics where the Winter frown'd,
Stretch'd upon these banks of broom,
We command the landscape round.

Nature in the prospect yields
Humble dales and mountains bold,
Meadows, woodlands, heaths—and fields
Yellow'd o'er with waving gold.

Goats upon that frowning steep
Fearless with their kidlings brouse;
Here a flock of snowy sheep,
There a herd of motley cows.

On the uplands ev'ry glade
Brightens in the blaze of day;
O'er the vales the sober shade
Softens to an ev'ning gray. . . .

Linnets on the crowded sprays
Chorus—and the woodlarks rise,
Soaring with a song of praise
Till the sweet notes reach the skies.

Torrents in extended sheets
Down the cliffs dividing break;
'Twixt the hills the water meets,
Settling in a silver lake. . .

On the isles, with osiers drest,
Many a fair-plum'd halcyon breeds;
Many a wild bird hides her nest,
Corer'd in yon' crackling reeds. . . .
                    John Cunningham.

36. A WYLD ROMANTIC DELL

... Soothd by the murmurs of a plaintive streame,
A wyld romantic dell its fragrance shed;
Safe from the thonder showre and scorching beame
Their faerie charmes the summer bowres displaid;
Wyld by the bancks the bashfull couslips spread,
And from the rock above each ivied seat
The spotted foxgloves hung the purple head,
And lowlie vilets kist the wanderer's feet:
Sure never Hyblas bees roovd through a wilde so sweet.

As winds the streamlet surpentine along,
So leads a solemn walk its bowry way,
The pale-leaved palms and darker limes among,
To where a grotto lone and secret lay;
The yellow broome, where chirp the linnets gay,
Waves round the cave; and to the blue-streakd skyes
A shatterd rock towres up in fragments gray:
The she-goat from its height the lawnskepe eyes,
And calls her wanderd young, the call each banck replies. ...
                                                                    W. J. Mickle.

37. PARADISE

... Ye that dwell with cherub-turtles
    Mated in that upmost light,
Or parade amongst the myrtles,
    On your steeds of speckl'd white. ...
                                        Christopher Smart.

38. ORIENTAL ODOURS

STRAWBERRY HILL, *June* 10, 1765. Eleven at night. I AM just come out of the garden in the most oriental of all evenings, and from breathing odours beyond those of Araby. The acacias, which the Arabians have the sense to worship, are covered with blossoms, the honeysuckles dangle from every tree in festoons, the seringas are thickets of sweets, and the new-cut hay in the fields tempers the balmy gales with simple freshness; while a thousand sky-rockets launched into the air at Ranelagh or Marybone illuminate the scene, and give it an air of Haroun Alraschid's paradise. I was not quite so content by daylight; some foreigners dined here, and though they admired our verdure, it mortified me by its brownness—we have not had a drop of rain this month to cool the tip of our daisies. *Horace Walpole.*

39. THE STARS

... Stars of the superior class,
   Which in magnitude surpass,
   From the time they rose and shone,
   Have their names and places known.

   Mazaroth his circuit runs,
   With Arcturus and his sons;
   Pleiad twinkles o'er the streams
   Of Orion's bolder beams.

   But what glories in array
   Brighten all the milky way,
   Where innumerables vie,
   Told alone by God Most High!...
                   Christopher Smart.

40. THE NATIVITY OF OUR LORD AND SAVIOUR JESUS CHRIST

   WHERE is this stupendous stranger,
     Swains of Solyma, advise,
   Lead me to my Master's manger,
     Shew me where my Saviour lies?

O Most Mighty! O Most Holy!
   Far beyond the seraph's thought,
Art thou then so mean and lowly
   As unheeded prophets taught?

O the magnitude of meekness!
   Worth from worth immortal sprung;
O the strength of infant weakness,
   If eternal is so young!

If so young and thus eternal,
   Michael tune the shepherd's reed,
Where the scenes are ever vernal,
   And the loves be love indeed!

See the God blasphemed and doubted
   In the schools of Greece and Rome;
See the pow'rs of darkness routed,
   Taken at their utmost gloom.

Nature's decorations glisten
   Far above their usual trim;
Birds on box and laurel listen,
   As so near the cherubs hymn.

Boreas now no longer winters
   On the desolated coast;
Oaks no more are riv'n in splinters
   By the whirlwind and his host.

Spinks and ouzles sing sublimely,
   "We too have a Saviour born";
Whiter blossoms burst untimely
   On the blest Mosaic thorn.

God all-bounteous, all-creative,
   Whom no ills from good dissuade,
Is incarnate, and a native
   Of the very world he made.
                    Christopher Smart.

41. THE CASTLE OF OTRANTO

I HAD time but to write a short note with the "Castle of Otranto," as your messenger called upon me at four o'clock, as I was going to dine abroad. Your partiality to me and Strawberry have, I hope, inclined you to excuse the wildness of the story. . . . Shall I ever confess to you, what was the origin of this romance! I waked one morning, in the beginning of last June, from a dream, of which, all I could recover was, that I had thought myself in an ancient castle (a very natural dream for a head filled like mine with Gothic story), and that on the uppermost bannister of a great staircase I saw a gigantic hand in armour. In the evening I sat down, and began to write, without knowing in the least what I intended to say or relate. . . . I was so engrossed with my tale, which I completed in less than two months, that one evening, I wrote from the time I had drunk my tea, about six o'clock, till half an hour after one in the morning, when my hand and fingers were so weary, that I could not hold the pen to finish the sentence, but left Matilda and Isabella talking, in the middle of a paragraph. . . .

Horace Walpole.

42. FLOWERS AND VEGETABLES

. . . All round the borders where the pansie blue,
  Crocus and polyanthus speckld fine,
  And daffodils in fayre confusion grew
Emong the rose-bush roots and eglantine;
These now their place to cabbages resign,
  And tawdrie pease supply the lillys stead;
Rough artichokes now bristle where the vine
In purple clusters round the windows spread,
And laisie coucumbers on dung recline the head. . . .

W. J. Mickle.

43. SWANS LILIES AND KOVES

...Ye swans that sail and lave
  In Jordan's hallow'd wave,
    Ah sweet! ah pensive! ah serene!
  Thou rose of maiden flush,
  Like Joseph's guiltless blush,
    And herb of ever-grateful green;

Ye lilies of perfume,
That triumph o'er the loom,
  And gaudy greatness far outshine;
And thou the famous tree,
Whose name is chastity,
  And all the brilliants of the mine;

Ye doves of silver down
That plume the seraph's crown,
  All, all the praise of Jesus sing,
The joy of heav'n and earth,
And Christ's eternal worth,
  The pearl of God, the Father's ring....
          Christopher Smart.

44. MILTON'S PARADISE ON EARTH

IT is more extraordinary, that having so long ago stumbled on the principle of modern gardening, we should have persisted in retaining its reverse, symmetrical and unnatural gardens. That parks were rare in other countries, Hentzner, who travelled over a great part of Europe, leads us to suppose, by observing that they were common in England. In France they retain the name, but nothing is more different both in compass and disposition. Their parks are usually square or oblong enclosures regularly planted with walls of chestnuts or limes....

One man, one great man we had, on whom nor education nor custom could impose their prejudices; who, *on evil days though fallen, and with darkness and solitude compassed round,* judged that the mistaken and fantastic ornaments he had seen in gardens were unworthy of the almighty hand that planted the delights of Paradise. He seems with the prophetic eye of taste . . . to have conceived, to have foreseen modern gardening; as lord Bacon announced the discoveries since made by experimental philosophy. The description of Eden is a warmer and more just picture of the present style than Claud Lorrain could have painted from Hagley or Stourhead. The first lines I shall quote exhibit Stourhead on a more magnificent scale.

> Thro 'Eden went a river large,
> Nor chang'd his course, but thro' the shaggy hill
> Pass'd underneath ingulph'd; for God had thrown
> That mountain as his garden-mound, high rais'd
> Upon the rapid current—

Hagley seems pictured in what follows,

> Which thro' veins
> Of porous earth with kindly thirst updrawn,
> Rose a fresh fountain, and with many a rill
> Water'd the garden—

What colouring, what freedom of pencil, what landscape in these lines

> —from that sapphire fount the crisped brooks
> Rolling on orient pearl and sands of gold,
> With mazy error, under pendent shades
> Ran nectar, visiting each plant, and fed
> Flow'rs worthy of Paradise, which not nice art
> In beds and curious knots, but *nature's* boon
> Pour'd forth profuse on hill and dale and plain,
> Both where the morning sun first warmly smote
> The open field, and where the unpierc'd shade
> Imbrown'd the noon-tide bow'rs—*Thus was this place*
> *A happy rural seat of various view.*

Read this transporting description, paint to your mind the scenes that follow, contrast them with the savage but respectable terror with which the poet guards the bounds of his Paradise, fenced

> —with the champain head
> Of a steep wilderness, whose hairy sides
> With thicket overgrown, grotesque and wild,
> Access denied; and overhead upgrew

> Insuperable height of loftiest shade,
> Cedar, and pine, and fir, and branching palm,
> A sylvan scene, and, as the ranks ascend,
> Shade above shade, a woody theatre
> Of stateliest view—

and then recollect that the author of this sublime vision had never seen a glimpse of any thing like what he has imagined; that his favourite ancients had dropped not a hint of such divine scenery. *Horace Walpole.*

45. EVENING

... And now, perchd prowdlie on the topmost spray,
  The sootie blackbird chaunts his vespers shrill;
  While twilight spreads his robe of sober grey,
  And to their bowres the rooks loud cawing wing their way:

  And bright behind the Cambrian mountains hore
  Flames the read beam; while on the distant east,
  Led by her starre, the horned Moone looks o'er
  The bending forest, and with rays increast
  Ascends; while trembling on the dappled west
  The purple radiance shifts and dies away;
  The willows with a deeper green imprest
  Nod o'er the brooks; the brooks with gleamy ray
  Glide on, and holy peace assumes her woodland sway....
  W. J. Mickle.

46. THE WALL-FLOWER

  "Why loves my flower, the sweetest flower
    That swells the golden breast of May,
  Thrown rudely o'er this ruin'd tower
    To waste her solitary day?

  "Why, when the mead, the spicy vale,
    The grove and genial garden call,
  Will she her fragrant soul exhale,
    Unheeded on the lonely wall?

"For never sure was beauty born
    To live in death's deserted shade!
Come, lovely flower, my banks adorn,
    My banks for life and beauty made."

Thus Pity wak'd the tender thought
    And by her sweet persuasion led,
To seize the hermit flower I sought,
    And bear her from her stony bed.

I sought—but sudden on mine ear
    A voice in hollow murmurs broke,
And smote my heart with holy fear—
    The Genius of the Ruin spoke.

"From thee be far th' ungentle deed,
    The honours of the dead to spoil,
Or take the sole remaining meed,
    The flower that crowns their former toil!

"Nor deem that flower the gardener's foe,
    Or fond to grace this barren shade;
'Tis Nature tells her to bestow
    Her honours on the lonely dead.

"For this obedient zephyrs bear
    Her light seeds round yon turret's mould,
And undispers'd by tempests there,
    They rise in vegetable gold. . . ."
                                                John Langhorne.

47. FROM PETRARCH

Wail'd the sweet warbler to the lonely shade;
    Trembled the green leaf to the summer gale;
    Fell the fair stream in murmurs down the dale,
Its banks, its flow'ry banks with verdure spread,
    Where, by the charm of pensive Fancy led,

All as I fram'd the love-lamenting tale,
   Came the dear object whom I still bewail,
Came from the regions of the cheerless dead:
   "And why," she cried, "untimely wilt thou die?
Ah why, for pity, shall those mournful tears,
   Start in wild sorrow from that languid eye?
Cherish no more those visionary fears,
   For me, who range yon light-invested sky!
For me, who triumph in eternal years."

John Langhorne
(translation from *Petrarch*).

48. GOD'S CREATURES

. . . They knew him well, and could not err,
    To him they all appeal'd;
The beast of sleek or shaggy fur,
And found their natures to recur
    To what they were in Eden's field.

For all that dwell in depth or wave
    And ocean—every drop—
Confess'd his mighty pow'r to save,
When to the floods his peace he gave,
    And bade careering whirlwinds stop.

And all things meaner from the worm
    Probationer to fly;
To him that creeps his little term,
And countless rising from the sperm
    Shed by sea-reptiles, where they ply.

These all were bless'd beneath his feet,
    Approaching them so near;
Vast flocks that have no mouths to bleat,
With yet a spirit to intreat,
    And in their rank divinely dear. . . .

Christopher Smart.

49. THE CAT

. . . For I will consider my Cat Jeoffrey.
For he is the servant of the Living God, duly and daily serving him.
For at the first glance of the glory of God in the East he worships in his way.
For is this done by wreathing his body seven times round with elegant quickness.
For then he leaps up to catch the musk, which is the blessing of God upon his prayer.
For he rolls up on prank to work it in.
For having done duty and received blessing he begins to consider himself.
For this he performs in ten degrees.
For first he looks upon his fore-paws to see if they are clean.
For secondly he kicks up behind to clear a way there.
For thirdly he works it upon stretch with his fore paws extended.
For fourthly he sharpens his paws by wood.
For fifthly he washes himself.
For sixthly he rolls upon wash.
For Seventhly he fleas himself, that he may not be interrupted upon the beat.
For Eighthly he rubs himself against a post.
For Ninthly he looks up for his instructions.
For Tenthly he goes in quest of food.
For having consider'd God and himself he will consider his neighbour.
For if he meets another cat he will kiss her in kindness.
For when he takes his prey he plays with it to give it chance.
For one mouse in seven escapes by his dallying.
For when his day's work is done his business more properly begins.
For he keeps the Lord's watch in the night against the adversary.
For he counteracts the powers of darkness by his electrical skin & glaring eyes.

For he counteracts the Devil, who is death, by brisking about the life.
For in his morning orisons he loves the sun and the sun loves him.
For he is of the tribe of Tiger.
For the Cherub Cat is a term of the Angel Tiger. . . .

Christopher Smart.

50. MOONRISE

. . . The sweets, that bending o'er their banks,
    From sultry Day declin'd,
Revive in little velvet ranks,
    And scent the western wind.

The Moon, preceded by the breeze
    That bade the clouds retire,
Appears amongst the tufted trees
    A Phoenix nest on fire.

But soft—the golden glow subsides!
    Her chariot mounts on high!
And now, in silent pomp, she rides
    Pale regent of the sky! . . .

John Cunningham.

51. SILVER IN MY MINES

. . . For there is silver in my mines and I bless God that it is there rather than in my coffers. . . .

Christopher Smart.

52. THE FIRST FLASH

A THOUGHT conceiv'd in the first warmth, an effect with which we are struck at the first view, is never so well express'd as by the strokes that are drawn at that instant.

Solomon Gessner.

53. THE LAKE DISTRICT

Oct: 3. The hills here are cloth'd all up their steep sides with oak, ash, birch, holly, &c: some of it has been cut 40 years ago, some within these 8 years, yet all is sprung again green, flourishing, & tall for its age, in a place where no soil appears but the staring rock, & where a man could scarce stand upright.

Met a civil young farmer overseeing his reapers (for it is oat-harvest here) who conducted us to a neat white house in the village of Grange, w ch is built on a rising ground in the midst of a valley, round it the mountains form an aweful amphitheatre, and thro' it obliquely runs the Darwent clear as glass, and shewing under it's bridge every trout that passes, beside the village rises a round eminence of rock, cover'd entirely with old trees, & over that more proudly towers *Castle-crag*, invested also with wood on its sides, & bearing on its naked top some traces of a fort said to be Roman. . . .

I went no farther than the Farmer's (better than 4 m: from Keswick) at *Grange*: his mother & he brought us butter, that Siserah would have jump'd at, tho' not in a lordly dish, bowls of milk, thin oaten-cakes, & ale; & we had carried a cold tongue thither with us. our farmer was himself the Man, that last year plundered the Eagle's eirie: all the dale are up in arms on such an occasion, for they lose abundance of lambs yearly, not to mention hares, partridge, grous, &c: he was let down from the cliff in ropes to the shelf of rock, on wch the nest was built, the people above shouting & hollowing to fright the old birds, w ch flew screaming round, but did not dare to attack him. he brought off the eaglet (for there is rarely more than one) & an addle egg. the nest was roundish and more than a yard over, made of twigs twisted together, seldom a year passes but they take the brood or eggs, & sometimes they shoot one, sometimes the other Parent, but the survivor has always found a mate (probably in Ireland) & they breed near the old place, by his description I learn, that this species is the *Erne* (the Vultur *Albicilla* of Linnæus in his last edition, but in yours *Falco Albicilla*) so consult him & Pennant about it.

Walk'd leisurely home the way we came, but saw a new

landscape: the features indeed were the same in part, but many new ones were disclosed by the mid-day Sun, and the tints were entirely changed, take notice this was the best or perhaps the only day for going up Skiddaw, but I thought it better employed: it was perfectly serene, & hot as midsummer.

In the evening walk'd alone down to the Lake by the side of *Crow-Park* after sun-set & saw the solemn colouring of night draw on, the last gleam of sunshine fading away on the hill-tops, the deep serene of the waters, & the long shadows of the mountains thrown across them, till they nearly touched the hithermost shore, at distance heard the murmur of many waterfalls not audible in the day-time, wished for the Moon, but she was *dark to me & silent, hid in her vacant interlunar cave.* *Thomas Gray.*

54. THE SEARCH FOR PEARLS

> ... For I pray God to bless improvements in gardening till London be a city of palm-trees.
> For I pray to give his grace to the poor of England, that Charity be not offended & that benevolence may increase.
> For in my nature I quested for pearls, but God, God, hath sent me to sea for pearls.... *Christopher Smart.*

55. AN IRON FORGE ON THE WYE

MINES are frequent in rocky places; and they are full of ideas suited to such occasions. To these may sometimes be added the operations of engines; for machinery, especially when its powers are stupendous, or its effects formidable, is an effort of art, which may be accommodated to the extravagances of nature.

A scene at the New Weir on the Wye, which in itself is truly great and awful, so far from being disturbed, becomes more interesting and important, by the business to which it is destined. It is a chasm between two high ranges of hill, which rise almost perpendicularly from the water; the rocks an the sides are mostly heavy masses; and their colour is generally brown; but here and there a pale craggy shape starts up to a vast heighth above the rest, unconnected, broken, and bare: large trees frequently force out their way amongst them; and many of them stand far back in the covert, where their natural dusky hue is deepened by the shadow which overhangs them. The river too, as it retires, loses itself in woods which close immediately above, then rise thick and high, and darken the water. In the midst of all this gloom is an iron forge, covered with a black cloud of smoak, and surrounded with half-burned ore, with coal, and with cinders; the fuel for it is brought down a path, worn into steps, narrow and steep, and winding among precipices, and near it is an open space of barren moor, about which are scattered the huts of the workmen. It stands close to the cascade of the Weir, where the agitation of the current is encreased by large fragments of rocks, which have been swept down by floods from the banks, or shivered by the tempests from the brow; and the sullen sounds, at stated intervals, from the strokes of the great hammers in the forge, deadens the roar of the waterfall. Just below it, while the rapidity of the stream still continues, a ferry is carried across it; and lower down the fishermen use little round boats, called truckles, the remains perhaps of ancient British navigation, which the least motion will overset, and the slightest touch may destroy. All the employments of the people seem to require either exertion or caution; and the ideas of force or of danger which attend them, give to the scene an animation unknown to a solitary, though perfectly compatible with the wildest romantic situation.

Thomas Whately.

56. FLOWERS

... For there is no Height in which there are not flowers.
For flowers have great virtues for all the senses.
For the flower glorifies God and the root parries the adversary.
For the flowers have their angels even the words of God's Creation.
For the warp & woof of flowers are worked by perpetual moving spirits.

For flowers are good both for the living and the dead.
For there is a language of flowers.
For there is a sound reasoning upon all flowers.
For elegant phrases are nothing but flowers.
For flowers are particularly the poetry of Christ.
For flowers are medicinal.
For flowers are musical in ocular harmony.
For the right names of flowers are yet in heaven, God make
    gardners better nomenclators.
For the Poorman's nosegay is an introduction to a Prince. . . .
                                    Christopher Smart.

57. CAWNA

... Cawna, o Cawna! deck'd in sable charms,
    What distant region holds thee from my arms?
    Cawna, the pride of Afric's sultry vales,
    Soft as the cooling murmur of the gales,
    Majestic as the many-colour'd snake,
    Trailing his glories through the blossom'd brake;
    Black as the glossy rocks where Eascal roars
    Foaming thro 'sandy wastes to Jaghir's shores;
    Swift as the arrow, hasting to the breast,
    Was Cawna, the companion of my rest.
    The sun sat low'ring in the Western sky,
    The swelling tempest spread around the eye;
    Upon my Cawna's bosom I reclin'd,
    Catching the breathing whispers of the wind:
    Swift from the wood a prowling tiger came,
    Dreadful his voice, his eyes a glowing flame;
    I bent the bow, the never-erring dart
    Pierc'd his rough armour, but escap'd his heart;
    He fled, tho' wounded, to a distant waste,
    I urg'd the furious flight with fatal haste;
    He fell, he dy'd—spent in the fiery toil,
    I strip'd his carcase of the furry spoil,
    And, as the varied spangles met my eye,
    "On this," I cried, "shall my lov'd Cawna lie."

The dusky midnight hung the skies in grey;
Impell'd by love, I wing'd my airy way;
In the deep valley and the mossy plain,
I sought my Cawna, but I sought in vain,
The pallid shadows of the azure waves
Had made my Cawna and my children slaves. . . .
                    Thomas Chatterton.

58. THE WANDERING JEW

THOUGH the sea-horse on the ocean
    Own no dear domestic cave,
Yet he slumbers without motion
    On the still and halcyon wave.

If, on windy days, the raven
    Gambol like a dancing skiff,
Not the less he loves his haven
    On the bosom of a cliff.

If almost with eagle pinion
    O'er the Alps the chamois roam,
Yet he has some small dominion,
    Which, no doubt, he calls his home.

Day and night my woes redouble:
    Never nearer to the goal.
Night and day I feel the trouble
    Of the wanderer in my soul.

59. ROCKY HOLLOW LANES

AMONG the singularities of this place, the two rocky hollow lanes, the one to Alton, and the other to the forest, deserve our attention. These roads, running through the malm lands, are, by the traffic of ages and the fretting of water, worn down through the first stratum of our freestone, and partly through the second; so that they look more like water-courses than roads; and are bedded with naked rag for furlongs together.

In many places they are reduced sixteen or eighteen feet beneath the level of the fields; and after floods, and in frosts, exhibit very grotesque and wild appearances, from the tangled roots that are twisted among the strata, and from the torrents rushing down their broken sides; and especially when those cascades are frozen into icicles, hanging in all the fanciful shapes of frost-work. These rugged gloomy scenes affright the ladies when they peep down into them from the paths above, and make timid horsemen shudder while they ride along them; but delight the naturalist with their various botany and particularly with the curious *Filices* with which they abound.

Gilbert White.

60. FROM "ST. PHILIP AND ST. JAMES"

... Beeches, without order seemly,
    Shade the flow'rs of annual birth,
And the lily smiles supremely
    Mention'd by the Lord on earth.

Cowslips seize upon the fallow,
    And the cardamine in white,
Where the corn-flow'rs join the mallow,
    Joy and health and thrift unite.

Study sits beneath her arbour,
    By the bason's glossy side;
While the boat from out its harbour
    Exercise and pleasure guide.

Pray'r and praise be mine employment,
    Without grudging or regret,
Lasting life and long enjoyment,
    Are not here, and are not yet.

Hark! aloud the black-bird whistles,
    With surrounding fragrance blest,
And the goldfinch in the thistles
    Makes provision for her nest.

> Ev'n the hornet hives his honey,
>   Bluecap builds his stately dome,
> And the rocks supply the coney
>   With a fortress and a home.
>
> But the servants of their Saviour,
>   Which with gospel-peace are shod,
> Have no bed but what the paviour
>   Makes them in the porch of God....
>   *Christopher Smart.*

61. THE HEART, GENIUS, AND INSPIRATION

i

Do not conceal from me thy secret recesses. I will make friendship, and erect a covenant with thee. Know, my heart, that no friendship is wiser and more abounding in blessings, than the friendship and intimacy of a heart with itself. He who is not his own confidant, can never become a friend of God and virtue.

ii

He knows himself greatly who never opposes his genius.

iii

The poet, who composes not before the moment of inspiration, and as that leaves him, ceases—composes, and he alone, for all men, all classes, all ages.   *J. C. Lavater.*

62. GOD IN ALL HIS WORKS

GOD, indeed, is himself the beauty and the benefit of all his works. As they cannot exist but in him and by him, so his impression is upon them, and his impregnation is through them.

Though the elements, and all that we know of nature and creature, have a mixture of natural and physical evil, God is, however, throughout, an internal, though often a hidden principle of good, and never wholly departs from his right of dominion and operation in his creatures; but is, and is alone, the beauty and beneficence, the whole glory and graciousness that can possibly be in them.

As the apostle says, "The invisible things of God are made manifest by the things that are seen." He is the secret and central light that kindles up the sun, his dazzling representative; and he lives, enlightens, and comforts in the diffusion of his beams.

His spirit inspires and actuates the air, and is in it a breath of Me to all his creatures. He blooms in the blossom, and unfolds in the rose. He is fragrance in flowers, and flavour in fruits. He holds infinitude in the hollow of his hand, and opens his world of wonders in the minims of nature. He is the virtue of every heart that is softened by a sense of pity or touch of benevolence. He coos in the turtle and bleats in the lamb; and through the paps of the stern bear and implacable tigress, he yields forth the milk of loving-kindness to their little ones. Even, my Harry, when we hear the delicious enchantment of music, it is but an external sketch and faint echo of those sentimental and rapturous tunings that rise up, throughout the immensity of our God, from eternity to eternity.

Thus all things are secretly pregnant with their God. And the lover of sinners, the universal Redeemer, is a principle of good within them, that contends with the malignity of their lapsed state. And thus as the apostle speaks—"All nature is in travail, and groaneth," to be delivered from the evil; till the breath of the love of God shall kindle upon the final fire, out of which the new heavens and new earth shall come forth, as gold seven times refined, to shine for ever and ever.

Henry Brooke.

63. TYGERS

... On Tiber's banks where scarlet jas'mines bloom,
   And purple aloes shed a rich perfume:
   Where, when the Sun is melting in his heat,
   The reeking tygers find a cool retreat;
   Bask in the sedges, lose the sultry beam,
   And wanton with their shadows in the stream. ...

Thomas Chatterton.

64. GORDALE SCAR

Oct. 13, to visit *Gordale-scar*. Wd N: E: day gloomy and cold, it lay but 6 m: from Settle, but that way was directly over a Fell, and it might rain, so I went round in a chaise the only way one could get near it in a carriage, w ch made it full thirteen miles: and half of it such a road! but I got safe over it, so there's an end; and came to Malham (pronounce Maum) a village in the bosom of the mountains, seated in a wild and dreary valley; from thence I was to walk a mile over very rough ground, a torrent rattling along on the left hand: on the cliffs above hung a few goats: one of them danced and scratched an ear with its hind foot in a place where I would not have stood stockstill for all beneath the moon: as I advanced the crags seem'd to close in; but discovered a narrow entrance turning to the left between them. I followed my guide a few paces, and lo, the hills open'd again into no large space, and then all further way is bar'd by a stream, that at the height of above 50 feet gushes from a hole in the rock, and spreading in large sheets over its broken front, dashes from steep to steep, and then rattles away in a torrent down the valley, the rock on the left rises perpendicular with stubbed Yew trees and shrubs, staring from its side to the height of at least 300 feet: but those are not the things: it is that to the right under which you stand to see the fall, that forms the principal horror of the place, from its very base it begins to slope forwards over you in one black and solid mass without any crevice in its surface; and overshadows half the area below with its dreadful canopy, when I stood at (I believe) full 4 yards distance from its foot, the drops wch perpetually distill from its brow, fell on my head, and in one part of the top more exposed to the weather there are loose stones that hang in air, and threaten visibly some idle Spectator with instant destruction: it is safer to shelter yourself close to its bottom, and trust the mercy of that enormous mass, which nothing but an earthquake can stir, the gloomy uncomfortable day well suited the savage aspect of the place and made it still more formidable.

I stay'd there (not without shuddering) a quarter of an hour, and thought my trouble richly paid, for the impression will last for Life: at the ale-house where I dined in Malham, Vivares, the landscape painter, had lodged for a week or more: Smith and Bellers had also been there; and two prints of Gordale have been engraved by them: I returned to my comfortable Inn: night fine: but windy and frosty.

Thomas Gray.

65. TAME DELINEATION

THE last branch of uninteresting subjects, that kind of landscape which is entirely occupied with the tame delineation of a given spot.... The landscape of Titian, of Mola, of Salvator, of the Poussins, Claude, Rubens, Elzheimer, Rembrandt, and Wilson, spurns all relation with this kind of map-work. To them nature disclosed her bosom in the varied light of rising, meridian, setting suns; in twilight, night, and dawn. Height, depth, solitude, strike, terrify, absorb, bewilder, in their scenery. We tread on classic or romantic ground, or wander through the characteristic groups of rich congenial objects.

J. H. Fuseli.

66. AUTUMN AND WINTER

... When golden Autumn, wreath'd in ripen'd corn,
    From purple clusters press'd the foamy wine,
    Thy genius did his sallow brows adorn,
    And made the beauties of the season thine.

    With rustling sound the yellow foliage flies,
    And wantons with the wind in rapid whirls.
    The gurgling riv'let to the valley hies,
    Whilst on the bank the spangled serpent curls ...

    Pale rugged Winter bending o'er his tread,
    His grizzled hair bedropt with icy dew;
    His eyes, a dusky light, congeal'd and dead;
    His robe, a tinge of light ethereal blue;

His train, a motley'd, sanguine, sable cloud,
He limps along the russet dreary moor;
Whilst rising whirlwinds, blasting, keen, and loud,
Roll the white surges to the sounding shore. . . .
Thomas Chatterton.

67. A TURKISH ODE OF MESTHI

Hear how the nightingales on ev'ry spray,
Hail in wild notes the sweet return of May!
The gale, that o'er yon waving almond blows,
The verdant bank with silver blossoms strows:
The smiling season decks each flow'ry glade.
Be gay: too soon the flow'rs of Spring will fade.

What gales of fragrance scent the vernal air!
Hills, dales, and woods their loveliest mantles wear.
Who knows what cares await that fatal day,
When ruder gusts shall banish gentle May?
Ev'n death, pernps, our valleys will invade.
Be gay: too soon the flow'rs of Spring will fade.

The tulip now its varied hue displays,
And sheds, like Ahmed's eye, celestial rays.
Ah, nation ever faithful, ever true,
The joys of youth, while May invites, pursue!
Will not these notes your tim'rous minds persuade?
Be gay: too soon the flow'rs of Spring will fade.

The sparkling dewdrops o'er the lilies play
Like orient pearls, or like the beams of day.
If love and mirth your wanton thoughts engage,
Attend, ye nymphs! (A poet's words are sage.)
While thus you sit beneath the trembling shade,
Be gay: too soon the flow'rs of Spring will fade.

The fresh-blown rose like Zerneb's cheek appears,
When pearls, like dewdrops, glitter in her ears.

The charms of youth at once are seen and past,
And nature says, "They are too sweet to last."
So blooms the rose, and so the blushing maid!
Be gay: too soon the flow'rs of Spring will fade.

See yon anemonies their leaves unfold
With rubies flaming, and with living gold!
While crystal show'rs from weeping clouds descend,
Enjoy the presence of thy tuneful friend.
Now, while the wines are brought, the sofa's lay'd,
Be gay: too soon the flow'rs of Spring will fade.

The plants no more are dried, the meadows dead,
No more the rose-bud hangs her pensive head.
The shrubs revive in valleys, meads, and bow'rs,
And ev'ry stalk is diadem'd with flow'rs:
In silken robes each hillock stands array'd.
Be gay: too soon the flow'rs of Spring will fade.

Clear drops each morn impearl the rose's bloom,
And from its leaf the Zephyr drinks perfume.
The dewy buds expand their lucid store,
Be this our wealth: ye damsels, ask no more.
Though wise men envy, and though fools upbraid.
Be gay: too soon the flow'rs of Spring will fade.

The dewdrops, sprinkled by the musky gale,
Are chang'd to essence ere they reach the dale.
The mild blue sky a rich pavilion spreads,
Without our labour, o'er our favour'd heads.
Let others toil in war, in arts, or trade.
Be gay: too soon the flow'rs of Spring will fade.

Late gloomy winter chill'd the sullen air,
Till Soliman arose, and all was fair.
Soft in his reign the notes of love resound,
And pleasure's rosy cup goes freely round.
Here on the bank, which mantling vines o'ershade,
Be gay: too soon the flow'rs of Spring will fade.

May this rude lay from age to age remain,
A true memorial of this lovely train.
Come, charming maid, and hear thy poet sing,
Thyself the rose, and He the bird of spring:
Love bids him sing, and Love will be obey'd.
Be gay: too soon the flow'rs of Spring will fade.
Sir William Jones Jones.

68. SHAKESPEARE AND SOPHOCLES

SAKESPEARE is to Sophocles what the incessant flashes of a tempestuous night are to daylight. *J. H. Fuseli.*

69. TO THE EVENING STAR

THOU fair-hair'd angel of the evening,
Now, while the sun rests on the mountains, light
Thy bright torch of love; thy radiant crown
Put on, and smile upon our evening bed I
Smile on our loves, and while thou drawest the
Blue curtains of the sky, scatter thy silver dew
On every flower that shuts its sweet eyes
In timely sleep. Let thy west wind sleep on
The lake; speak silence with thy glimmering eyes,
And wash the dusk with silver. Soon, full soon,
Dost thou withdraw; then the wolf rages wide,
And the lion glares thro' the dun forest:
The fleeces of thy flocks are cover'd with
Thy sacred dew: protect them with thine influence.
William Blake.

70. AN AFRICAN SONG

HASTE, ye purple gleams of light,
   Haste and gild the spacious skies;
Haste, ye eagles, take your flight,
   Haste and bid the morning rise.

Now the eastern curtain draws;
  Now the red'ning splendor gleams,
Now the purple plum'd maccaws
  Skim along the silver streams.

Now the fragrant-scented thorn,
  Trembles with the gummy dew;
Now the pleasures of the morn,
  Swell upon the eager view.

Whither does my archer stay?
  Whither is my Narva fled?
What can keep his soul away,
  From the transports of Mored?
            Thomas Chatterton.

71. MIDDLETON DALE

MIDDLETON dale is a cleft between rocks, ascending gradually from a romantic village, till it merges, at about two miles distance, on the vast moor-lands of the Peake; it is a dismal entrance to a desart; the hills above it are bare; the rocks are of a grey colour; their surfaces are rugged; and their shapes savage; frequently terminating in craggy points; sometimes assembling vast unwieldy bulwarks; or rising in heavy buttresses, one above another; and here and there a mishapen mass bulging out, hangs lowering over its base. No traces of men are to be seen, except in a road which has no effect on such a scene of desolation, and in the lime kilns constantly smoking on the side; but the labourers who occasionally attend them live at a distance; there is not a hovel in the dale; and some scanty withering bushes are all its vegetation; for the soil between the rocks produces as little as they do; it is disfigured with all the tinges of brown and red, which denote barrenness; in some places it has crumbled away, and strata of loose dark stones only appear; and in others, long lines of dross and rubbish shoveled out of mines, have fallen down the steeps. In these mines, the veins of lead on one side of the dale, are observed always to have corresponding veins, in exactly the same direction, on the other: and the rocks, though differing widely in different places, yet always continue in one style for some way together, and seem to have a relation to each other; both these appearances make it probable, that Middleton dale is a chasm rent in the mountain by some convulsion of nature, beyond the memory of man, or perhaps before the island was peopled: the scene, though it does not prove the fact, yet justifies the supposition; and it gives credit to the tales of the country people, who, to aggravate its horrors, always point to a precipice, down which they say, that a poor girl of the village threw herself headlong, in despair at the neglect of the man whom she loved: and shew a cavern where a skeleton was once discovered; but of what wretch is unknown; his. bones were the only memorial left of him: all the dreariness however of the place, which accords so well with such traditions, abates upon the junction of another valley, the sides of which are still of rock, but mixed and crowned with fine wood; and Middleton dale becomes more mild by sharing in its beauties: near this junction a clear stream issues from under the hill, and runs down the dale, receiving as it proceeds many rills and springs, all as transparent as itself.

Thomas Whately.

72. AUTUMN FRUITS

... Whanne Autumpne blake and sonne-brente doe appere,
 With hys goulde honde guylteynge the falleynge lefe,
 Bryngeynge oppe Wynterr to folfylle the yere,
 Beerynge uponne hys backe the riped shefe;
 Whan al the hyls wythe woddie sede ys whyte;
Whanne levynne-fyres and lemes do mete from far the syghte;

 Whann the fayre apple, rudde as even skie,
 Do bende the tree unto the fructyle grounde;
 When joicie peres, and berries of blacke die,
 Doe daunce yn ayre, and call the eyne arounde;
 Thann, bee the even foule, or even fayre,
Meethynckes mie hartys joie ys steynced wyth somme care. . . .

Thomas Chatterton.

73. THE YELLOW BARN

The morning's fair, the lusty Sun
With ruddy cheeks begins to run;
And early birds, that wing the skies,
Sweetly sing to see him rise.
　　I am resolved, this charming day,
In the open field to stray;
And have no roof above my head,
But that whereon the gods do tread.
Before the yellow barn I see
A beautiful variety
Of strutting cocks, advancing stout,
And flirting empty chaff about,
Hens, ducks, and geese, and all their brood,
And turkeys gobbling for their food;
While rustics thresh the wealthy floor,
And tempt them all to crowd the door.
　　What a-fair face does Nature show!
Augusta, wipe thy dusty brow;
A landscape wide salutes my sight,
Of shady vales, and mountains bright;
And azure heavens I behold,
And clouds of silver and of gold.
And now into the fields I go,
Where thousand flaming flowers grow;
And every neighbouring hedge I greet,
With honeysuckles smelling sweet. . . .
　　　　　　　　　　John Dyer.

74. PRAISE

. . . I speak for all—for them that fly,
　　And for the race that swim;
For all that dwell in moist and dry,
　　Beasts, reptiles, flow'rs and gems to vie
　　　When gratitude begins her hymn.

Praise him ye doves, and ye that pipe
   Ere buds begin to stir;
Ev'n every finch of every stripe,
And thou of filial love the type,
   O stork! that sit'st upon the fir.

Praise him thou sea, to whom he gave
   The shoal of active mutes;
(Fit tenants of thy roaring wave)
Who comes to still the fiends, that rave
   In oracles and school disputes. . . .

Praise him ye family that weave
   The crimson to be spread
There where communicants receive,
And ye, that form'd the eye to grieve,
   Hid in green bush or wat'ry bed.

Praise him ye flow'rs that serve the swarm
   With honey for their cells;
Ere yet the vernal day is warm,
To call out myriads to perform
   Their gambols on your cups and bells.

Praise him ye gems of lively spark;
   And thou the pearl of price;
In that great depth or caverns dark,
Nor yet are wrested from the mark
   To serve the turns of pride and vice.

Praise him ye cherubs of his breast,
   The mercies of his love,
Ere yet from guile and hate profest
The phenix makes his fragrant nest
   In his own paradise above.
                Christopher Smart.

75. ELEGY

... Once, ere the gold-hair'd Sun shot the new ray
    Through the grey twilight of the dubious morn,
To woodlands, lawns, and hills, I took my way,
    And listen'd to the echoes of the horn;

Dwelt on the prospect, sought the varied view,
    Trac'd the meanders of the bubbling stream;
From joy to joy, uninterrupted flew,
    And thought existence but a fairy dream.

Now thro 'the gloomy cloister's length'ning way,
    Thro' all the terrour superstition frames,
I lose the minutes of the ling'ring day,
    And view the night light up her pointed flames.

I dare the danger of the mould'ring wall,
    Nor heed the arch that totters o'er my head:
O! quickly may the friendly ruin fall,
    Release me of my love, and strike me dead. . . .
                        Thomas Chatterton.

76. SCENES AT HAFOD

i

CONTINUE the walk, till arriving near a bold piece of smooth rock, formed like a seat, the path takes to the left: and after continuing round the brow of that remarkably smooth, tumulously formed hill (of which I before took notice, from the church of Eglwys-newydd, and which seems to be marked out for a Druid's temple), the astonished eye is all at once presented with a command of the valley, that beggars all description—a mighty and magnificent theatre of varied forests, on both sides ascending majestically from the river Ystwyth, which rushes through the valley in the most pleasingly irregular lines; bordered here and there with rich stripes of pasturage; often bending its blue course till lost behind the projecting points of land covered with woods, and again breaking out in the distances; the whole crowned with smooth, verdant caps, towards whose summits vegetation diminishes; occasionally broken by gray mossy rocks that protrude from the soil; the whole interspersed with rude shepherds' cottages, and deliciously sprinkled over with flocks and herds: in a word you see at one view, from a proud eminence, the whole range of this exquisite valley, extending to Lord Lisburne's woods; on the right, capt by Grogwinian's fall; while to the left, the bare mossy mountains of Sputty-Ystwyth, terminate the scene, and mingle with the vapours of the horizon.

The impression this view made upon my mind *is indelible*; yet I saw it without any advantageous concomitants. What then must be the effects of sunshine—vapours—autumnal foliage—a fine aurora—or a clear moonlight! what, in the language of Ossian, "When the blast has entered the womb of the mountain-cloud and scattered its curling gloom around," for here on this globose promontory, a bard might indeed sit, and draw all his fine images from nature!

ii

. . . a rugged cave, worn, during the lapse of ages, under the opposite projecting rocks; whose beetling brows, crowned with trees, almost overhang and darkly shade the deep pools whence they sprang; to the edges of which are clinched the fantastic roots of aged oaks; from whose sides depend slender bands of ivy, waving with every breeze, or dipping in the wells beneath; wildly shooting across the whole, long, crooked branches of oaks vibrate suspended; and, with their scanty but elegant leaves, chequer the shades of the moist caves below;

"And holy horrors solemnize the shade."

George Cumberland.

77. EATING YELLOW HORNED POPPY
Papaver cornicidatwn luteun, Park. *Yellow horned Poppy.*

It grows in plenty on the coast near *Dublin*. The following account of its effects is given in No. 242 of the *Philosophical Transactions*. "A certain person made a pye of the roots of this plant, supposing them to be roots of the Eryngo, of which he had before eaten pyes which were very pleasant, and eating it while it was hot, became delirious, and having voided a stool in a white chamber pot, fancied it to be gold, breaking the pot in pieces, and desiring what he imagined to be gold might be preserved as such. Also his man and maid servant eating of the same pye, fancied of what they saw to be gold; and a child in the cradle having tasted of the same pye, was much dozed, and turned its mouth to and fro: this they continued for some days, and then recovered." *John Rutty.*

78. FLOWERS AND SPICE

... Chalma, whose excellence is known from far;
   From Lupa's rocky hill to Calabar.
   The guardian god of Afric and the isles,
   Where Nature in her strongest vigour smiles;
   Where the blue blossom of the forky thorn,
   Bends with the nectar of the op'ning morn:
   Where ginger's aromatic, matted root,
   Creep through the mead, and up the mountain shoot. ...
Thomas Cliatterton.

79. NOTES IN MAY

May 12-18. The fern owl, or churn owl returns, and chatters in the Hanger.

Sowed in the three-light annual frame African and French marrigolds, China asters, pendulous Amaranths, Orange-gourds.

A man brought me a large trout weighing three pounds, which he found in the waste current at the tail of Bins pond, in water so shallow that it could not get back again to the Selborne stream.

Took the blackbird's nest a second time; it had squab young.

Set the second Bantam hen over the saddle cupboard in the stable with eleven dark eggs.

A solitary hen red-start in the garden.

Timothy travels about the garden.

Made rhubarb tarts, and a rhubarb pudding, which was very good. *Gilbert White.*

80. THE COMING NIGHT

> . . . Here, stretch'd upon this heav'n ascending hill,
> I'll wait the horrors of the coming night;
> I'll imitate the gently plaintive rill,
> And by the glare of lambent vapours write.
>
> Wet with the dew, the yellow'd hawthorns bow;
> The rustic whistles through the echoing cave;
> Far o'er the lea the breathing cattle low,
> And the full Avon lifts the darken'd wave. . . .
>
> Thomas Chatterton.

81. TINTERN ABBEY

In the ruins of Tintern abbey, the original construction of the church is perfectly marked; and it is principally from this circumstance that they are celebrated as a subject of curiosity and contemplation. The walls are almost entire; the roof only is fallen in; but most of the columns which divided the isles are still standing; of those which have dropped down the bases remain, every one exactly in its place; and in the middle of the nave four lofty arches, which once supported the steeple, rise high in the air above all the rest, each reduced now to a narrow rim of stone, but completely preserving its form. The shapes even of the windows are little altered; but some of them are quite obscured, others partially shaded, by tufts of ivy, and those which are most clear, are edged with its slender tindrils, and lighter foliage, wreathing about the sides and the divisions; it winds round the pillars; it clings to the walls; and in one of the isles, clusters at the top in bunches so thick and so large, as to darken the space below. The other isles, and the great nave, are exposed to the sky; the floor is entirely overspread with turf; and to keep it clear from weeds and bushes, is now its highest preservation. Monkish tomb-stones, and the monuments of benefactors long since forgotten, appear above the greensward; the bases of the pillars which have fallen, rise out of it; and maimed effigies, and sculpture worn with age and weather, Gothic capitals, carved cornices, and various fragments, are scattered about, or lie in. heaps piled up together. Other shattered pieces, though disjointed and mouldering, still occupy their original places; and a staircase much impaired, which led to a tower now no more, is suspended at a great heighth, uncovered and inaccessible. Nothing is perfect; but memorials of every part still subsist; all certain, but all in decay; and suggesting, at once, every idea which can occur in a seat of devotion, solitude, and desolation. Upon such models fictitious ruins should be formed; and if any parts are entirely lost, they should be such as the imagination can easily supply from those which are still remaining. *Thomas Whately.*

82. THE ARTIST'S CHARACTER

EVERY artist has, or ought to have, a character or system of his own; if, instead of referring that to the test of nature, you judge him by your own packed notions, or arraign him at the tribunal of schools which he does not recognize—you degrade the dignity of art, and add another fool to the herd of Dilettanti. *J. H. Fuseli.*

83. NATURAL MAN

MAN is so much a creature of art, that it is a matter of nice discernment to separate what is artificial in him from what is purely natural. But, unless we know what man is by *nature,* we cannot be said to know the *natural history* of man. And it is really surprising, that in an age in which natural history has been so diligently cultivated, this part of it, so much more interesting to us than any other, should have been neglected. His nature, as far as concerns the structure and organization of his body, has been sufficiently studied: But is not the natural state of his better part, the mind, much more deserving our enquiry? For my part, I do not know any speculation more curious, or more interesting, than to inquire what kind of animal the man of God and nature is, in contradistinction to what man has made himself. *Lord Monboddo.*

84. THE ORANG OUTANG

I HAVE dwelt thus long upon the Orang Outang, because, if I make him out to be a man, I prove, by fact as well as argument, this fundamental proposition, upon which my whole theory hangs, that language is not natural to man. And, secondly, I likewise prove that the natural state of man, such as I suppose it, is not a mere hypothesis, but a state which at present actually exists. That my facts and arguments are so convincing as to leave no doubt of the humanity of the Orang Outang, I will not take upon me to say; but thus much I will venture to affirm, that I have said enough to make the philosopher consider it as problematical, and a subject deserving to be inquired into. For, as to the vulgar, I can never expect that they should acknowledge any relation to those inhabitants of the woods of Angola; but that they should continue, thro' a false pride, to think highly derogatory from human nature, what the philosopher, on the contrary, will think the greatest praise of man, that, from the savage state, in which the Orang Outang lives, he should, by his own sagacity and industry, have arrived at the state in which we now see him. *Lord Monboddo.*

85. TO THE MUSES

WHETHER on Ida's shady brow,
   Or in the chambers of the East,
The chambers of the sun, that now
   From antient melody have ceas'd;

Whether in Heav'n ye wander fair,
   Or the green corners of the earth,
Or the blue regions of the air,
   Where the melodious winds have birth;

Whether on chrystal rocks ye rove,
   Beneath the bosom of the sea
Wandr'ing in many a coral grove,
   Fair Nine, forsaking Poetry!

> How have you left the antient love
> That bards of old enjoy'd in you!
> The languid strings do scarcely move!
> The sound is forc'd, the notes are few!
>
> *William Blake.*

86. THE TORTOISE

April 12, 1772. While I was in Sussex last autumn, my residence was at the village near Lewes, from whence I had formerly the pleasure of writing to you. On the 1st of November, I remarked that the old tortoise, formerly mentioned, began first to dig the ground in order to the forming its hybernaculum, which it had fixed on just beside a great tuft of hepaticas. It scrapes out the ground with its fore feet, and throws it up over its back with its hind; but the motion of its legs is ridiculously slow, little exceeding the hour-hand of a clock, and suitable to the composure of an animal said to be a whole month in performing one feat of copulation. Nothing can be more assiduous than this creature night and day in scooping the earth and forcing its great body into the cavity; but, as the noons of that season proved unusually warm and sunny, it was continually interrupted, and called forth, by the heat in the middle of the day; and though I continued there till the 13th of November, yet the work remained unfinished. Harsher weather, and frosty mornings, would have quickened its operations. No part of its behaviour ever struck me more than the extreme timidity it always expresses with regard to rain; for though it has a shell that would secure it against the wheel of a loaded cart, yet does it discover as much solicitude about rain as a lady dressed in all her best attire, shuffling away on the first sprinklings, and running its head up in a corner. If attended to, it becomes an excellent weather-glass; for as sure as it walks elate, and as it were on tip-toe, feeding with great earnestness in a morning, so sure will it rain before night. It is totally a diurnal animal, and never pretends to stir after it becomes dark. The tortoise, like other reptiles, has an arbitrary stomach as well as lungs; and can refrain from eating as well as breathing for a great part of the year. When first awakened it eats nothing; nor again in the autumn before it retires; through the height of the summer it feeds voraciously, devouring all the food that comes its way. I was much taken with its sagacity in discerning those that do it kind offices: for, as soon as the good old lady comes in sight who has waited on it for more than thirty years, it hobbles towards its benefactress with awkward alacrity; but remains inattentive to strangers. Thus, not only "the ox knoweth his owner, and the ass his master's crib" but the most abject reptile and torpid of beings distinguishes the hand that feeds it, and is touched with the feelings of gratitude!

P.S. In about three days after I left Sussex the tortoise retired into the ground under the hepaticas.

Gilbert White.

87. THE ARTIST IN LOVE WITH ART

THERE is no reputation for him to whom a taste for his art does not become his ruling passion, to whom the hours he employs in its cultivation are not the most delicious of his life, to whom the study of it does not constitute his real existence, and his primary happiness; to whom the society of artists is not, of all others, the most pleasing, to him whose watchings, or dreams in the night, are not occupy'd with the ideas of his art, who in the morning does not fly with fresh transport to his painting-room. *Solomon Gessner.*

88. LANDSCAPE AND PORTRAIT

I'M sick of Portraits and wish very much to take my viol-da-gamba and walk off to some sweet village, where I can paint landskips and enjoy the fag-end of life in quietness and ease. But these fine ladies and their tea-drinkings, dancings, husband-huntings, etc., etc., etc., will fob me out of the last ten years, and I fear miss getting husbands too. But we can say nothing to these things, you know, Jackson, we must jogg on and be content with the jingling of the bells, only, damn it, I hate a dust, the kicking up a dust, and being confined in harness to follow the track whilst others ride in the waggon, under cover, stretching their legs in the straw at ease, and gazing at green trees and blue skies without half my *Taste*. That's damned hard. My comfort is I have five viols-da-gamba, three Jayes and two Barak Normans. *Thomas Gainsborough.*

89. RUBENS

THE male forms of Rubens are the brawny pulp of slaughtermen, his females are hillocks of roses: overwhelmed muscles, dislocated bones and distorted joints are swept along in a gulph of colours, as herbage, trees and shrubs are whirled, tossed, or absorbed by vernal inundation. *J. H. Fuseli.*

90. RAPHAEL

RAPHAEL is, and ever will be, an *apostolic* man; in other words, he is with regard to painters, what the apostles were with regard to the rest of mankind. *J. C. Lavater.*

91. LASSIE WI' THE LINT-WHITE LOCKS

LASSIE wi' the lint-white locks,
 Bonnie lassie, artless lassie,
Wilt thou wi' me tent the flocks?
 Wilt thou be my dearie O?

Now nature deeds the flowery lea,
And a 'is young and sweet like thee;
O wilt thou share its joys wi' me,
 And say thou'lt be my dearie O?

The primrose bank, the wimpling burn,
The cuckoo on the milk-white thorn,
The wanton lambs at early morn
 Shall welcome thee, my dearie O.

And when the welcome simmer-shower
Has cheer'd ilk drooping little flower,
We'll to the breathing woodbine bower
 At sultry noon, my dearie O.

> When Cynthia lights, wi 'silver ray,
> The weary shearer's hameward way,
> Thro' yellow waving fields we'll stray,
>   And talk o' love, my dearie O.
>
> And when the howling wintry blast
> Disturbs my lassie's midnight rest;
> Enclaspèd to my faithfu' breast,
>   I'll comfort thee, my dearie O.
>
> Robert Burns.

92. THE ENTRANCE TO ITALY

1780. *July* 31*st.*—My heart beat quick when I saw some hills, not very distant, which I was told lay in the Venetian State, and I thought an age, at least, had elapsed before we were passing their base. The road was never formed to delight an impatient traveller; loose pebbles and rolling stones render it, in the highest degree, tedious and jolting. I should not have spared my execrations, had it not traversed a picturesque valley, overgrown with juniper, and strewed with fragments of rock, precipitated, long since, from the surrounding eminences, blooming with cyclamens.

I clambered up several of these crags,

Fra gli odoriferi ginepri,

to gather the flowers I have just mentioned, and found them deliciously scented. Fratillarias and the most gorgeous flies, many of which I here noticed for the first time, were fluttering about and expanding their wings to the sun. There is no describing the number I beheld, nor their gaily varied colouring. I could not find in my heart to destroy their felicity; to scatter their bright plumage and snatch them for ever from the realm of light and flowers. Had I been less compassionate, I should have gained credit with that respectable corps, the torturers of butterflies; and might, perhaps, have enriched their cabinets with some unknown captives. However, I left them imbibing the dews of heaven, in free possession of their native rights; and having changed horses at Tremolano, entered at length my long-desired Italy.

The pass is rocky and tremendous, guarded by the fortress of Covalo, in possession of the empress queen, and only fit, one should think, to be inhabited by her eagles. There is no attaining this exalted hold but by means of a cord let down many fathoms by the soldiers, who live in dens and caverns, which serve also as arsenals, and magazines for powder; whose mysteries I declined prying into, their appearance being a little too aerial for my earthly frame. A black vapour, tingling their entrance, completed the romance of the prospect, which I shall never forget.

For two or three leagues there was little variation in the scenery; cliffs, nearly perpendicular on both sides, and the Brenta foaming and thundering below. Beyond the rocks began to be mantled with vines and gardens. Here and there a cottage shaded with mulberries made its appearance, and we often discovered, on the banks of the river, ranges of white buildings, with courts and awnings, beneath which numbers of women and children were employed in manufacturing silk. As we advanced the stream gradually widened, and the rocks receded; woods were more frequent and cottages thicker strown.

About five in the evening we left the country of crags and precipices, of mists and cataracts, and were entering the fertile territory of the Bassanese. It was now I beheld groves of olives, and vines clustering the summits of the tallest elms; pomegranates in every garden, and vases of citron and orange before almost every door. The softness and transparency of the air soon told me I was arrived in happier climates; and I felt sensations of joy and novelty run through my veins, upon beholding this smiling land of groves and verdure stretched out before me. A few hazy vapours, I can hardly call them clouds, rested upon the extremities of the landscape; and through their medium the sun cast an oblique and dewy ray. Peasants were returning home, singing as they went, and calling to each other over the hills; whilst the women were milking goats before the wickets of the cottage.

William Beckford.

93. A WAR SONG TO ENGLISHMEN

PREPARE, prepare the iron helm of war,
Bring forth the lots, cast in the spacious orb;
Th' Angel of Fate turns them with mighty hands,
And casts them out upon the darken'd earth!
    Prepare, prepare.

Prepare your hearts for Death's cold hand I prepare
Your souls for flight, your bodies for the earth!
Prepare your arms for glorious victory!
Prepare your eyes to meet a holy God!
    Prepare, prepare.

Whose fatal scroll is that? Methinks 'tis mine!
Why sinks my heart, why faultereth my tongue?
Had I three lives, I'd die in such a cause,
And rise, with ghosts, over the well-fought field.
    Prepare, prepare.

The arrows of Almighty God are drawn!
Angels of Death stand in the low'ring heavens!
Thousands of souls must seek the realms of light,
And walk together on the clouds of heaven!
    Prepare, prepare.

Soldiers, prepare! Our cause is Heaven's cause;
Soldiers, prepare I Be worthy of our cause:
Prepare to meet our fathers in the sky:
Prepare, O troops, that are to fall to-day!
    Prepare, prepare.

Alfred shall smile, and make his harp rejoice:
The Norman William, and the learned Clerk,
And Lion Heart, and black-brow'd Edward with
His loyal queen shall rise, and welcome us!
    Prepare, prepare.
                        William Blake.

94. AFTON WATER

Flow gently, sweet Afton, among thy green braes,
Flow gently, I'll sing thee a song in thy praise;
My Mary's asleep by thy murmuring stream,
Flow gently, sweet Afton, disturb not her dream.

Thou stock-dove whose echo resounds thro' the glen,
Ye wild whistling blackbirds in yon thorny den,
Thou green-crested lapwing, thy screaming forbear,
I charge you disturb not my slumbering fair.

How lofty, sweet Afton, thy neighbouring hills,
Far mark'd with the courses of clear winding rills;
There daily I wander as noon rises high,
My flocks and my Mary's sweet cot in my eye.

How pleasant thy banks and green valleys below,
Where wild in the woodlands the primroses blow;
There oft as mild ev'ning weeps over the lea,
The sweet-scented birk shades my Mary and me.

Thy crystal stream, Afton, how lovely it glides,
And winds by the cot where my Mary resides;
How wanton thy waters her snowy feet lave,
As gathering sweet flow'rets she stems thy clear wave.

Flow gently, sweet Afton, among thy green braes,
Flow gently, sweet river, the theme of my lays;
My Mary's asleep by thy murmuring stream,
Flow gently, sweet Afton, disturb not her dream.
                                                Robert Burns.

95. LOVE AND POETRY

There is certainly some connection between Love, and Music & Poetry; and therefore, I have always thought it a fine touch of Nature, that passage in a modern love composition

> "As towards her cot he joggd along
> Her name was frequent in his song—"

For my own part I never had the least thought or inclination of turning Poet till I got once heartily in Love, and then Rhyme and Song were, in a manner, the spontaneous language of my heart.   *Robert Burns.*

96. THE BEE EATER

December 12, 1775. We had in this village, more than twenty years ago, an idiot boy, whom I well remember, who, from a child, showed a strong propensity to bees; they were his food, his amusement, his sole object: and as people of this cast have seldom more than one point in view, so this lad exerted all his few faculties on this one pursuit. In the winter he dozed away his time, within his father's house by the fireside, in a kind of torpid state, seldom departing from the chimney-corner; but in the summer he was all alert, and in quest of his game in the fields, and on sunny banks. Honey bees, humble bees, and wasps, were his prey wherever he found them: he had no apprehensions from their stings, but would seize them *nudis manibus,* and at once disarm them of their weapons, and suck their bodies for the sake of their honey bags. Sometimes he would fill his bosom between his shirt and his skin with a number of these captives: and sometimes would confine them in bottles. He was a very *Merops apiaster,* or bee-bird; and very injurious to men that kept bees; for he would slide into their bee gardens, and, sitting down before the stools, would rap with his finger on the hives, and so take the bees as they came out. He has been known to overturn hives for the sake of honey, of which he was passionately fond. Where metheglin was making he would linger round the tubs and vessels, begging a draught of what he called bee-wine. As he ran about he used to make a humming noise with his lips, resembling the buzzing of bees. This lad was lean and sallow, and of a cadaverous complexion; and, except in his favourite pursuit, in which he was wonderfully adroit, discovered no manner of understanding. Had his capacity been better, and directed to the same object, he had perhaps abated much of our wonder at the feats of a more modern exhibitor of bees; and we may justly say of him now,

> "*Thou,*
> *Had thy presiding star propitious shone,*
> *Shouldst* Wildman *be.*"

When a tall youth, he was removed from hence to a distant village, where he died, as I understand, before he arrived at manhood. *Gilbert White.*

97. THE ROBIN IN WINTER

> ... No noise is here, or none that hinders thought.
> The redbreast warbles still, but is content
> With slender notes, and more than half suppress'd:
> Pleas'd with his solitude, and flitting light
> From spray to spray, where'er he rests he shakes
> From many a twig the pendent drops of ice,
> That tinkle in the wither'd leaves below. . . .
> *William Cowper.*

98. ENTHUSIASM FROM THE WINDS OF HEAVEN

THERE is scarcely any earthly object gives me more—I don't know if I should call it pleasure, but something which exalts me, something which enraptures me—than to walk in the sheltered side of a wood or high plantation, in a cloudy, winter day, and hear a stormy wind howling among the trees & raving o'er the plain. It is my best season for devotion;—my mind is rapt up in a kind of enthusiasm to Him who, in the pompous language of Scripture, "walks on the wings of the wind." *Robert Burns.*

99. THE STRICKEN DEER

> ... I was a stricken deer, that left the herd
> Long since; with many an arrow deep infixt
> My panting side was charged, when I withdrew
> To seek a tranquil death in distant shades.

There was I found by one who had himself
Been hurt by th' archers. In his side he bore,
And in his hands and feet, the cruel scars.
With gentle force soliciting the darts,
He drew them forth, and heal'd and bade me live.
Since then, with few associates, in remote
And silent woods I wander, far from those
My former partners of the peopled scene;
With few associates, and not wishing more.
Here much I ruminate, as much I may,
With other views of men and manners now
Than once, and others of a life to come,
I see that all are wand'rers, gone astray
Each in his own delusions; they are lost
In chase of fancied happiness, still woo'd
And never won. Dream after dream ensues;
And still they dream that they shall still succeed,
And still are disappointed. Rings the world
With the vain stir. I sum up half mankind,
And add two-thirds of the remaining half,
And find the total of their hopes and fears
Dreams, empty dreams. . . .
. . . 'Twere well, says one sage erudite, profound,
Terribly arch'd and aquiline his nose,
And overbuilt with most impending brows,
'Twere well, could you permit the world to live
As the world pleases. What's the world to you?—
Much. I was born of woman, and drew milk,
As sweet as charity, from human breasts.
I think, articulate, I laugh and weep,
And exercise all functions of a man.
How then should I and any man that lives
Be strangers to each other? Pierce my vein,
Take of the crimson stream meand'ring there,
And catechize it well; apply thy glass,
Search it, and prove now if it be not blood
Congenial with thine own: and, if it be,
What edge of sublety canst thou suppose
Keen enough, wise and skilful as thou art,

To cut the link of brotherhood, by which
One common Maker bound me to the kind?
True; I am no proficient, I confess,
In arts like yours. I cannot call the swift
And perilous lightnings from the angry clouds,
And bid them hide themselves in earth beneath;
I cannot analyse the air, nor catch
The parallax of yonder luminous point,
That seems half quench'd in the immense abyss:
Such pow'rs I boast not—neither can I rest
A silent witness of the headlong rage
Or heedless folly by which thousands die,
Bone of my bone, and kindred souls to mine. . . .
William Cowper.

100. THE BEAMS OF LOVE

. . . And we are put on earth a little space
That we may learn to bear the beams of love. . . .
William Blake.

101. SCIENCE AND PRAYER

. . . Philosophy, baptiz'd
In the pure fountain of eternal love,
Has eyes indeed; and, viewing all she sees
As meant to indicate a God to man,
Gives *him* his praise, and forfeits not her own.
Learning has borne such fruit in other days
On all her branches: piety has found
Friends in the friends of science, and true pray'r
Has flow'd from lips wet with Castalian dews. . . .
William Cowper.

102. A GLORY

ON the thirteenth of February 1780, as I was returning to Chester, and ascending, at Rhealt, the mountain, which forms the eastern boundary of the Vale of Clwyd, I observed a rare and curious phaenomenon. . . .

In the road above me, I was struck with the peculiar appearance of a very white shining cloud, that lay remarkably close to the ground. The sun was nearly setting, but shone extremely bright. I walked up to the cloud, and my shadow was projected into it; when a very unexpected, and beautiful scene was presented to my view. The head of my shadow was surrounded at some distance by a circle of various colours, whose centre appeared to be near the situation of the eye, and whose circumference extended to the shoulders. The circle was complete, except what the shadow of my body intercepted. It exhibited the most vivid colours, red being outermost: as far as can be recollected, all the colours appeared in the same order and proportion that the rain-bow presents to our view. It resembled, very exactly, what in pictures is termed a *glory* around the head of our Saviour, and of saints: not indeed that luminous radiance, which is painted close to the head, but an arch of concentric colours, which is placed separate and distinct from it. As I walked forward, this *glory* approached or retired, just as the inequality of the ground shortened or lengthened my shadow. The cloud being sometimes in a small valley below me, sometimes on the same level, or on higher ground, the variation of the shadow, and *glory* became extremely striking and singular.

To add to the beauty of the scene, there appeared, at a considerable distance to the right and left the arches of a white shining bow. These arches were in the form of, and broader than a rain-bow; but were not completely joined into a semicircle above, on account of the shallowness of the cloud. When my chaise came up,. . . the postillion was alarmed to an uncommon degree, by this very singular apparition: which, indeed, might excite terror or delight in the beholder according to the disposition of mind with which it was viewed.

John Haygarth, F.R.S.

103. DRAWING AFTER NATURE

My natural inclination led me to landscapes; I sought with ardour the means of satisfying my desire, and embarrassed in the route I should take, I said to myself, there is but one

model, there is but one master; and I determined to draw after nature.
Solomon Gessner.

104. FLOWERING SHRUBS

> ... Laburnum, rich
> In streaming gold; syringa, iv'ry pure;
> The scentless and the scented rose; this red,
> And of a humbler growth, the other tall,
> And throwing up into the darkest gloom
> Of neighb'ring cypress, or more sable yew,
> Her silver globes, light as the foamy surf
> That the wind severs from the broken wave;
> The lilac, various in array, now white,
> Now sanguine, and her beauteous head now set
> With purple spikes pyramidal, as if
> Studious of ornament, yet unresolv'd
> Which hue she most approv'd, she chose them all;
> Copious of flowers the woodbine, pale and wan,
> But well compensating her sickly looks
> With never-cloying odours, early and late;
> Hypericum, all bloom, so thick a swarm
> Of flow'rs, like flies clothing her slender rods,
> That scarce a leaf appears; mezerion, too,
> Though leafless, well attir'd, and thick beset
> With blushing wreaths, investing ev'ry spray;
> Althaea with the purple eye; the broom,
> Yellow and bright, as bullion unalloy'd,
> Her blossoms; and, luxuriant above all,
> The jasmine, throwing wide her elegant sweets,
> The deep dark green of whose unvarnish'd leaf
> Makes more conspicuous, and illumines more
> The bright profusion of her scatter'd stars. ...
> *William Cowper.*

105. SUBLIMITY

I DO not wish to build a cottage but to erect a pyramid.
J. H. Fuseli.

106. WATERSOUCHY THE DUTCHMAN

THIS promising heir of the Watersouchies had just entered into his fifth year, when his father ventured for the first time to take him to the Bootersacs and his other relations. These good people, enchanted with the neatness of his person and the correctness of his behaviour, never failed to load him with toys, sugar plumbs, and gingerbread; but a spruce set of Aesop's Fables, minutely engraved, and some designs for Brussels point, were the presents in which he chiefly delighted. These delicate drawings drew his whole attention, and they were not long in his hands before he attempted to imitate them, with a perseverance and exactness, surprising at his years. These infantine performances were carefully framed and glazed, and hung up in Madam Watersouchy's apartment, where they always produced the highest admiration. Amongst those who were principally struck with their merit was the celebrated Francis Van Cuyck de Mierhop, a noble artist from Ghent, who, during his residence at Amsterdam, frequently condescended to pass his evenings at Watersouchy's. Mierhop could boast of illustrious descent, to which his fortune was by no means equal, and having a peculiar genius for painting eatables, old women, and other pieces of still life, applied himself to the art, and made a considerable figure. Watersouchy's table was quite an academy in the branches he wished to cultivate, daily exhibiting the completest old women, the most portly turbots, the plumpest soles, and, in a word, the best conditioned fish imaginable, of every kind. Mierhop availed himself of his friend's invitations to study legs of mutton, sirloins of beef, and joints of meat in general. It was for Madam Watersouchy he painted the most perfect fillet of veal, that ever made the mouth of man to water, and she prided herself not a little upon the original having appeared at her table.

The air of Amsterdam agreeing with Mierhop's constitution, and Watersouchy's table not less with his palate, he was quite inspired during his residence there, and took advantage of these circumstances to immortalize himself, by an immense and most inviting picture, in which he introduced a whole entertainment. No part was neglected.—The vapour smoking over the dishes judiciously concealed the extremities of the repast, and gave the finest play to the imagination. This performance was placed with due solemnity in the Butchershall at Ghent, of which respectable corps he had been chosen protector.

Whilst he remained at Amsterdam, young Watersouchy was continually improving, and arrived to such perfection in copying point lace, that Mierhop entreated his father to cultivate these talents, and to place his son under the patronage of Gerard Dow, ever renowned for the exquisite finish of his pieces. Old Watersouchy stared at the proposal, and solemnly asked his wife, to whose opinion he always paid a deference, whether painting was a genteel profession for their son. Mierhop, who overheard their conversation, smiled disdainfully at the question, and Madam Watersouchy answered, that she believed it was one of your liberal arts.

William Beckford

107. DOCTOR JOHNSON

Lo the Bat with Leathern wing,
Winking & blinking,
Winking & blinking,
Winking & blinking,
Like Doctor Johnson.

"Oho," said Dr. Johnson
To Scipio Africanus,
"If you don't own me a Philosopher,
I'll kick your Roman Anus."

"Aha," to Dr. Johnson
Said Scipio Africanus,
"Lift up my Roman Petticoat
And kiss my Roman Anus."

William Blake.

108. FUSELI'S "NIGHTMARE"

... So on his NIGHTMARE through the evening fog
Flits the squab Fiend o'er fen, and lake, and bog;
Seeks some love-wilder'd Maid with sleep oppress'd,
Alights, and grinning sits upon her breast.
—Such as of late amid the murky sky
Was marked by FUSELI's poetic eye;
Whose daring tints, with SHAKESPEAR's happiest grace,
Gave to the airy phantom form and place.—
Back o'er her pillow sinks her blushing head,
Her snow-white limbs hang helpless from the bed;
While with quick sighs, and suffocative breath,
Her interrupted heart-pulse swims in death.
—Then shrieks of captur'd towns, and widow's tears,
Pale lovers stretch'd upon their blood-stain'd biers,
The headlong precipice that thwarts her flight,
The trackless desert, the cold starless night,
And stern-eyed Murderer with his knife behind,
In dread succession agonize her mind.
O'er her fair limbs convulsive tremors fleet,
Start in her hands, and struggle in her feet;
In vain to scream with quivering lips she tries,
And strains in palsy'd lips her tremulous eyes;
In vain she *wills* to run, fly, swim, walk, creep;
The WILL presides not in the bower of SLEEP.
—On her fair bosom sits the Demon-Ape,
Erect, and balances his bloated shape;
Rolls in their marble orbs his Gorgon-eyes
And drinks with leathern ears her tender cries....
Erasmus Darwin.

109. THE FLAMING HEART

THE caliph . . . approached the vases with faltering footsteps, and was ready to sink with terror when he heard the groans of Soliman. As he proceeded, a voice from the livid lips of the prophet articulated these words: "In my lifetime I filled a magnificent throne; having, on my right hand, twelve thousand seats of gold, where the patriarchs and prophets heard my doctrines; on my left the sages and doctors, upon as many thrones of silver, were present at all my decisions. Whilst I thus administered justice to innumerable multitudes, the birds of the air, hovering over me, served as a canopy against the rays of the sun. My people flourished, and my palace rose to the clouds. I erected a temple to the Most High, which was the wonder of the universe: but I basely suffered myself to be seduced by the love of women, and a curiosity that could not be restrained by sublunary things. I listend to the counsels of Aherman and the daughter of Pharaoh, and adored fire and the hosts of heaven. I forsook the holy city, and commanded the genii to rear the stupendous palace of Istakhar and the terrace of the watch-towers, each of which was consecrated to a star. There, for a while, I enjoyed myself in the zenith of glory and pleasure. Not only men but supernatural beings were subject also to my will. I began to think, as these unhappy monarchs around had already thought, that the vengeance of Heaven was asleep; when, at once, the thunder burst my structures asunder, and precipitated me hither: where, however, I do not remain like other inhabitants, totally destitute of hope; for an angel of light hath revealed that in consideration of the piety of my early youth my woes shall come to an end, when this cataract shall for ever cease to flow. Till then I am in torments, ineffable torments! An unrelenting fire preys on my heart."

Having uttered this exclamation, Soliman raised his hands towards heaven, in token of supplication; and the caliph discerned through his bosom, which was as transparent as crystal, his heart enveloped in flames. At a sight so full of horror, Nouronihar fell back, like one petrified, into the arms of Vathek, who cried out with a convulsive sob: "O Giaour! whither hast thou brought us! allow us to depart, and I will relinquish all thou hast promised. O Mahomet! remains there no more mercy?" "None! none!" replied the malicious dive. "Know, miserable prince! thou art now in the abode of vengeance and despair. Thy heart, also, will be kindled like those of the other votaries of Eblis. A few days are allotted thee previous to this fatal period: employ them as thou wilt; recline on these heaps of gold; command the infernal potentates; range at thy pleasure through these immense subterranean domains: no barrier shall be shut against thee. As for me, I have fulfilled my mission: I will now leave thee to thyself." At these words he vanished.

The caliph and Nouronihar remained in the most abject affliction. Their tears were unable to flow, and scarcely could they support themselves. At length, taking each other despondingly by the hand, they went faltering from this fatal hall, indifferent which way they turned their steps. Every portal opened at their approach. The dives fell prostrate before them. Every reservoir of riches was disclosed to their view; but they no longer felt the incentives of curiosity, of pride, or avarice. With like apathy they heard the chorus of genii, and saw the stately banquets prepared to regale them. They went wandering on from chamber to chamber, hall to hall, and gallery to gallery; all without bounds or limit; all distinguishable by the same lowering gloom; all adorned with the same awful grandeur; all traversed by persons in search of repose and consolation, but who sought them in vain, for everyone carried within him a heart tormented in flames.

William Beckford
(translated by *Samuel Henley*).

110. SCROGGAM

THERE was a wife wonn'd in Cockpen,
 Scroggam;
She brew'd gude ale for gentlemen,
Sing auld Cowl, lay you down by me,
Scroggam, my dearie, ruffum.

The gudewife's dochter fell in a fever,
 Scroggam;
The priest o' the parish fell in anither,
Sing auld Cowl, lay you down by me,
Scroggam, my dearie, ruffum.

> They laid the twa i' the bed thegither,
>   Scroggam;
> That the heat o' the tane might cool the tither,
> Sing auld Cowl, lay you down by me,
> Scroggam, my dearie, ruffum.
>
> Robert Burns.

111. THE BASTILLE

> ... Then shame to manhood, and opprobrious more
>   To France than all her losses and defeats,
>   Old or of later date, by sea or land,
>   Her house of bondage, worse than that of old
>   Which God aveng'd on Pharaoh—the Bastille!
>   Ye horrid tow'rs, th' abode of broken hearts;
>   Ye dungeons and ye cages of despair,
>   That monarchs have supplied from age to age
>   With music such as suits their sov'reign ears—
>   The sighs and groans of miserable men!
>   There's not an English heart that would not leap
>   To hear that ye were fall'n at last; to know
>   That ev'n our enemies, so oft employ'd
>   In forging chains for us, themselves were free....
>   There, like the visionary emblem seen
>   By him of Babylon, life stands a stump,
>   And filletted about with hoops of brass,
>   Still lives, though all its pleasant boughs are gone,
>   To count the hour-bell and expect no change....
>
> William Cowper.

112. A LATE SPRING

ALL my apricots were cut off by that violent weather in the beginning of March. So deep was the snow, and so starved the birds, that the poor ring doves came into our gardens to crop the leaves and sprouts of the cabbages! Hay is become very scarce and dear indeed! My rick is now almost as slender as the waste of a virgin: and it would have been much for the reputation of the two last brides that I have married, had their wastes been as slender. . . . The first swallow that I heard of was on April 6th, the first nightingale April 13th. The great straddle-bob, Orion, that in the winter seems to bestride my brew-house, is seen now descending of an evening, on one side foremost behind the hanger. The almanack announces Venus to be an evening star, but I have not seen her yet.

Gilbert White.

113. PROTECTIVE COLOURING

THE colour of insects and many smaller animals contribute to conceal them from the larger ones which prey upon them. Caterpillars which feed on leaves are generally green; and earth-worms the colour of the earth which they inhabit; butterflies which frequent flowers are coloured like them; small birds which frequent hedges have greenish backs like the leaves, and light coloured bellies like the sky, and are hence less visible to the hawk, who passes under them or over them. Those birds which are much amongst flowers, as the goldfinch (Fringella Carduelis), are furnished with vivid colours. The lark, partridge, hare, are the colour of dry vegetables, or earth on which they rest. And frogs vary their colour with the mud of the streams which they frequent; and those which live on trees are green. Fish which are generally suspended in water, and swallows, which are generally suspended in air, have their backs the colour of the distant ground, and their bellies of the sky. In the colder climates many of these become white during the existence of the snows.

Erasmus Darwin.

114. THE RIGS O' BARLEY

It was upon a Lammas night,
  When corn rigs are bonnie,
Beneath the moon's unclouded light
  I held awa to Annie:

The time flew by wi' tentless heed,
    Till 'tween the late and early,
Wi' sma' persuasion she agreed
    To see me thro' the barley.

The sky was blue, the wind was still,
    The moon was shining clearly;
I set her down wi' right good will
    Amang the rigs o 'barley;
I kent her heart was a' my ain;
    I loved her most sincerely;
I kissed her owre and owre again
    Amang the rigs o' barley.

I locked her in my fond embrace;
    Her heart was beating rarely;
My blessings on that happy place,
    Amang the rigs o' barley!
But by the moon and stars so bright,
    That shone that hour so clearly,
She aye shall bless that happy night
    Amang the rigs o' barley.

I hae been blythe wi' comrades dear;
    I hae been merry drinking;
I hae been joyfu 'gatherin' gear;
    I hae been happy thinking:
But a' the pleasures e'er I saw,
    Tho 'three times doubled fairly,
That happy night was worth them a',
    Amang the rigs o' barley.

Corn rigs, an' barley rigs,
    An' corn rigs are bonnie:
I'll ne'er forget that happy night,
    Amang the rigs wi' Annie.
              Robert Burns.

115. HERMITAGES IN THE SAVAGE WILDERNESS

I COULD not give you any account of my return from Loretto till this day. I arrived here on the sixth of May. I was for fifteen days in perpetual motion! The journey was beyond all description curious and picturesque; much more so than is the route from hence to Florence. There is a strange mixture of savage wildness and of domestic scenery, of plain and precipice, such as the eye delights to wander over. I can safely swear to you, that the tints of these mountains by far exceed all I have ever observed under your Tuscan skies; and as for your Verucola, which I once thought a dreary desert, I shall henceforth deem it a fair garden, in comparison with the scenes I have now explored in these Alpine solitudes. O God! how often have I sighed to possess, how often since called to mind, those solitary hermitages which I passed on my way!—How often wished that fortune had reserved for me such a destiny!   *Salvator Rosa (translated by Lady Morgan)*.

116. VIA COELI: THE ENTRANCE TO THE GRANDE CHARTREUSE

IN an hour's time we were drawing near, and could discern the opening of a narrow valley overhung by shaggy precipices, above which rose lofty peaks, covered to their very summits with wood. We could now distinguish the roar of torrents, and a confusion of strange sounds, issuing from dark forests of pine. I confess at this moment I was somewhat startled. I experienced some disagreeable sensations, and it was not without a degree of unwillingness that I left the gay pastures and enlivening sunshine, to throw myself into this gloomy and disturbed region. How dreadful, thought I, must be the despair of those who enter it never to return!

But after the first impression was worn away all my curiosity redoubled; and desiring our guide to put forward with greater speed, we made such good haste, that the meadows and cottages of the plain were soon left far behind, and we found ourselves on the banks of the torrent, whose agitation answered the ideas which its sounds had inspired. Into the midst of these troubled waters we were obliged to plunge with our horses, and, when landed on the opposite shore, were by no means displeased to have passed them.

We had now closed with the forests, over which the impending rocks diffused an additional gloom. The day grew obscured by clouds, and the sun no longer enlightened the distant plains, when we began to ascend towards the entrance of the desert, marked by two pinnacles of rock far above us, beyond which a melancholy twilight prevailed. Every moment we approached nearer and nearer to the sounds which had alarmed us; and, suddenly emerging from the woods, we discovered several mills and forges, with many complicated machines of iron, hanging over the torrent, that threw itself headlong from a cleft in the precipices; on one side of which I perceived our road winding along, until it was stopped by a venerable gateway. A rock above one of the forges was hollowed into the shape of a round tower, of no great size, but resembling very much an altar in figure; and what added greatly to the grandeur of the object, was a livid flame palpitating upon it, which the gloom of the valley rendered perfectly discernible.

The road, at a small distance from this remarkable scene, became so narrow, that, had my horse started, I should have been but too well acquainted with the torrent that raged beneath; dismounting, therefore, I walked towards the edge of the great fall, and there, leaning on a fragment of cliff, looked down into the foaming gulph, where the waters were hurled along over broken pines, pointed rocks, and stakes of iron. Then, lifting up my eyes, I took in the vast extent of the forests, frowning on the brows of the mountains.

It was here first I felt myself seized by the genius of the place, and penetrated with veneration of its religious gloom; and, I believe, uttered many extravagant exclamations; but, such was the dashing of the wheels, and the rushing of the waters at the bottom of the forges, that what I said was luckily undistinguishable.

I was not yet, however, within the consecrated inclosure, and therefore not perfectly contented; so, leaving my fragment, I paced in silence up the path which led to the great portal. When we arrived before it, I rested a moment, and looking against the stout oaken gate, which closed up the entrance to this unknown region, felt at my heart a certain awe, that brought to my mind the sacred terror of those, in ancient days, going to be admitted into the Eleusinian mysteries.

My guide gave two knocks; after a solemn pause, the gate was slowly opened, and all our horses having passed through it, was again carefully closed.

I now found myself in a narrow dell, surrounded on every side by peaks of the mountains, rising almost beyond my sight, and shelving downwards till their bases were hidden by the foam and spray of the water, over which hung a thousand withered and distorted trees. The rocks seemed crowded upon me, and, by their peculiar situation, threatening to obstruct every ray of light; but, notwithstanding the menacing appearance of the prospect, I still kept following my guide, up a craggy ascent, partly hewn through a rock, and bordered by the trunks of ancient fir trees, which formed a fantastic barrier, till we came to a dreary and exposed promontory, impending directly over the dell.

The woods are here clouded with darkness, and the torrents rushing with additional violence are lost in the gloom of the caverns below; every object, as I looked downwards from my path, that hung midway between the base and the summit of the cliff, was horrid and woeful. The channel of the torrent sunk deep amidst frightful crags, and the pale willows and wreathed roots spreading over it, answered my ideas of those dismal abodes, where, according to the druidical mythology, the ghosts of conquered warriors were bound. I shivered whilst I was regarding these regions of desolation, and quickly lifting up my eyes to vary the scene, I perceived a range of whitish cliffs glistening with the light of the sun, to emerge from these melancholy forests.

On a fragment that projected over the chasm, and concealed for a moment its terrors, I saw a cross on which was written VIA COELI. The cliffs being the heaven to which I now aspired, we deserted the edge of the precipice, and ascending, came to a retired nook of rocks, in which several copious rills had worn irregular grottoes. Here we reposed an instant, and were enlivened with a few sunbeams, piercing the thickets and gilding the waters that bubbled from the rock, over which hung another cross, with this short sentence, which the situation rendered wonderfully pathetic, O SPES UNICA! the fervent exclamation of some wretch disgusted with the world whose only consolation was found in this retirement.

William Beckford.

117. THE LASS THAT MADE THE BED TO ME

WHEN Januar' wind was blawing cauld,
    As to the north I took my way,
The mirksome night did me enfauld,
    I knew na where to lodge till day.

By my good luck a maid I met,
    Just in the middle o' my care;
And kindly she did me invite
    To walk into a chamber fair.

I bow'd fu' low unto this maid,
    And thank'd her for her courtesie;
I bow'd fu' low unto this maid,
    And bade her mak a bed to me.

She made the bed baith large and wide,
    Wi' twa white hands she spread it down;
She put the cup to her rosy lips,
    And drank, "Young man, now sleep ye soun'."

She snatch'd the candle in her hand,
    And frae my chamber went wi' speed;
But I call'd her quickly back again
    To lay some mair below my head.

A cod she laid below my head,
    And served me wi 'due respect;
And, to salute her wi' a kiss,
    I put my arms about her neck.

"Haud aff your hands, young man," she says,
   "And dinna sae uncivil be:
If ye hae ony love for me,
   O wrang na my virginitie!"

Her hair was like the links o' gowd,
   Her teeth were like the ivorie;
Her cheeks like lilies dipt in wine,
   The lass that made the bed to me.

Her bosom was the driven snaw,
   Two drifted heaps sae fair to see;
Her limbs the polish'd marble stane,
   The lass that made the bed to me.

I kiss'd her owre and owre again,
   And aye she wist na what to say;
I laid her between me and the wa',—
   The lassie thought na lang till day.

Upon the morrow when we rose,
   I thank'd her for her courtesie;
But aye she blush'd, and aye she sigh'd
   And said "Alas! ye've ruin'd me."

I clasp'd her waist, and kiss'd her syne,
   While the tear stood twinkling in her e'e,
I said "My lassie, dinna cry,
   For ye aye shall make the bed to me."

She took her mither's Holland sheets,
   And made them a in sarks to me:
Blythe and merry may she be,
   The lass that made the bed to me.

The bonnie lass made the bed to me,
   The braw lass made the bed to me:
I'll ne'er forget the day I die,
   The lass that made the bed to me!

Robert Burns.

118. OF THE HAND OF GLORY

*Which is made use of by housebreakers, to enter
into houses at night, without fear of opposition*

TAKE the hand, left or right, of a person hanged, and exposed on the highway; wrap it up in a piece of a shroud, or winding-sheet, in which let it be well squeezed, to get out any small quantity of blood that may have remained in it; then put it into an earthen vessel, with zimat, saltpetre, salt, and long pepper, the whole well powdered; leave it fifteen days in that vessel; afterwards take it out, and expose it to the noon-tide sun in the dog-days, till it is thoroughly dry; and if the sun is not sufficient, put it into an oven heated with fern and vervain: then compose a kind of candle with the fat of a hanged man, virgin wax, and sisame of Lapland. The Hand of Glory is used as a candlestick to hold this candle when lighted. Its properties are, that wheresoever any one goes with this dreadful instrument, the persons to whom it is presented will be deprived of all power of motion. . . . The Hand of Glory would cease to take effect, and thieves could not make use of it, if the threshold of the door of the house by which they might enter, were anointed with an unguent composed of the gall of a black cat, the fat of a white hen, and the blood of a screech-owl; which mixture must necessarily be prepared during the dog-days. *Francis Grose.*

119. THE SETTING OF THE MOON

. . . The wan moon is setting ayont the white wave,
And time is setting with me, oh! . . .
Robert Burns,

120. THE RUINED ABBEY IN THE FOREST

HE approached, and perceived the Gothic remains of an abbey: it stood on a kind of rude lawn, overshadowed by high and spreading trees, which seemed coeval with the building, and diffused a romantic gloom around. The greater part of the pile appeared to be sinking into ruins, and that which had withstood the ravages of time showed the remaining features of the fabric more awful in decay. The lofty battlements, thickly enwreathed with ivy, were half demolished, and become the residence of birds of prey. Huge fragments of the eastern tower, which was almost demolished, lay scattered amid the high grass, that waved slowly to the breeze. "The thistle shook its lonely head, the moss whistled to the wind." A Gothic gate, richly ornamented with fretwork, which opened into the main body of the edifice, but which was now obstructed with brushwood; remained entire. Above the vast and magnificent portal of this gate arose a window of the same order, whose pointed arches still exhibited fragments of stained glass, once the pride of monkish devotion. La Motte, thinking it possible it might yet shelter some human being, advanced to the gate and lifted a massy knocker. The hollow sounds rung through the emptiness of the place. After waiting a few minutes he forced back the gate, which was heavy with iron work, and creaked harshly on its hinges.

He entered what appeared to have been the chapel of the abbey, where the hymn of devotion had once been raised, and the tear of penitence had once been shed; sounds which could now only be recalled by imagination—tears of penitence which had been long since fixed in fate. La Motte paused a moment, for he felt a sensation of sublimity rising into terror—a suspension of mingled astonishment and awe! He surveyed the vastness of the place, and as he contemplated its ruins, fancy bore him back to past ages. "And these walls," said he,"where once superstition lurked, and austerity anticipated an earthly purgatory, now tremble over the mortal remains of the beings who reared them!"

The deepening gloom reminded La Motte that he had no time to lose; but curiosity prompted him to explore farther, and he obeyed the impulse. As he walked over the broken pavement, the sound of his steps ran in echoes through the place, and seemed like the mysterious accents of the dead reproving the sacrilegious mortal who thus dared to disturb their holy precincts.

From this chapel he passed into the nave of the great church, of which one window, more perfect than the rest, opened upon a long vista of the forest, and through this was seen the rich colouring of evening, melting by imperceptible gradations into the solemn gray of upper air. Dark hills, whose outline appeared distinctly upon the vivid glow of the horizon, closed the perspective. Several of the pillars, which had once supported the roof, remained, the proud effigies of sinking greatness, and seemed to nod at every murmur of the blast over the fragments of those that had fallen a little before them. La Motte sighed. The comparison between himself and the gradation of decay which these columns exhibited was but too obvious and affecting. "A few years," said he, "and I shall become like the mortals on whose relics I now gaze, and like them, too, I may be the subject of meditation to a succeeding generation, which shall totter but a little while over the object they contemplate, ere they also sink into the dust."

Ann Radcliffe.

121. A PAPER GARDEN

Mrs. Delany has finished nine hundred and seventy accurate and elegant representations of different vegetables with the parts of their flowers, fructification, etc., according with the classification of Linneus, in what she terms paper-mosaic. She began this work at the age of 74, when her sight would no longer serve her to paint, in which she much excelled: between her age of 74 and 82, at which time her eyes quite failed her, she executed the curious Hortus siccus above mentioned, which I suppose contains a greater number of plants than were ever before drawn from the life by any one person. Her method consisted in placing the leaves of each plant, with the petals and all the other parts of the flower, on coloured paper, and cutting them with scissors accurately to the natural size and form, and then pasting them on a dark ground; the effect of which is wonderful, and their accuracy less liable to fallacy than drawings. *Erasmus Darwin.*

122. THE MUSE OF BURNS

... "With future hope I oft would gaze,
Fond, on thy little early ways,
Thy. rudely-caroll'd chiming phrase,
    In uncouth rhymes,—
Fired at the simple artless lays
    Of other times.

"I saw thee seek the sounding shore,
Delighted with the dashing roar;
Or when the North his fleecy store
    Drove thro' the sky,
I saw grim Nature's visage hoar
    Struck thy young eye.

"Or when the deep green-mantled Earth
Warm-cherished ev'ry flow'ret's birth,
And joy and music pouring forth
    In ev'ry grove,
I saw thee eye the gen'ral mirth
    With boundless love.

"When ripen'd fields and azure skies
Call'd forth the reapers' rustling noise,
I saw thee leave their ev'ning joys,
    And lonely stalk,
To vent thy bosom's swelling rise
    In pensive walk.

"When youthful love, warm-blushing, strong,
Keen-shivering shot thy nerves along,
Those accents, grateful to thy tongue,
    Th' adored Name,
I taught thee how to pour in song,
    To soothe thy flame.

"I saw thy pulse's maddening play
Wild send thee pleasure's devious way,
Misled by fancy's meteor ray,
    By passion driven;
But yet the light that led astray
    Was light from Heaven.

"I taught thy manners-painting strains,
The loves, the ways of simple swains,
Till now o'er all my wide domains
    Thy fame extends;
And some, the pride of Coiia's plains,
    Become thy friends.

"Thou canst not learn, nor can I show,
To paint with Thomson's landscape-glow;
Or wake the bosom-melting throe
    With Shenstone's art;
Or pour with Gray the moving flow
    Warm on the heart.

"Yet all beneath th' unrivall'd rose
The lowly daisy sweetly blows;
Tho' large the forest's monarch throws
    His army shade,
Yet green the juicy hawthorn grows
    Adown the glade.

"Then never murmur nor repine;
Strive in thy humble sphere to shine;
And trust me, not Potosi's mine,
    Nor king's regard,
Can give a bliss o'ermatching thine,
    A rustic Bard.

"To give my counsels all in one,
Thy tuneful flame still careful fan;
Preserve the dignity of Man
    With Soul erect;
And trust the Universal Plan
    Will all protect.

> "And wear thou this": She solemn said,
> And bound the holly round my head:
> The polish'd leaves and berries red
>   Did rustling play;
> And, like a passing thought, she fled
>   In light away.
>
> Robert Burns.

123. GOD'S GIFTS IN MEN

ONCE I saw a Devil in a flame of fire, who arose before an Angel that sat on a cloud, and the Devil utter'd these words:

"The worship of God is: Honouring his gifts in other men, each according to his genius, and loving the greatest men best: those who envy or calumniate great men hate God; for there is no other God."

The Angel hearing this became almost blue; but mastering himself he grew yellow, & at last white, pink, & smiling.

William Blake.

124. THE LAPWING

> O LAPWING, thou fliest around the heath,
> Nor seest the net that is spread beneath.
> Why dost thou not fly among the corn fields?
> They cannot spread nets where a harvest yields.
>
> William Blake.

125. LIBERTY AND RUINS

SOLITARY Ruins, sacred Tombs, ye mouldering and silent Walls, all hail! To you I address my Invocation. While the vulgar shrink from your aspect with secret terror, my heart finds in the contemplation a thousand delicious sentiments, a thousand admirable recollections. Pregnant, I may truly call you, with useful lessons, with pathetic and irresistible advice, to the man who knows how to consult you. A while ago the whole world bowed the neck in silence before the tyrants that oppressed it; and yet in that hopeless moment you already proclaimed the truths that tyrants hold in abhorrence: mixing the dust of the proudest kings with that of the meanest slaves, you called upon us to contemplate this example of EQUALITY. From your caverns, whither the musing and anxious love of LIBERTY led me, I saw escape its venerable shade, and with unexpected felicity direct its flight, and marshal my steps, the way to renovated France.

Tombs, what virtue and potency do you exhibit! Tyrants tremble at your aspect, you poison with secret alarm their impious pleasures; they turn from you with impatience, and, coward-like, endeavour to forget you amid the sumptuousness of their palaces. It is you that brings home the rod of justice to the powerful oppressor; it is you that wrest the ill-gotten gold from the merciless extortioner, and avenge the cause of him that has none to help; you compensate the narrow enjoyments of the poor by dashing with care the goblet of the rich: to the unfortunate you offer a last and inviolable asylum; in fine, you give to the soul that just equilibrium of strength and tenderness, which constitutes the wisdom of the sage and the science of life. *C.F.Volney.*

126. FRAGMENT

SPIRIT, who lov'st Britannia's Isle
Round which the Fiends of Commerce smile.
William Blake.

127. CLAUDE

THE peculiar excellence of the painter, who most studied the beautiful in landscape, is characterized by *il riposo di Claudio*; and when the mind of man is in the delightful state of repose, of which Claude's pictures are the image,—when he feels that mild and equal sunshine of the soul, which warms and cheers, but neither inflames nor irritates,—his heart seems to dilate with happiness, he is disposed to every act of kindness and benevolence, to love and cherish all around him . . . . A mind in such a state, is like the surface of a pure and tranquil lake *Uvedale Price.*

128. AN EVENING WALK

... But now the clear bright Moon her zenith gains,
And, rimy without speck, extend the plains:
The deepest cleft the mountain's front displays
Scarce hides a shadow from her searching rays;
From the dark-blue faint silvery threads divide
The hills, while gleams below the azure tide;
Time softly treads; throughout the landscape breathes
A peace enlivened, not disturbed, by wreaths
Of charcoal-smoke, that, o'er the fallen wood,
Steal down the hill, and spread along the flood.

    The song of mountain-streams, unheard by day,
Now hardly heard, beguiles my homeward way.
Air listens, like the sleeping water, still,
To catch the spiritual music of the hill,
Broke only by the slow clock tolling deep,
Or shout that wakes the ferry-man from sleep,
The echoed hoof nearing the distant shore;
The boat's first motion—made with dashing oar;
Sound of closed gate, across the water borne,
Hurrying the timid hare through rustling corn;
The sportive outcry of the mocking owl;
And at long intervals the mill-dog's howl;
The distant forge's swinging thump profound;
Or yell, in the deep woods, of lonely hound.
                              William Wordsworth.

129. HOLLOW ROADS

IT is a singular circumstance, that some of the most striking varieties of form, of colour, and of light and shade, should . . . be owing to the indiscriminate hacking of the peasant, nay, to the very decay that is occasioned by it. When opposed to the tameness of the poor pinioned trees of a gentleman's plantation drawn up strait and even together, there is often a sort of spirit and animation in the manner in which old neglected pollards stretch out their immense limbs right across one of these hollow roads, and in every wild and irregular direction: on some the large knots and protuberances add to the ruggedness of their twisted trunks; in others, the deep hollow of the inside, the mosses on the bark, the rich yellow of the touchwood, with the blackness of the more decayed substance, afford such variety of tints, of brilliant and mellow lights, with deep and peculiar shades, as the finest timber tree (however beautiful in other respects) with all its health and vigour, cannot exhibit. . . . The ground itself, in these lanes, is as much varied in form, tint and light and shade, as the plants that grow upon it; this, as usual, instead of owing any thing to art, is, on the contrary, occasioned by accident and neglect. The winter torrents, in some places, wash down the mould from the upper grounds, and form projections of various shapes, which, from the fatness of the soil, are generally enriched with the most luxuriant vegetation; in other parts, they tear the banks into deep hollows, discovering the different strata of earth, and the shaggy roots of trees; these hollows are frequently overgrown with wild roses, with honeysuckles, periwincles, and other trailing plants, whose flowers and pendent branches have quite a different effect when hanging loosely over one of these recesses, opposed to its deep shade, and mixed with the fantastic roots of trees, and the varied tints of the soil, from those that are cut into bushes, or crawl along the uniform slope of a mowed or dug shrubbery. *Uvedale Price.*

130. PROVERBS OF HELL

IN seed time learn, in harvest teach, in winter enjoy.
Drive your cart and your plow over the bones of the dead.
The road of excess leads to the palace of wisdom.
Prudence is a rich, ugly old maid courted by Incapacity.
He who desires but acts not, breeds pestilence.
The cut worm forgives the plow.
Dip him in the river who loves water.
A fool sees not the same tree that a wise man sees.
He whose face gives no light, shall never become a star.

Eternity is in love with the productions of time.
The busy bee has no time for sorrow.
The hours of folly are measur'd by the clock; but of wisdom no clock can measure.
All wholesome food is caught without a net or trap.
Bring out number, weight and measure in a year of dearth.
No bird soars too high, if he soars with his own wings.
A dead body revenges not injuries.
The most sublime act is to set another before you.
If the fool would persist in his folly he would become wise.
Folly is the cloke of knavery.
Shame is Pride's cloke.
Prisons are built with stones of Law, Brothels with bricks of Religion.
The pride of the peacock is the glory of God.
The lust of the goat is the bounty of God.
The wrath of the lion is the wisdom of God.
The nakedness of woman is the work of God.
Excess of sorrow laughs. Excess of joy weeps.
The roaring of lions, the howling of wolves, the raging of the stormy sea, and the destructive sword, are portions of eternity, too great for the eye of man.
The fox condemns the trap, not himself.
Joys impregnate. Sorrows bring forth.
Let man wear the fell of the lion, woman the fleece of the sheep.
The bird a nest, the spider a web, man friendship.
The selfish, smiling fool, and the sullen, frowning fool shall be both thought wise, that they may be a rod.
What is now proved was once only imagin'd.
The rat, the mouse, the fox, the rabbet watch the roots; the lion, the tyger, the horse, the elephant watch the fruits.
The cistern contains: the fountain overflows.
One thought fills immensity.
Always be ready to speak your mind, and a base man will avoid you.
Every thing possible to be believ'd is an image of truth.
The eagle never lost so much time as when he submitted to learn of the crow.

The fox provides for himself, but God provides for the lion.
Think in the morning. Act in the noon. Eat in the evening. Sleep in the night.
He who has suffer'd you to impose on him, knows you.
As the plow follows words, so God rewards prayers.
The tygers of wrath are wiser than the horses of instruction.
Expect poison from the standing water.
You never know what is enough unless you know what is more than enough.
Listen to the fool's reproach! it is a kingly title!
The eyes of fire, the nostrils of air, the mouth of water, the beard of earth.
The weak in courage is strong in cunning.
The apple tree never asks the beech how he shall grow; nor the lion, the horse, how he shall take his prey.
The thankful receiver bears a plentiful harvest.
If others had not been foolish, we should have been so.
The soul of sweet delight can never be defil'd.
When thou seest an Eagle, thou seest a portion of Genius; lift up thy head!
As the caterpiller chooses the fairest leaves to lay her eggs on, so the priest lays his curse on the fairest joys.
To create a little flower is the labour of ages.
Damn braces. Bless relaxes.
The best wine is the oldest, the best water the newest.
Prayers plow not! Praises reap not!
Joys laugh not! Sorrows weep not!
The head Sublime, the heart Pathos, the genitals Beauty, the hands and feet Proportion.
As the air to a bird or the sea to a fish, so is contempt to the contemptible.
The crow wish'd every thing was black, the owl that every thing was white.
Exuberance is Beauty.
If the Lion was advised by the fox, he would be cunning.
Improvement makes straight roads; but the crooked roads without Improvement are the roads of Genius.
Sooner nurse an infant in its cradle than nurse unacted desires.

Where man is not, nature is barren.
Truth can never be told so as to be understood, and not be believ'd.
Enough! or Too much.

William Blake.

131. ETHINTHUS

... Ethinthus, queen of waters, how thou shinest in the sky!
My daughter, how do I rejoice I for thy children flock around
Like the gay fishes on the wave, when the cold moon drinks
    the dew....

William Blake.

132. LOGAN BRAES

O LOGAN, sweetly didst thou glide
That day I was my Willie's bride;
And years sinsyne hae o'er us run,
Like Logan to the simmer sun.
But now thy flow'ry banks appear
Like drumlie winter, dark and drear,
While my dear lad maun face his faes,
Far, far frae me and Logan Braes.

Again the merry month o' May
Has made our hills and valleys gay;
The birds rejoice in leafy bowers,
The bees hum round the breathing flowers;
Blithe morning lifts his rosy eye,
And evening's tears are tears of joy:
My soul, delightless, a' surveys,
While Willie's far frae Logan Braes.

Within yon milk-white hawthorn bush,
Amang her nestlings, sits the thrush;
Her faithfu 'mate will share her toil,
Or wi' his song her cares beguile:

But I, wi' my sweet nurslings here,
Nae mate to help, nae mate to cheer,
Pass widow'd nights and joyless days,
While Willie's far frae Logan Braes.

O wae upon you, men o' state,
That brethren rouse to deadly hate!
As ye mak mony a fond heart mourn,
Sae may it on your heads return!
How can your flinty hearts enjoy
The widow's tears, the orphan's cry?
But soon may peace bring happy days,
And Willie hame to Logan Braes!

Robert Burns.

133. THE ESCURIAL

I RELUCTANTLY left this beautiful court, and was led into a low gallery, roofed and wainscotted with cedar, lined on both sides by ranges of small doors of different-coloured Brazil-wood, looking in appearance at least, as solid as marble. Four sacristans and as many lay-brothers, with large lighted flambeaux of yellow wax in their hands, and who, by the by, never quitted us more the remainder of our peregrinations, stood silent as death, ready to unlock those mysterious entrances.

The first they opened exhibited a buffet, or *credence*, three stories high, set out with many a row of grinning skulls, looking as pretty as gold and diamonds could make them; the second, every possible and impossible variety of odds and ends, culled from the carcases of martyrs; the third, enormous ebony presses, the secrets of which I begged for pity's sake might not be intruded upon for my recreation, as I began to be heartily wearied of sight-seeing; but when my conductors opened the fourth mysterious door, I absolutely shrank back, almost sickened by a perfume of musk and ambergris.

A spacious vault was now disclosed to me—one noble arch, richly panelled: had the pavement of this strange looking chamber been strewn with saffron, I should have thought myself transported to the enchanted courser's forbidden stable we read of in the tale of the Three Calenders.

The Prior, who is not easily pleased, seemed to have suspicions that the seriousness of my demeanour was not entirely orthodox; I overheard him saying to Roxas, "shall I show him the Angel's feather? you know we do not display this our most valued, incomparable relic to everybody, nor unless upon special occasions." — "The occasion is sufficiently special," answered my partial friend; "the letters I brought to you are your warrant, and I beseech your reverence to let us look at this gift of Heaven, which I am extremely anxious myself to adore and venerate."

Forth stalked the Prior, and drawing out from a remarkably large cabinet an equally capacious sliding shelf — (the source, I conjecture, of the potent odour I complained of) — displayed, lying stretched out upon a quilted silken mattress, the most glorious specimen of plumage ever beheld in terrestrial regions — a feather from the wing of the Archangel Gabriel, full three feet long, and of a blushing hue more soft and delicate than that of the loveliest rose. I longed to ask at what precise moment this treasure beyond price had been dropped — whether from the air — on the open ground, or within the walls of the humble tenement of Nazareth; but I repressed all questions of an indiscreet tendency — the why and wherefore, the when and how, for what and to whom such a palpable manifestation of archangelic beauty and wingedness had been vouchsafed.

We all knelt in silence, and when we rose up, after the holy feather had been again deposited in its perfumed lurking-place, I fancied the Prior looked doubly suspicious, and uttered a sort of *humph* very doggedly; nor did his ill-humour evaporate upon my desiring to be conducted to the library. "It is too late for you to see the precious books and miniatures by daylight," replied the crusty old monk, "and you would not surely have me run the risk of dropping wax upon them. No, no, another time, another time, when you come earlier. For the present, let us visit the tombs of the Catholic kings; there our flambeaux will be of service, without doing injury."

He led the way through a labyrinth of cloisters, gloomy as the grave; till, ordering a grated door to be thrown open, the light of our flambeaux fell upon a flight of most beautiful marble steps, polished as a mirror, leading down between walls of the rarest jaspers to a portal of no great size, but enriched with balusters of rich bronze, sculptured architraves, and tablets of inscriptions, in a style of the greatest magnificence.

As I descended the steps, a gurgling sound, like that of a rivulet, caught my ear. "What means this?" said I. "It means," answered the monk, "that the sepulchral cave on the left of the stairs, where repose the bodies of many of our Queens and Infantas, is properly ventilated, running water being excellent for that purpose." I went on, not lulled by these rippling murmurs, but chilled when I reflected through what precincts flows this river of death.

Arrived at the bottom of the stairs, we passed through the portal just mentioned, and entered a circular saloon, not more than five-and-thirty feet in diameter, characterized by extreme elegance, not stern solemnity. The regal sarcophagi, rich in golden ornaments, ranged one above the other, forming panels of the most decorative kind; the lustre of exquisitely sculptured bronze, the pavement of mottled alabaster: in short, this graceful dome, covered with scrolls of the most delicate foliage, appeared to the eye of my imagination more like a subterranean boudoir, prepared by some gallant young magician for the reception of an enchanted and enchanting princess, than a temple consecrated to the king of terrors.

William Beckford.

134. WHA IS THAT AT MY BOWER DOOR?

WHA is that at my bower door?
  O what is it but Findlay.
Then gae your gate, ye'se nae be here!
  Indeed maun I, quo' Findlay.
What mak ye sae like a thief?
  O come and see, quo' Findlay;
Before the morn ye'll work mischief;
  Indeed will I, quo' Findlay.

        Gif I rise and let you in;
           Let me in, quo 'Findlay;
        Ye'll keep me waukin wi' your din;
           Indeed will I, quo' Findlay.
        In my bower if ye should stay;
           Let me stay, quo 'Findlay;
        I fear ye'll bide till break o' day;
           Indeed will I, quo' Findlay.

        Here this night if ye remain;
           I'll remain, quo' Findlay;
        I dread ye'll learn the gate again;
           Indeed will I, quo' Findlay.
        What may pass within this bower—
           Let it pass, quo' Findlay;
        Ye maun conceal till your last hour;
           Indeed will I, quo' Findlay.
                                Robert Burns.

135. ELEGY ON THE DEATH OF PEG NICHOLSON

        PEG NICHOLSON was a gude bay mare,
           As ever trode on airn;
        But now she's floating down the Nith,
           An 'past the mouth o' Cairn.

        Peg Nicholson was a gude bay mare,
           An 'rode thro' thick an' thin;
        But now she's floating down the Nith,
           An' wanting even the skin.

        Peg Nicholson was a gude bay mare,
           An' ance she bare a priest;
        But now she's floating down the Nith,
           For Solway fish a feast.

        Peg Nicholson was a gude bay mare,
           An 'the priest he rode her sair;
        An' meikle oppress'd an' bruised she was,
           As priest-rid cattle are.
                                Robert Burns.

136. HEAVEN AND HELL

WITHOUT Contraries is no progression. Attraction and Repulsion, Reason and Energy, Love and Hate, are necessary to human existence.

From these contraries spring what the religious call Good and Evil. Good is the passive that obeys Reason. Evil is the active springing from Energy.

Good is Heaven. Evil is Hell. *William Blake.*

137. THE LAW OF NATURE

I CONCLUDE . . . that all the social virtues consist in the performance of actions useful both to society and to the individual:

That they may all be traced to the physical object of the preservation of man:

That nature, having implanted in our bosoms the necessity of this preservation, imposes all the consequences arising from it as a law, and prohibits as a crime whatever counteracts the operation of this principle:

That we have within us the germ of all virtue and of all perfection: that we have only to attend to the means of exciting it into action:

That we are happy in exact proportion to the obedience we yield to those laws which nature has established with a view to our preservation:

That all wisdom, all perfection, all law, all virtue, all philosophy consist in the practice of the following axioms, which are founded upon our natural organization:

> Preserve thyself.
> Instruct, thyself.
> Moderate thyself.
> Live for thy fellow-creatures, in order that they may
> live for thee. *C.F.Volney*

138. THE MORNING COMES

. . . The morning comes, the night decays, the watchmen leave
 their stations;
The grave is burst, the spices shed, the linen wrapped up;

The bones of death, the cov'ring clay, the sinews shrunk & dry'd
Reviving shake, inspiring move, breathing, awakening,
Spring like redeemed captives when their bonds & bars are burst.
Let the slave grinding at the mill run out into the field,
Let him look up into the heavens & laugh in the bright air;
Let the inchained soul, shut up in darkness and in sighing,
Whose face has never seen a smile in thirty weary years,
Rise and look out; his chains are loose, his dungeon doors are open;
And let his wife and children return from the oppressor's scourge.
They look behind at every step & believe it is a dream,
Singing: "The Sun has left his blackness & has found a fresher morning,
And the fair Moon rejoices in the clear & cloudless night;
For Empire is no more, and now the Lion & Wolf shall cease." . . .
William Blake.

139. THE BOOK-WORMS

> THROUGH and through the inspired leaves,
>   Ye maggots, make your windings;
> But, oh! respect his lordship's taste,
>   And spare his golden bindings.
Robert Burns.

140. CROMEK

> A PETTY Sneaking Knave I knew —
> O Mr. Cromek, how do ye do?
William Blake.

141. THE TOAD-EATER

> WHAT of earls with whom you have supt,
>   And of dukes that you dined with yestreen?
> Lord! an insect's an insect at most,
>   Though it crawls on the curls of a Queen.
Robert Burns.

142. I CRY:LOVE, LOVE

... "I cry: Love! Love! Love! happy happy Love! free as
   the mountain wind!
Can that be Love that drinks another as a sponge drinks water,
That clouds with jealousy his nights, with weepings all the day,
To spin a web of age around him, grey and hoary, dark,
Till his eyes sicken at the fruit that hangs before his sight?
Such is self-love that envies all, a creeping skeleton
With lamplike eyes watching around the frozen marriage bed.

"But silken nets and traps of adamant will Oothoon spread,
And catch for thee girls of mild silver, or of furious gold,
I'll lie beside thee on a bank & view their wanton play
In lovely copulation, bliss on bliss, with Theotormon:
Red as the rosy morning, lustful as the first born beam,
Oothoon shall view his dear delight, nor e'er with jealous cloud
Come in the heaven of generous love, nor selfish blightings
   bring.

"Does the sun walk in glorious raiment on the secret floor
Where the cold miser spreads his gold; or does the bright
   cloud drop
On his stone threshold? does his eye behold the beam that
   brings
Expansion to the eye of pity? or will he bind himself
Beside the ox to thy hard furrow? does not that mild beam blot
The bat, the owl, the glowing tyger, and the king of night?
The sea fowl takes the wintry blast for a covring to her limbs,
And the wild snake the pestilence to adorn him with gems
   & gold;
And trees & birds & beasts & men behold their eternal joy.
Arise, you little glancing wings, and sing your infant joy!
Arise, and drink your bliss, for every thing that lives is
   holy!" ...   *William Blake.*

143. THE UPAS TREE

... There is a poison tree in the island of Java, which is said by its effluvia to have depopulated the country for 12 or 14 miles round the place of its growth. It is called, in the Malayan language, Bohon-Upas; with the juice of it the most poisonous arrows are prepared; and, to gain this, the condemned criminals are sent to the tree with proper direction both to get the juice and to secure themselves from the malignant exhalations of the tree; and are pardoned if they bring back a certain quantity of the poison. But by the registers there kept not one in four are said to return. Not only animals of all kinds, both quadrupeds, fish, and birds, but all kinds of vegetables also are destroyed by the effluvia of the noxious tree; so that, in a district of 12 or 14 miles round it, the face of the earth is quite barren and rocky intermixed only with the skeletons of men and animals, affording a scene of melancholy beyond what poets have described or painters delineated.

Erasmus Darwin.

144. MISCELLANEOUS SUPERSTITIONS

... The toad has a stone in its head, very efficacious in the cure of divers diseases; but it must be taken out of the animal whilst alive.

The ass has a cross on its back, ever since Christ rode on one of those animals....

The haddock has the mark of St. Peter's thumb, ever since St. Peter took the tribute penny out of the mouth of a fish of that species.

The mandrake grows on gibbets whereon malefactors are exposed, being produced by droppings from the dead body. It resembles the human figure, either male or female; and, when eradicated, sends forth a loud shriek. Pulling up a mandrake is generally fatal to the person that does it, who rarely long survives....

Storks are found in republicks only. During Oliver Cromwell's protectorship, it is pretended they were in England.

Most persons break the shells of eggs, after they have eaten the meat. This was originally done to prevent their being used as boats by witches. *Francis Grose.*

145. THE PRICE OF EXPERIENCE

. . . I am made to sow the thistle for wheat, the nettle for a
    nourishing dainty.
I have planted a false oath in the earth; it has brought forth
    a poison tree.
I have chosen the serpent for a councellor, & the dog
For a schoolmaster to my children.
I have blotted out from light & living the dove & nightingale,
And I have caused the earth worm to beg from door to door.

I have taught the thief a secret path into the house of the
    just.
I have taught pale artifice to spread his nets upon the morning.
My heavens are brass, my earth is iron, my moon a clod of clay,
My sun a pestilence burning at noon & a vapour of death in
    night.

What is the price of Experience? Do men buy it for a song?
Or wisdom for a dance in the street? No, it is bought with the
    price
Of all that a man hath, his house, his wife, his children.
Wisdom is sold in the desolate market where none come to
    buy,
And in the wither'd field where the farmer ploughs for bread
    in vain.

It is an easy thing to triumph in the summer's sun
And in the vintage & to sing on the waggon loaded with corn.
It is an easy thing to talk of patience to the afflicted,
To speak the laws of prudence to the houseless wanderer,
To listen to the hungry raven's cry in wintry season
When the red blood is fill'd with wine & with the marrow of
    lambs.

It is an easy thing to laugh at wrathful elements,
To hear the dog howl at the wintry door, the ox in the slaughter
    house moan;
To see a god on every wind & a blessing on every blast;
To hear sounds of love in the thunder storm that destroys our
    enemies' house;
To rejoice in the blight that covers his field, & the sickness that
    cuts off his children,
While our olive & vine sing & laugh round our door, & our
    children bring fruit & flowers.

Then the groan & the dolor are quite forgotten, & the slave
    grinding at the mill,
And the captive in chains, & the poor in prison, & the soldier
    in the field
When the shatter'd bone hath laid him groaning among the
    happier dead.

It is an easy thing to rejoice in the tents of prosperity:
Thus could I sing & thus rejoice: but it is not so with me. . . .
William Blake.

146. CHARACTERS OF FIRE

i

IN the cavern at Colebrook Dale, where the mineral tar exudes, the eyes of the horse, which was drawing a cart from within towards the mouth of it, appeared like two balls of phosphorus, when he was above 100 yards off, and for a long time before any other part of the animal was visible. In this case I suspect the luminous appearance to have been owing to the light which had entered the eye, being reflected from the back surface of the vitreous humour, and thence emerging again in parallel rays from the animal's eye as it does from the back surface of the drops of the rainbow, and from the water drops which lie, perhaps without contact, on cabbage leaves, and have the brilliancy of quicksilver. This accounts for this luminous appearance being best seen in those animals which have large apertures in their iris, as in cats and horses, and is the only part visible in obscure places, because this is a better reflecting surface than any other part of the animal. If any of these emergent rays from the animal's eye can be supposed to have been reflected from the choroid coat through the semi-transparent retina, this would account for the coloured glare of the eyes of dogs or cats and rabbits in dark corners.

ii

IN some seas, as particularly about the coast of Malabar, as a ship floats along, it seems during the night to be surrounded with fire, and to leave a long tract of light behind it. Whenever the sea is gently agitated, it becomes converted into little stars, every drop as it breaks emits light, like bodies electrified in the dark. Mr. Bomare says, that when he was at the port of Cettes in Languedoc, and bathing with a companion in the sea after a very hot day, they both appeared covered with fire after every immersion, and that laying his wet hand on the arm of his companion, who had then not dipped himself, the exact mark of his hand and fingers was seen in characters of fire. As numerous microscopic insects are found in this shining water, its light is generally ascribed to them, though it seems probable that fish slime in hot countries may become in such a state of incipient putrefaction as to give light, especially when by agitation it is more exposed to the air; otherwise it is not easy to explain why agitation should be necessary to produce this marine light. *Erasmus Darwin.*

147. SIR JOSHUA REYNOLDS

I CONSIDER Reynolds's Discourses to the Royal Academy as the Simulations of the Hypocrite who smiles particularly where he means to Betray. His Praise of Rafael is like the Hysteric Smile of Revenge. His Softness & Candour, the hidden trap & the poisoned feast. . . . I always consider'd True Art & True Artists to be particularly Insulted & Degraded by the Reputation of these Discourses, As much as they were Degraded by the Reputation of Reynolds's Paintings, & that Such Artists as Reynolds are at all times Hired by the Satans for the Depression of Art—A Pretence of Art, To destroy Art.

The Rich Men of England form themselves into a Society to Sell & Not to Buy Pictures. The Artist who does not throw his Contempt on such Trading Exhibitions, does not know either his own Interest or his Duty.

> When Nations grow Old, The Arts grow Cold
> And Commerce settles on every Tree,
> And the Poor & the Old can live upon Gold,
> For all are Born Poor, Aged Sixty three.

Reynolds's Opinion was that Genius May be Taught & that all Pretence to Inspiration is a Lie & a Deceit, to say the least of it. For if it is a Deceit, the whole Bible is Madness. This Opinion originates in the Greeks calling the Muses Daughters of Memory.

The Enquiry in England is not whether a Man has Talents & Genius, But whether he is Passive & Polite & a virtuous Ass & obedient to Noblemen's Opinions in Art & Science. If he is, he is a Good Man. If Not, he must be Starved.

I do not believe that Rafael taught Mich. Angelo, or that Mich. Angelo taught Rafael, any more than I believe the Rose teaches the Lilly how to grow, or the Apple tree teaches the Pear tree how to bear Fruit. I do not believe the tales of Anecdote writers when they militate against Individual character.

Reynolds Thinks that Man Learns all that he knows. I say on the Contrary that Man Brings All that he has or can have Into the World with him. Man is Born Like a Garden ready Planted & Sown. This World is too Poor to produce one Seed.

William Blake.

PART II: THE PEAK

Lately our poets loiter'd in green lanes,
Content to catch the ballads of the plains;
I fancied I had strength enough to climb
A loftier station at no distant time,
And might securely from intrusion doze
Upon the flowers thro' which Ilissus flows.
In those pale olive grounds all voices cease,
And from afar dust fills the paths of Greece.
My slumber broken and my doublet torn,
I find the laurel also bears a thorn.
                                        W. S. Landor.

148. THE FRENCH REVOLUTION

Oh! pleasant exercise of hope and joy!
For mighty were the auxiliars which then stood
Upon our side, we who were strong in love!
Bliss was it in that dawn to be alive,
But to be young was very heaven!—Oh! times,
In which the meagre, stale, forbidding ways
Of custom, law, and statute, took at once
The attraction of a country in romance!
When Reason seemed the most to assert her rights,
When most intent on making of herself
A prime Enchantress—to assist the work
Which then was going forward in her name I
Not favoured spots alone, but the whole earth,
The beauty wore of promise, that which sets
(As at some moment might not be unfelt
Among the bowers of Paradise itself)
The budding rose above the rose full blown.
What temper at the prospect did not wake
To happiness unthought of? The inert
Were roused, and lively natures rapt away!
They who had fed their childhood upon dreams,
The playfellows of fancy, who had made
All powers of swiftness, subtilty, and strength
Their ministers,—who in lordly wise had stirred
Among the grandest objects of the sense,
And dealt with whatsoever they found there
As if they had within some lurking right
To wield it;—they, too, who, of gentle mood,
Had watched all gentle motions, and to these
Had fitted their own thoughts, schemers more mild,
And in the region of their peaceful selves;—
Now was it that both found, the meek and lofty
Did both find, helpers to their heart's desire,
And stuff at hand, plastic as they could wish;
Were called upon to exercise their skill,
Not in Utopia, subterranean fields,

Or some secreted island, Heaven knows where!
But in the very world, which is the world
Of all of us,—the place where in the end
We find our happiness, or not at all!
William Wordsworth.

149. THE PLANT

S<small>EEK'ST</small> thou The Highest—The Greatest? The plant will
   teach thee the lesson.
What it unconsciously is—be thou in purpose the same.
Translated from Schiller by J. H. Merivale.

150. JOY IN THE FLOWERS

... Thou perceivest the Flowers put forth their precious Odours,
And none can tell how from so small a center comes such
   sweets,
Forgetting that within that Center Eternity expands
Its ever during doors that Og & Anak fiercely guard.
First, e'er the morning breaks, joy opens in the flowery bosoms,
Joy even to tears, which the Sun rising dries; first the Wild
   Thyme
And Meadow-sweet, downy & soft waving among the reeds,
Light springing on the air, lead the sweet Dance: they wake
he Honeysuckle sleeping on the Oak; the flaunting beauty
Revels along upon the wind; the White-thorn, lovely May,
Opens her many lovely eyes listening; the Rose still sleeps,
None dare to wake her; soon she bursts her crimson curtain'd
   bed
And comes forth in the majesty of beauty; every Flower,
The Pink, the Jessamine, the Wall-flower, the Carnation,
The Jonquil, the mild Lilly, opes her heavens; every Tree
And Flower & Herb soon fill the air with an innumerable
   Dance,
Yet all in order sweet & lovely....
William Blake.

151. THE METAPHYSICIAN

"How low the world beneath me lies—
I scarce can see those human atoms roll.
How near my Art exalts me to the pole
    That props the fabric of the skies!"
  Thus, sitting on his turret roof astride,
Exclaims the Tiler—so that little mighty man,
Hans Metaphysicus, from closet six feet wide.
    Say on, thou creature of a span!
That tower, from whence thine eye looks down with such
    disdain,
  Whereof—whereon is't built? The cause explain,
How thou thyself didst mount. Its height—so vast in shew—
What serves it, but to peep into the vale below?
              Translated from Schiller by J. H. Merivale.

152. FORGIVENESS OF SINS

MANY Persons, such as Paine & Voltaire, with some of the Ancient Greeks, say: "we will not converse concerning Good & Evil; we will live in Paradise & Liberty." You may do so in Spirit, but not in the Mortal Body as you pretend, till after the Last Judgement; for in Paradise they have no Corporeal & Mortal Body—that originated with the Fall & was call'd Death & cannot be removed but by a Last Judgement. While we are in the world of Mortality we Must Suffer. The Whole Creation Groans to be deliver'd; there will always be as many Hypocrites born as Honest Men, & they will always have superior Power in Mortal Things. You cannot have Liberty in this World without what you call Moral Virtue, & you cannot have Moral Virtue without the Slavery of that half of the Human Race who hate what you call Moral Virtue. . . . The Bible never tells us that devils torment one another thro' Envy; it is thro' this that they torment the Just—but for what do they torment one another? I answer: For the Coercive Laws of Hell, Moral Hypocrisy. They torment a Hypocrite when he is discover'd; they punish a failure in the tormentor who has suffer'd the Subject of his torture to Escape. In Hell all is Self Righteousness; there is no such thing there as Forgiveness of Sin; he who does Forgive Sin is Crucified as an Abettor of Criminals, & he who performs Works of Mercy in any shape whatever, is punish'd &, if possible, destroy'd, not thro 'envy or Hatred or Malice, but thro' Self Righteousness that thinks it does God service, which God is Satan. They do not Envy one another: They contemn & despise one another: Forgiveness of Sin is only at the Judgement Seat of Jesus the Saviour, where the Accuser is cast out, not because he Sins, but because he torments the Just & makes them do what he condemns as Sin & what he knows is opposite to their own Identity.

It is not because Angels are Holier than Men or Devils that makes them Angels, but because they do not expect Holiness from one another, but from God only.

The Player is a liar when he says: "Angels are happier than Men because they are better." Angels are happier than Men & Devils because they are not always Prying after Good & Evil in one another & eating the Tree of Knowledge for Satan's Gratification.

Thinking as I do that the Creator of this World is a very Cruel Being, & being a Worshipper of Christ, I cannot help saying: "the Son, O how unlike the Father!" First God Almighty comes with a Thump on the Head. Then Jesus Christ comes with a balm to heal it.

The Last Judgement is an Overwhelming of Bad Art & Science. Mental Things are alone Real; what is call'd Corporeal, Nobody knows of its Dwelling Place: it is in Fallacy, & its Existence an Imposture. Where is the Existence Out of Mind or Thought? Where is it but in the Mind of a Fool? Some People flatter themselves that there will be No Last Judgement & that Bad Art will be adopted & mixed with Good Art, That Error or Experiment will make a Part of Truth, & they Boast that it is its Foundation; these People flatter themselves: I will not Flatter them. Error is Created. Truth is Eternal. Error, or Creation, will be Burned up, & then, & not till Then, Truth or Eternity will appear. It is burnt up the Moment Men cease to behold it. I assert for

My Self that I do not behold the outward Creation & that to me it is hindrance & not Action; it is as the dirt upon my feet, No part of Me. "What," it will be Question'd, "When the Sun rises, do you not see a round disk of fire somewhat like a Guinea?" O no, no, I see an Innumerable company of the Heavenly host crying, "Holy, Holy, Holy is the Lord God Almighty." I question not my Corporeal or Vegetative Eye any more than I would Question a Window concerning a Sight. I look thro' it & not with it. *William Blake.*

153. IMAGINATION AND THE DREAM OF LIFE

i

I KNOW of no other Christianity and of no other Gospel than the liberty both of body & mind to exercise the Divine Arts of Imagination, Imagination, the real & eternal World of which this Vegetable Universe is but a faint shadow, & in which we shall live in our Eternal or Imaginative Bodies when these Vegetable Mortal Bodies are no more.

William Blake

ii

.... Believe thou, O my soul,
Life is a vision shadowy of Truth;
And vice, and anguish, and the wormy grave,
Shapes of a dream I The veiling clouds retire,
And lo I the Throne of the redeeming God
Forth flashing unimaginable day
Wraps in one blaze earth, heaven, and deepest hell. . . .

S. T. Coleridge.

154. HUMILITY AND DOUBT

... God wants not Man to Humble himself:
That is the trick of the ancient Elf.
This is the Race that Jesus ran:
Humble to God, Haughty to Man,
Cursing the Rulers before the People
Even to the Temple's highest Steeple;

And when he Humbled himself to God,
Then descended the Cruel Rod.
"If thou humblest thyself, thou humblest me;
Thou also dwell'st in Eternity.
Thou art a man, God is no more,
Thy own humanity learn to adore,
For that is my Spirit of Life." . . .
Can that which was of woman born
In the absence of the Morn,
When the Soul fell into Sleep
And Archangels round it weep,
Shooting out against the Light
Fibres of a deadly night,
Reasoning upon its own dark Fiction,
In doubt which is Self Contradiction?
Humility is only doubt,
And does the Sun & Moon blot out,
Rooting over with thorns & stems
The buried Soul & all its Gems.
This Life's dim windows of the Soul
Distorts the Heavens from Pole to Pole
And leads you to Believe a Lie
When you see with, not thro', the Eye
That was born in a night to perish in a night,
When the Soul slept in the beams of Light. . . .
      William Blake.

155. THE EOLIAN HARP

My pensive Sara! thy soft cheek reclined
Thus on mine arm, most soothing sweet it is
To sit beside our Cot, our Cot o'ergrown
With white-flower'd Jasmin, and the broad-leav'd Myrtle,
(Meet emblems they of Innocence and Love!)
And watch the clouds, that late were rich with light,
Slow saddening round, and mark the star of eve
Serenely brilliant (such should Wisdom be)
Shine opposite! How exquisite the scents
Snatch'd from yon bean-field! And the world so hush'd!

The stilly murmur of the distant Sea
Tells us of silence.
                    And that simplest Lute,
Placed length-ways in the clasping casement, hark!
How by the desultory breeze caress'd,
Like some coy maid half yielding to her lover,
It pours such sweet upbraiding, as must needs
Tempt to repeat the wrong! And now, its strings
Boldlier swept, the long sequaceous notes
Over delicious surges sink and rise,
Such a soft floating witchery of sound
As twilight Elfins make, when they at eve
Voyage on gentle gales from Fairy-Land,
Where Melodies round honey-dropping flowers,
Footless and wild, like birds of Paradise,
Nor pause, nor perch, hovering on untam'd wing!

   And thus, my Love! as on the midway slope
Of yonder hill I stretch my limbs at noon,
Whilst through my half-clos'd eye-lids I behold
The sunbeams dance, like diamonds, on the main,
And tranquil muse upon tranquillity;
Full many a thought uncall'd and undetain'd,
And many idle flitting phantasies,
Traverse my indolent and passive brain,
As wild and various as the random gales
That swell and flutter on this subject Lute I

   And what if all of animated nature
Be but organic Harps diversely fram'd,
That tremble into thought, as o'er them sweep
Plastic and vast, one intellectual breeze,
At once the Soul of each, and God of all?. . . .
                                   S. T. Coleridge.

156. LIGHT FROM PLANTS

In Sweden a very curious phenomenon has been observed on certain flowers, by M. Haggern, lecturer in natural history.

One evening he perceived a faint flash of light repeatedly dart from a marigold. Surprised at such an uncommon appearance, he resolved to examine it with attention; and, to be assured it was no deception of the eye, he placed a man near him, with orders to make a signal at the moment when he observed the light. They both saw it constantly at the same moment.

The light was most brilliant on marigolds of an orange or flame colour; but scarcely visible on pale ones. The flash was frequently seen on the same flower two or three times in quick succession; but more commonly at intervals of several minutes; and when several flowers in the same place emitted their light together, it could be observed at a considerable distance.

This phenomenon was remarked in the months of July and August at sun-set, and for half an hour when the atmosphere was clear; but after a rainy day, or when the air was loaded with vapours nothing of it was seen.

The following flowers emitted flashed, more or less vivid, in this order:—

1. The marigold, *calendula officinalis*.
2. Monk's-hood, *tropæolum majus*.
3. The orange-lily, *lilian bulbiferum*.
4. The Indian pink, *tagetes patula et erecta*.

From the rapidity of the flash, and other circumstances, it may be conjectured that there is something of electricity in this phenomenon. *S. T. Coleridge.*

157. A SYMPATHY WITH NATURE

TODAY, for the first time in my life, I have had a distinct sympathy with nature. I was lying on the top of a rock to leeward; the wind was high, and everything in motion; the branches of an oak tree were waving and murmuring to the breeze; yellow clouds, deepened by grey at the base, were rapidly floating over the western hills; the whole sky was in motion; the yellow stream below was agitated by the breeze; everything was alive, and myself part of the series of visible impressions; I should have felt pain in tearing a leaf from one of the trees.
Humphry Davy.

158. WATERCOLOURS AT DOVER

September 3 [1797].—Walked on the beach, watching the retiring and returning waves, and attending to the bursting thunder of the surge.

Afterwards stood on a fortified point below the castle, immediately and high over the beach, commanding a vast marine horizon, with a long tract of the French coast, a white line bounding the blue waters. Below, on the right, Dover curves picturesquely along the sea-bay; the white and green cliffs rising closely over it, except near the castle, where they give place to hills, that open to a green valley, with enclosures and a pretty village, beyond which it winds away. The most grand and striking circumstances, as we stood on the point, were—the vast sea-view—the long shades on its surface of soft green, deepening exquisitely into purple; but, above all, that downy tint of light blue, that sometimes prevailed over the whole scene, and even faintly tinged the French coast, at a distance. Sometimes, too, a white sail passed in a distant gloom, while all between was softly shadowed; the cliffs above us broken and encumbered with fortifications; the sea viewed beyond them, with vessels passing from behind; the solemn sound of the tide breaking immediately below, and answered, as it were, at measured intervals, along the whole coast; this circumstance inexpressibly grand; the sound more solemn and hollow than when heard on the beach below. A fleet of merchantmen, with a convoy, passed and spread itself over the channel.

Afternoon.—Walked towards Shakespeare's Cliff; the fleet still in view. Looked down from the edge of the cliffs on the fine red gravel margin of the sea. Many vessels on the horizon and in mid-channel. The French coast, white and high, and clear in the evening gleam. Evening upon the sea becoming melancholy, silent and pale. A leaden-coloured vapour rising upon the horizon, without confounding the line of separation; the ocean whiter, till the last deep twilight falls, when all is one gradual, inseparable, undistinguishable, grey.

Ann Radcliffe.

159. COPIERS OF NATURE

MEN think they can copy Nature as correctly as I copy Imagination; this they will find impossible, and all the copies or pretended copiers of Nature, from Rembrandt to Reynolds, prove that Nature becomes to its victim nothing but blots and blurs.
William Blake.

160. SNOW AT ALFOXDEN

[*February*] 17*th.*—A deep snow upon the ground. Wm. and Coleridge walked to Mr. Bartholomew's, and to Stowey. Wm. returned, and we walked through the wood into the Coombe to fetch some eggs. The sun shone bright and clear. A deep stillness in the thickest part of the wood, undisturbed except by the occasional dropping of the snow from the holly boughs; no other sound but that of the water, and the slender notes of a redbreast, which sang at intervals on the outskirts of the southern side of the wood. There the bright green moss was bare at the roots of the trees, and the little birds were upon it. The whole appearance of the wood was enchanting; and each tree, taken singly, was beautiful. The branches of the hollies pendent with their white burden, but still showing their bright red berries, and their glossy green leaves. The bare branches of the oaks thickened by the snow.
Dorothy Wordsworth.

161. TOMB-FLIES

WHEN the French, in their war with Pedro of Aragon, took Gerona, a swarm of white flies is said to have proceeded from the body of St. *Narcis,* in the church of St. *Phelin* (I copy the names as they stand in the Catalan author) which stung the French and occasioned such a mortality, that they evacuated the city. This is so extraordinary a miracle that there is probably some truth in it, because miracle-mongers have never the least invention, and because a Cnrious fact in confirmation of it is to be found in the Monthly Magazine for December, 1805. "In preparing for the foundation of the New Church at Lewes, it became necessary to disturb the mouldering bones of the long defunct, and in the prosecution of that unavoidable business a leaden coffin was taken up, which, on being opened, exhibited a complete skeleton of a body that had been interred about sixty years, whose leg and thigh bones, to the utter astonishment of all present, were covered with myriads of flies (of a species, perhaps, totally unknown to the naturalist) as active and strong on the wing as gnats flying in the air, on the finest evening in summer. The wings of this non-descript are white, and for distinction's sake, the spectators gave it the name of the coffin-fly. The lead was perfectly sound, and presented not the least chink or crevice for the admission of air. The moisture of the flesh had not yet left the bones, and the fallen beard lay on the under jaw."

Such a swarm of white flies very probably proceeded from the Saint's coffin; that he produced them by virtue of his saintship, and that they produced the infection among the French, would be believed in that age by all parties.

Robert Southey.

162. A DREAM OF GUILT

[Earl Osmond, who plans to marry his niece, Angela, against her will, had been in love with her mother, Evelina, his sister-in-law. He had killed Evelina when she threw herself between his dagger and her husband, whom Osmond was about to murder.]

OSMOND rushes in wildly.

OSM. Save me! Save me! They are at hand! Oh! let them not enter! (*Sinks into the arms of* SAIB.)

SAIB. What can this mean? See how his eyes roll! How violently he trembles!

HASSAN. Speak, my lord. Do you not know us?

OSM. (*recovering himself*). Ha! Whose voice? Hassan's? And Saib too here? Oh! was it then but a dream? Did I not hear those dreadful, those damning words? Still, still they ring in my ears. Hassan! Hassan! Death must be bliss in flames or on the rack, compared to what I have this night suffered.

Has. Compose yourself, my lord. Can a mere dream unman you thus?

Osm. A mere dream, say'st thou? Hassan, 'twas a dream of such horror, did such dreams haunt my bitterest foe, I should wish him no severer punishment. Mark you not, how the ague of fear still makes my limbs tremble? Roll not my eyes as if still gazing on the spectre? Are not my lips convulsed, as they were yet pressed by the kiss of corruption? Oh!' twas a sight that might have bleached joy's rosy cheek for ever, and strewed the snows of age upon youth's auburn ringlets! Hassan, thou said'st 'twas but a dream—I was deceived by fancy. Hassan, thou said'st true; there is not, there cannot be a world to come.

Has. My lord!—

Osm. Answer me not. Let me not hear the damning truth. Tell me not, that flames await me! that for moments of bliss, I must endure long ages of torture. Say, that with my body must perish my soul. For, oh! should my fearful dream be prophetic—Hark, fellows! Instruments of my guilt, listen to my punishment. Methought I wandered through the low browed caverns, where repose the reliques of my ancestors. My eye dwelt with awe upon their tombs, with disgust on mortality's surrounding emblems. Suddenly a female form glided along the vault: it was Angela! She smiled upon me and beckoned me to advance. I flew towards her; my arms were already unclosed to clasp her—when suddenly her figure changed, her face grew pale, a stream of blood gushed from her bosom—Hassan, 'twas Evelina!

Saib and Has. Evelina!

Osm. Such as when she sank at my feet expiring, while my hand grasped the dagger still crimsoned with her blood. "We meet again this night!" murmured her hollow voice. "Now rush to my arms, but first see what you have made me. Embrace me, my bridegroom. We must never part again!" While speaking her form withered away: the flesh fell from her bones; her eyes burst from their sockets:

a skeleton, loathsome and meagre, clasped me in her mouldering arms!

SAIB. Most horrible!

OSM. Her infected breath was mingled with mine; her rotting fingers pressed my hand, and my face was covered with her kisses. Oh! then, then how I trembled with disgust! And then blue dismal flames gleamed along the walls; the tombs were rent asunder; bands of fierce spectres rushed round me in frantic dance; furiously they gnashed their teeth while they gazed upon me, and shrieked in loud yell— "Welcome, thou fratricide! Welcome, thou lost for ever!" Horror burst the bands of sleep; distracted I flew hither: but my feelings—words are too weak, too powerless to express them.
M. G. Lewis.

163. MALIGNANT FAIRY

THE *Brown Man of the Muirs* is a Fairy of the most malignant order, the genuine *duergar*. Walsingham mentions a story of an unfortunate youth, whose brains were extracted from his skull during his sleep by this malicious being. Owing to this operation he remained insane for many years, till the Virgin Mary courteously restored his brains to their station.
John Leyden.

164. STRANGE TALE

ABOUT fifty years ago, an unfortunate female wanderer took up her residence in a dark vault, among the ruins of Dryburgh Abbey, which, during the day, she never quitted. When night fell, she issued from this miserable habitation, and went to the house of Mr. Haliburton of Newmains, the Editor's great-grandfather, or to that of Mr. Erskine of Sheilfired, two gentlemen of the neighbourhood. From their charity she obtained such necessaries as she could be prevailed upon to accept. At twelve, each night, she lighted her candle, and returned to her vault, assuring her friendly neighbours, that, during her absence, her habitation was arranged by a spirit, to whom she gave the uncouth name of *Fat lips*; describing him as a little man, wearing heavy iron shoes, with which he trampled the clay floor of the vault, to dispel the damps. This circumstance caused her to be regarded, by the well-informed, with compassion, as deranged in her understanding; and, by the vulgar, with some degree of terror. The cause of her adopting this extraordinary mode of life she would never explain. It was, however, believed to have been occasioned by a vow, that, during the absence of a man to whom she was attached, she would never look upon the sun. Her lover never returned. He fell during the civil war of 1745-6, and she never more would behold the light of day. *Sir Walter Scott.*

165. FRAGMENT FROM THE GREEK OF ALCMAN

THE mountain summits sleep: glens, cliffs, and caves
   Are silent—all the black earth's reptile brood,
   The bees, the wild beasts of the mountain wood:
In depths beneath the dark red ocean's waves
   Its monsters rest, whilst, wrapt in bower and spray,
   Each bird is hushed that stretched its pinions to the day.
Thomas Campbell.

166. THE LAKE OF RATZEBURG

YESTER-MORNING I saw the lesser lake completely hidden by mist; but the moment the sun peeped over the hill, the mist broke in the middle, and in a few seconds stood divided, leaving a broad road all across the lake; and between these two walls of mist the sunlight *burnt* upon the ice, forming a road of golden fire, intolerably bright! and the mist-walls themselves partook of the blaze in a multitude of shining colours. This is our second frost. About a month ago, before the thaw came on, there was a storm of wind; during the whole night, such were the thunders and howlings of the breaking ice, that they have left a conviction on my mind, that there are sounds more sublime than any sight *can* be, more absolutely suspending the power of comparison, and more utterly absorbing the mind's self-consciousness in its total attention to the object working upon it. Part of the ice which the vehemence of the wind had shattered, was driven shoreward and froze anew. On the evening of the next day, at sunset, the shattered ice thus frozen, appeared of a deep blue, and in shape like an agitated sea; beyond this the water, that ran up between the great islands of ice which had preserved their masses entire and smooth, shone of a yellow green; but all these scattered ice-islands, themselves, were of an intensely, bright blood colour—they seemed blood and light in union! On some of the largest of these islands, the fishermen stood pulling out their immense nets through the holes made in the ice for this purpose, and the men, their net-poles, and their huge nets, were a part of the glory; say rather, it appeared as if the rich crimson light had shaped itself into these forms, figures, and attitudes, to make a glorious vision in mockery of earthly things. *S. T. Coleridge.*

167. THRUSH AND BLACKTHORN

... The sporting white-throat on some twig's end borne,
Pour'd hymns to freedom and the rising morn;
Stopt in her song perchance the starting thrush
Shook a white shower from the blackthorn bush,
Where dew drops thick as early blossoms hung,
And trembled as the minstrel sweetly sung. ...
Robert Bloomfield.

168. THERE WAS A BOY

THERE was a Boy; ye knew him well, ye cliffs
And islands of Winander!—many a time,
At evening, when the earliest stars began
To move along the edges of the hills,
Rising or setting, would he stand alone,
Beneath the trees, or by the glimmering lake;
And there, with fingers interwoven, both hands
Pressed closely palm to palm and to his mouth

Uplifted, he, as through an instrument,
Blew mimic hootings to the silent owls,
That they might answer him.—And theywould shout
Across the watery vale, and shout again,
Responsive to his call,—with quivering peals,
And long halloos, and screams, and echoes loud
Redoubled and redoubled; concourse wild
Of mirth and jocund din! And, when there came a pause
Of silence such as baffled his best skill:
Then, sometimes, in that silence, while he hung
Listening, a gentle shock of mild surprise
Has carried far into his heart the voice
Of mountain-torrents; or the visible scene
Would enter unawares into his mind
With all its solemn imagery, its rocks,
Its woods, and that uncertain heaven, received
Into the bosom of the steady lake. . . .
                              William Wordsworth.

169. CHAROBA AT HER BATH

. . . Next to her chamber, closed by cedar doors,
A bath, of purest marble, purest wave,
On its fair surface bore its pavement high.
Arabian gold enchased its crystal roof,
With fluttering boys adorn'd and girls unrobed,
These, when you touch the quiet water, start
From their aerial sunny arch, and pant
Entangled mid each other's flowery wreaths,
And each pursuing is in turn pursued.
Here came at last, as ever wont at morn,
Charoba: long she linger'd at the brink,
Often she sighed, and, naked as she was,
Sat down, and leaning on the couch's edge,
On the soft inward pillow of her arm
Rested her burning cheek: she moved her eyes;
She blush'd; and blushing plung'd into the wave. . . .
                              W. S. Landor.

170. A STONE

THE flat pink-colour'd stone painted over in jagged circles and strange parallelograms with the greenish black-spotted lichens—
S. T. Coleridge.

171. INFLUENCE OF NATURAL OBJECTS

IN CALLING FORTH AND STRENGTHENING THE IMAGINATION IN BOYHOOD AND EARLY YOUTH

WISDOM and Spirit of the universe!
Thou Soul, that art the Eternity of thought!
And giv'st to forms and images a breath
And everlasting motion! not in vain,
By day or star-light, thus from my first dawn
Of childhood didst thou intertwine for me
The passions that build up our human soul;
Not with the mean and vulgar works of Man;
But with high objects, with enduring things,
With life and nature; purifying thus
The elements of feeling and of thought,
And sanctifying by such discipline
Both pain and fear,—until we recognize
A grandeur in the beatings of the heart.

   Nor was this fellowship vouchsafed to me
With stinted kindness. In November days,
When vapours rolling down the valleys made
A lonely scene more lonesome; among woods
At noon; and 'mid the calm of summer nights,
When, by the margin of the trembling lake,
Beneath the gloomy hills, I homeward went
In solitude, such intercourse was mine:
'Twas mine among the fields both day and night,
And by the waters, all the summer long.
And in the frosty season, when the sun
Was set, and visible for many a mile,

The cottage-windows through the twilight blazed,
I heeded not the summons: happy time
It was indeed for all of us; for me
It was a time of rapture! Clear and loud
The village-clock tolled six—I wheeled about,
Proud and exulting like an untired horse
That cares not for his home.—All shod with steel
We hissed along the polished ice, in games
Confederate, imitative of the chase
And woodland pleasures,—the resounding horn,
The pack loud-chiming, and the hunted hare.
So through the darkness and the cold we flew,
And not a voice was idle: with the din
Smitten, the precipices rang aloud;
The leafless trees and every icy crag
Tinkled like iron; while far-distant hills
Into the tumult sent an alien sound
Of melancholy, not unnoticed while the stars,
Eastward, were sparkling clear, and in the west
The orange sky of evening died away.

   Not seldom from the uproar I retired
Into a silent bay, or sportively
Glanced sideway,. leaving the tumultuous throng,
To cut across the reflect of a star;
Image that, flying still before me, gleamed
Upon the glassy plain: and oftentimes,
When we had given our bodies to the wind,
And all the shadowy banks on either side
Came sweeping through the darkness, spinning still
The rapid line of motion, then at once
Have I, reclining back upon my heels,
Stopped short; yet still the solitary cliffs
Wheeled by me—even as if the earth had rolled
With visible motion her diurnal round!
Behind me did they stretch in solemn train,
Feebler and feebler, and I stood and watched
Till all was tranquil as a summer sea.
William Wordsworth.

172. THE NYMPH

... 'Twas evening, though not sunset, and the tide
Level with these green meadows, seem'd yet higher:
'Twas pleasant; and I loosen'd from my neck
The pipe you gave me, and began to play.
O that I ne'er had learnt the tuneful art!
It always brings us enemies or love.
Well, I was playing, when above the waves
Some swimmer's head methought I saw ascend;
I, sitting still, survey'd it, with my pipe
Awkwardly held before my lips half-closed.
Gebir! it was a Nymph! a Nymph divine!
I cannot wait describing how she came,
How I was sitting, how she first assum'd
The sailor: of what happened, there remains
Enough to say, and too much to forget.
The sweet deceiver stept upon this bank
Before I was aware; for, with surprize
Moments fly rapid as with love itself.
Stooping to tune afresh the hoarsen'd reed,
I heard a rustling; and where that arose
My glance first lighted on her nimble feet.
Her feet resembled those long shells explored
By him who to befriend his steeds' dim sight
Would blow the pungent powder in their eye.
Her eyes too! O immortal Gods I her eyes
Resembled—what could they resemble—what
Ever resemble those! E'en her attire
Was not of wonted woof nor vulgar art:
Her mantle shew'd the yellow samphire-pod,
Her girdle, the dove-colour'd wave serene.
"Shepherd," said she, "and will you wrestle now
And with the sailor's hardier race engage?"
I was rejoiced to hear it, and contrived
How to keep up contention;—could I fail
By pressing not too strongly, yet to press?
"Whether a shepherd, as indeed you seem,

Or whether of the hardier race you boast,
I am not daunted, no: I will engage."
"But first," said she, "what wager will you lay?"
"A sheep," I answered; "add whate'er you will."
"I cannot," she replied, "make that return:
Our hided vessels, in their pitchy round
Seldom, unless from rapine, hold a sheep.
But I have sinuous shells, of pearly hue
Within, and they that lustre have imbibed
In the sun's palace porch; where when unyoked
His chariot wheel stands midway in the wave.
Shake one, and it awakens, then apply
Its polished lips to your attentive ear,
And it remembers its august abodes,
And murmurs as the ocean murmurs there.
And I have others given me by the nymphs,
Of sweeter sound than any pipe you have.—
But we, by Neptune, for no pipe contend;
This time a sheep I win, a pipe the next."
Now came she forward, eager to engage;
But first her dress, her bosom then, survey'd,
And heav'd it, doubting if she could deceive.
Her bosom seem'd, inclos'd in haze like heav'n,
To baffle touch; and rose forth undefined.
Above her knees she drew the robe succinct,
Above her breast, and just below her arms:
"This will preserve my breath, when tightly bound,
If struggle and equal strength should so constrain."
Thus, pulling hard to fasten it, she spoke,
And, rushing at me, closed. I thrill'd throughout
And seem'd to lessen and shrink up with cold.
Again, with violent impulse gushed my blood;
And hearing nought external, thus absorb'd,
I heard it, rushing through each turbid vein,
Shake my unsteady swimming sight in air.
Yet with unyielding though uncertain. arms,
I clung around her neck; the vest beneath
Rustled against our slippery limbs entwined:
Often mine, springing with eluded force,

Started aside, and trembled, till replaced:
And when I most succeeded, as I thought,
My bosom and my throat felt so comprest
That life was almost quivering on my lips,
Yet nothing was there painful! these are signs
Of secret arts, and not of human might,
What arts I cannot tell: I only know
My eyes grew dizzy, and my strength decay'd,
I was indeed o'ercome!—with what regret,
And more, with what confusion, when I reached
The fold, and yielding up the sheep, she cried,
"This pays a shepherd to a conquering maid."
She smil'd, and more of pleasure than disdain
Was in her dimpled chin, and liberal lip,
And eyes that languished, lengthening,—just like love.
She went away; I on the wicker gate
Leant, and could follow with my eyes alone.
The sheep she carried easy as a cloak.
But when I heard its bleating, as I did,
And saw, she hastening on, its hinder feet
Struggle, and from her snowy shoulder slip,
(One shoulder its poor efforts had unveil'd,)
Then, all my passions mingling fell in tears!
Restless than ran I to the highest ground
To watch her; she was gone; gone down the tide;
And the long moonbeam on the hard wet sand
Lay like a jasper column half-uprear'd. . . .
W. S. Landor.

173. LIONS OF ROMANCE

Il est vray que le lyon est sire and roy de toutes les bestes du monde, et est de si franche nature et de si haulte que sil trouvoit fitx de roy de loyal pere et de loyalle mere ja nul mal ne lid feroit (Lancelot du Lac, p. 2, ff. 127). The experiment was tried upon Lenvalles, son of King Eliezer, to prove his birth when he was three days old.

Beaumont and Fletcher have made a humorous view of this notion in the Mad Lover. When Memnon has lost his wits for love of the Princess, they endeavour to pass upon him a woman of a very different description for her. The lady begins by giving him a kiss. He, however, takes her "royal hand as more than he must purchase," and finding good cause for suspicion, exclaims,

> Fetch the Numidian lion I brought over, . . .
> If she be sprung from royal blood, the lion
> Will do you reverence; else—
> WOMAN. I beseech your lordship—
> MEMNON. He'll tear her all to pieces.

A century ago the lions in the Tower were named after the reigning kings; and "it has been observed," says a writer of that age, "that when a king dies, the lion of that name dies after him." . . . The true lion is jealous of the leopard, who "is a very tyrant, and advouterous in his kind; and he knoweth, sayth Pliny, when the lyonesse hath played him false play, and hath played the advoutresse with the libard, by a certain rammish * smell or sweate which ariseth of them both; yet if she washeth herselfe throughly, she may deceyve him. The leoparde hath his cabbage in the yearth, with two contrary wayes undermined to enter into it, or to run out of it at his pleasure; verie wide at the coming in, but as narrow and straight about the mid cabbage: whether his enemie the lion, running sometimes after him and apace, at the first coming in thither, is narrowly pent, insomuch that he cannot neyther get forward nor backwarde. That seeing the leoparde, he runneth apace out of the furder hole, and commeth to that whereas the lion first ran in, and having him hard pent, and his backe towards him, bighteth and scratcheth him with tooth and nayle, and so by art the leopard getteth the victory, and not by strength."

The greene Forest, or a naturale historie, &c. compiled by John Maplet, M. of Arte, student in Cambridge, entending hereby that God might especially be glorified, and the people furdered. London, 1567.   *R. Southey.*

---

* It is curious to see how this M. of Arte has debased the expressions of Pliny—odore pardi coitum sentit in adultera lea, totaque vi consurgit in poenam. Idcirco ea culpa flumine abluitur, aut longius comitatur. L. 8, § 17.

174. MEMORANDUM

MEM: not to adulterize my time by absenting myself from my wife. *S. T. Coleridge.*

175. COLERIDGE AND HIS CHILD

. . . Dear Babe, that sleepest cradled by my side,
Whose gentle breathings, heard in this deep calm,
Fill up the interspersed vacancies
And momentary pauses of the thought!
My babe so beautiful! It thrills my heart
With tender gladness, thus to look at thee,
And think that thou shalt learn far other lore
And in far other scenes! For I was reared
In the great city, pent 'mid cloisters dim,
And saw nought lovely but the sky and stars.
But thou, my babe! shalt wander like a breeze
By lakes and sandy shores, beneath the crags
Of ancient mountain, and beneath the clouds,
Which image in their bulk both lakes and shores
And mountain crags: so shalt thou see and hear
The lovely shapes and sounds intelligible
Of that eternal language, which thy God
Utters, who from eternity doth teach
Himself in all, and all things in himself.
Great universal Teacher! he shall mould
Thy spirit, and by giving make it ask.

 Therefore all seasons shall be sweet to thee,
Whether the summer clothe the general earth
With greenness, or the redbreast sit and sing
Betwixt the tufts of snow on the bare branch
Of mossy apple-tree, while the nigh thatch
Smokes in the sun-thaw; whether the eve-drops fall
Heard only in the trances of the blast,
Or if the secret ministry of frost
Shall hang them up in silent icicles,
Quietly shining to the quiet Moon.

S. T. Coleridge.

176. THE NOBLE

... There is
One great society alone on earth:
The noble Living and the noble Dead. . . .
William Wordsworth.

177. GLOW-BEAST

"The Valley of Chalchaquina, running 30 leagues in length from N. to S., is but of a small breadth, and almost enclosed on both sides by high ridges of mountains, that makes the borders of Peru and Chile. It is reported that in the night there is a sort of creature seen here which casts a mighty light from its head, and many are of opinion that light is caused by a carbuncle; but as yet this creature could never be taken or killed, because it suddenly baffles all the designs of men, leaving them in the dark by clouding that light." *

The existence of this animal is still believed. The Missionary Fr. Narciso y Barcel says, in a letter written in 1791, "I had scarcely reached Manoa before I began the commission with which his Excellency the Viceroy charged me, concerning the search of the carbuncle. I found a Pagan of the Pira nation, who had not only seen one, but has killed one and thrown it away, through ignorance, as a thing of no value. He assured me that there were two kinds, one about a quarter, the other about half a *vara* high. The curtain, or lid, with which it covers its splendor, is, he says, a thing of exquisite plumage, and that it has on its breast spots of singular beauty. He called it in his Pira language Inuyucoy. He promised to bring me one dead, since it is impossible to take it alive; I regaled him plentifully for the sake of encouraging him, and he set off in full confidence that he should not return without it. As soon as I get this precious jewel (*alhaja*), I will send it to his Excellency. (*Mercurio Peruano, Enero* 152.)

* *History of Paraguay, etc.*, by F. Nicholas del Techo.

D. Joseph Ignacio de Lequanda (*Mer. Peruan. N.* 249), relates some stories of this carbuncle animal, and evidently believes them. By his account, it opens this eye of light when it is in danger, and dazzles its enemy. At other times the eye is covered with its veil, or lid,—like Prince Arthur's shield.

The author of the verse-Argentina, D. Martin del Barco, says he had seen this beast, and often hunted it in vain and that happy man would be he who should catch one. Ruy Diaz Melgarejo, he adds, had been thus fortunate. He had caught a carbuncle-beast and taken out the stone,—but the canoe in which he embarked with it upset, and the jewel was lost. I, says D. Martin, saw him lamenting his evil fortune, and heard him say, that if he had not lost the carbuncle, he would have presented it to King Philip. (*Argentina, Canto* 3.)

R. Southey.

178. FRAGMENT

ENCINTUR'D with a twine of leaves,
That leafy twine his only dress I
A lovely boy was plucking fruits
By moonlight, in a wilderness.
The moon was bright, the air was free,
And fruits and flowers together grew
On many a shrub and many a tree:
And all put on a gentle hue,
Hanging in the shadowy air,
Like a picture rich and rare.
It was a climate where, they say,
The night is more belov'd than day.
But who that beauteous boy beguil'd,
That beauteous boy to linger here?
Alone, by night, a little child,
In place so silent and so wild—
Has he no friend, no loving mother near?

S. T. Coleridge.

179. THINGS SEEN

i

I HAVE never seen the evening star set behind the mountains, but it was as if I had lost a hope out of my soul, as if a love were gone, and a sad memory only remained. O it was my earliest affection, the evening star I One of my first utterances in verse was an address to it as I was returning from the New River, and it looked newly bathed as well as I. I remember that the substance of the sonnet was that the woman whom I could ever love would surely have been emblemed in the pensive serene brightness of that planet, that we were both constellated to it, and would after death return thither.

ii

BRIGHT reflections, in the canal, of the blue and green vitriol bottles in the druggists' shops in London.

iii

—the severity of the winter—the kingfisher its slow, short flight permitting you to observe all its colours, almost as if it had been a flower.

iv

September 15, 1801.—Observed the great half moon setting behind the mountain ridge, and watched the shapes its various segments presented as it slowly sunk—first the foot of a boot, all but the heel—then a little Δ—then a star of the first magnitude—indeed it was not distinguishable from the evening star at its largest—then rapidly a smaller, a small, a very small star—and, as it diminished in size, so it grew paler in tint. And now where is it? Unseen—but a little fleecy cloud hangs above the mountain ridge, and is rich in amber light.

S. T. Coleridge.

180. REBELLION

... The Sensual and the Dark rebel in vain,
Slaves by their own compulsion I In mad game
They burst their manacles and wear the name
   Of Freedom, graven on a heavier chain! ...
                              S. T. Coleridge.

181. THE LIFE OF MEN

YE Children of Man! whose life is a span,
Protracted with sorrow from day to day,
Naked and featherless, feeble and querulous,
Sickly calamitous creatures of clay!
Attend to the words of the Sovereign Birds,
(Immortal, illustrious, lords of the air)
Who survey from on high, with a merciful eye,
Your struggles of misery, labour, and care.
Whence you may learn and clearly discern
Such truths as attract your inquisitive turn;
Which is busied of late, with a mighty debate,
A profound speculation about the creation,
And organical life, and chaotical strife,
With various notions of heavenly motions,
And rivers and oceans, and valleys and mountains,
And sources of fountains, and meteors on high,
And stars in the sky.... We propose by and by,
(If you'll listen and hear) to make it all clear.
And Prodicus henceforth shall pass for a dunce,
When his doubts are explain'd and expounded at once.

   Before the creation of Æther and Light,
Chaos and Night together were plight,
In the dungeon of Erebus foully bedight.
Not Ocean, or Air, or stibstance was there,
Or solid or rare, or figure or form,
But horrible Tartarus rul'd in the storm:

At length, in the dreary chaotical closet
Of Erebus old, was a privy deposit,
By Night the primæval in secresy laid;
A Mystical Egg, that in silence and shade
Was brooded and hatch'd; till time came about:
And Love, the delightful, in glory flew out,
In rapture and light, exulting and bright,
Sparkling and florid, with stars in his forehead,
His forehead and hair, with a flutter and flare,
As he rose in the air, triumphantly furnish'd
To range his dominions, on glittering pinions,
All golden and azure, and blooming and burnish'd:
 He soon, in the murky Tartarean recesses,
With a hurricane's might, in his fiery caresses
Impregnated Chaos; and hastily snatch'd
To being and life, begotten and hatch'd,
The primitive Birds: but the Deities all,
The celestial Lights, the terrestial Ball,
Were later of birth, with the dwellers on earth,
More tamely combin'd, of a temperate kind;
When chaotical mixture approach'd to a fixture.
 Our antiquity prov'd; it remains to be shewn
That Love is our author, and master alone,
Like him, we can ramble, and gambol and fly
O'er ocean and earth, and aloft to the sky:
And all the world over, we're friends to the lover,
And when other means fail, we are found to prevail,
When a Peacock or Pheasant is sent as a present.
 All lessons of primary daily concern,
You have learnt from the Birds, and continue to learn,
Your best benefactors and early instructors;
We give you the warning of seasons returning.
 When the Cranes are arrang'd and muster afloat
In the middle air, with a creaking note,
Steering away to the Lybian sands;
Then careful farmers sow their lands;
The crazy vessel is haul'd ashore,
The sail, the ropes, the rudder and oar
Are all unshipp'd, and hous'd in store.

    The Shepherd is warn'd, by the Kite reappearing,
To muster his flock, and be ready for shearing.
    You quit your old cloak at the Swallow's behest.
In assurance of summer, and purchase a vest.
    For Delphi, for Ammon, Dodona, in fine
For every oracular temple and shrine,
The Birds are a substitute equal and fair,
For on us you depend, and to us you repair
For council and aid, when a marriage is made,
A purchase, a bargain, a venture in trade:
Unlucky or lucky, whatever has struck ye,
An Ox or an Ass, that may happen to pass,
A Voice in the street, or a Slave that you meet,
A Name or a Word by chance overheard,
If you deem it an Omen, you call it a *Bird*;
And if birds are your omens, it clearly will follow
That birds are a proper prophetic Apollo.

    Then take us as Gods, and you'll soon find the odds,
We'll serve for all uses, as Prophets and Muses;
We'll give ye fine weather, we'll live here together;
We'll not keep away, scornful and proud, a-top of a cloud,
(In Jupiter's way); but attend every day,
To prosper and bless, all you possess,
And all your affairs, for yourselves and your heirs.
And as long as you live, we shall give
You wealth and health, and pleasure and treasure,
In ample measure;
And never bilk, you of pidgeon's milk,
Or potable gold; you shall live to grow old,
In laughter and mirth, on the face of the earth,
Laughing, quaffing, carouzing, bouzing,
    Your only distress, shall be the excess
    Of ease and abundance and happiness.
                            Aristophanes
                        (translated by *J. H. Frere*).

182. BEACHY HEAD

July 23 [1800].—Walked to the shore and along it, with a hope of having some sight of the sea-front of Beachy Head from beneath it, though four or five miles off. The beach impassable by any sort of carriage. A shore of ruins under the cliffs, which gradually rise from what is called the Wish-House, a small white building standing sweetly near the beach, to the summit of the Cape. Large blocks of granite imbedded on the shore, and extending to the waves, which rage and foam over them, giving one dreadful ideas of shipwreck. Sometimes, patches of gravelly sand, or pebbles, soon ending against masses of granite, or chalk, between which it is difficult, and not always possible to walk; some of them must be stepped upon. Within half a mile of the great front, unable to proceed farther; sat down on a block, wearied out, desiring William to go on; he was soon hid by a turn of the cliffs. Almost frightened by the solitude and vastness of the scene, though *Chance*[*] was with me. Tide almost out; only sea in front; white cliffs rising over me, but not impending; strand all around a chaos of rocks and fallen cliffs far out into the waves; sea-fowl wheeling and screaming; all disappeared behind the point, beyond which is the great cliff; but we had doubled point after point, in the hope that this would be the next, and had been much deceived in the distances by these great objects; after one remote point gained, another and another succeeded, and still the great cliff was unattained; the white precipices beautifully varied with plants, green, blue, yellow, and poppy. Wheatears flew up often from the beach: *Chance* pursued them. At length William returned, having been nearly, but not quite, in front of the great promontory. Slowly and laboriously we made our way back along the beach, greatly fatigued, the day exceedingly hot, the horizon sulphurous, with lowering clouds; thunder rolled faintly at a distance. *Ann Radcliffe.*

[*] Her dog.

183. EVENING AT AMBLESIDE

Sunday, June 1st.—Rain in the night. A sweet mild morning. Read ballads. Went to church. Singers from Wytheburn. Walked upon the hill above the house till dinner time. Went again to church. After tea, went to Ambleside, round the Lakes. A very fine warm evening. I lay upon the steep of Loughrigg, my heart dissolved in what I saw: when I was not startled, but called from my reverie by a noise as of a child paddling without shoes. I looked up, and saw a lamb close to me. It approached nearer and nearer, as if to examine me, and stood a long time. I did not move. At last, it ran past me, and went bleating along the pathway, seeming to be seeking its mother. I saw a hare on the high road. . . .
Dorothy Wordsworth.

184. NATURE, LOVE, AND MAN

. . . Nor less do I remember to have felt,
Distinctly manifested at this time,
A human-heartedness about my love
For objects hitherto the absolute wealth
Of my own private being and no more;
Which I had loved, even as a blessed spirit
Or Angel, if he were to dwell on earth,
Might love in individual happiness.
But now there opened on me other thoughts
Of change, congratulation or regret,
A pensive feeling! It spread far and wide;
The trees, the mountains shared it, and the brooks,
The stars of Heaven, now seen in their old haunts—
White Sirius glittering o'er the southern crags,
Orion with his belt, and those fair Seven,
Acquaintances of every little child,
And Jupiter, my own beloved star!
Whatever shadmgs of mortality,
Whatever imports from the world of death
Had come among these objects heretofore,

Were, in the main, of mood less tender: strong,
Deep, gloomy were they, and severe; the scatterings
Of awe or tremulous dread, that had given way
In later youth to yearnings of a love
Enthusiastic, to delight and hope. . . .
William Wordsworth.

185. JUPITER

Monday [10 Nov. 1800].— . . . Jupiter over the hilltops, the only star, like a sun, flashed out at intervals from behind a black cloud, *Dorothy Wordsworth.*

186. THE SEEDS OF LIFE

September 1 [1800].—The beards of thistle and dandelions flying about the lonely mountains like life—and I saw them through the trees skimming the lake like swallows.
S. T. Coleridge.

187. LONDON

I OUGHT before this to have reply'd to your very kind invitation into Cumberland. With you and your Sister I could gang any where. But I am afraid whether I shall ever be able to afford so desperate a Journey. Seperate from the pleasure of your company, I dont much care if I never see a mountain in my life. I have passed all my days in London, until I have formed as many and intense local attachments, as any of your mountaineers can have done with dead nature. The Lighted shops of the Strand and Fleet Street, the innumerable trades, treadesmen and customers, coaches, waggons, playhouses, all the bustle and wickedness round about Covent Garden, the very women of the Town, the watchmen, drunken scenes, rattles,—life awake, if you awake, at all hours of the night, the impossibility of being dull in Fleet Street, the crowds, the very dirt and mud, the Sun shining upon houses and pavements, the print shops, the old book stalls, parsons cheap'ning books, coffee houses, steams of soups from kitchens, the pantomimes, London itself a pantomime and a masquerade, —all these things work themselves into my mind and feed me without a power of satiating me. The wonder of these sights impells me into nightwalks about the crowded streets, and I often shed tears in the motley Strand from fulness of joy at so much Life.—All these emotions must be strange to you. So are your rural emotions to me. But consider, what must I have been doing all my life, not to have lent great portions of my heart with usury to such scenes?—

My attachments are all local, purely local. I have no passion (or have had none since I was in love, and then it was the spurious engendering of poetry and books) to groves and vallies. The rooms where I was born, the furniture which has been before my eyes all my life, a book case which has followed me about (like a faithful dog, only exceeding him in knowledge) wherever I have moved, old tables, streets, squares, where I have sunned myself, my old school,—these are my mistresses. Have I not enough, without your mountains? I do not envy you. I should pity you, did I not know, that the Mind will make friends of any thing. Your sun and moon and skies and hills and lakes affect me no more, or scarcely come to me in more venerable characters, than as a gilded room with tapestry and tapers, where I might live with handsome visible objects. I consider the clouds above me but as a roof, beautifully painted, but unable to satisfy the mind, and at last, like the pictures of the apartment of a connoisseur, unable to afford him any longer a pleasure. So fading upon me, from disuse, have been the Beauties of Nature, as they have been confinedly called; so ever fresh and green and warm are all the inventions of men in this great city.

Charles Lamb.

188. A WATERFALL

November 12 [1799].—We ascend the hill to Scale Force. The first fall dashes in a thin, broad, white ribbon, from a stupendous height, uninterrupted though not impinged by the perpendicular rock, down which, or rather parallel with which, it falls. There is no pool at the bottom but a common shallow brook which flows over small flattish pebbles. But the chasm through which it flows is stupendous, so wildly wooded that the mosses and wet weeds and the perilous Tree increase the horror of the rocks which ledge only enough to interrupt not stop your fall! And the Tree, O God! to think of a poor wretch hanging with one arm from it! The lower fall, that is, from the brook, is broader, but very low in comparison, and only mark-worthy as combining admirably with the other. Before the great fall there are six falls, each higher than the other, the chasm still gradually deepening till the great fall, the height and depth of which are sudden and out of all comparison. I never saw trees on rock zigzag in their lines more beautifully—trees white in bark, and more than half overpatched with blackish moss—then the green moss upon the rock. *S. T. Coleridge.*

189. POEM

I CANNOT tell, not I, why she
Awhile so gracious, now should be
So grave: I cannot tell you why
The violet hangs its head awry.
It shall be cull'd, it shall be worn,
In spite of every sign of scorn,
Dark look, and overhanging thorn.
  W. S. Landor.

190. APRIL

Friday, 16th April (Good Friday).— . . . A sheep came plunging through the river, stumbled up the bank, and passed close to us. It had been frightened by an insignificant little dog on the other side. Its fleece dropped a glittering shower under its belly. Primroses by the road-side, pile wort that shone like stars of gold in the sun, violets, strawberries, retired and half-buried among the grass. When we came to the foot of Brothers Water, I left William sitting on the bridge, and went along the path on the right side of the lake through the wood. I was delighted with what I saw. The water under the boughs of the bare old trees, the simplicity of the mountains, and the exquisite beauty of the path. There was one grey cottage. I repeated *The Glow-worm*, as I walked along. I hung over the gate, and thought I could have stayed for ever. When I returned, I found William writing a poem descriptive of the sights and sounds we saw and heard. There was the gentle flowing of the stream, the glittering, lively lake, green fields without a living creature to be seen on them; behind us, a flat pasture with forty-two cattle feeding; to our left, the road leading to the hamlet. No smoke there, the sun shcone on the bare roofs. The people were at work, ploughing, harrowing, and sowing; . . . a dog barking now and then, cocks crowing, birds twittering, the snow in patches at the top of the highest hills, yellow palms, purple and green twigs on the birches, ashes with their guttering spikes quite bare. The hawthorn a bright green, with black stems under the oak. The moss of the oak glossy. We went on. Passed two sisters at work (they first passed us), one with two pitchforks in her hand, the other had a spade. We had some talk with them. They laughed long after we were gone, perhaps half in wantonness, half boldness. William finished his poem before we got to the foot of Kirkstone. There were hundreds of cattle in the vale. There we ate our dinner. The walk up Kirkstone was very interesting. The becks among the rocks were all alive. William showed me the little mossy streamlet which he had before loved when he saw its bright green track in the snow. The view above Ambleside very beautiful. There we sate and looked down on the green vale. We watched the crows at a little distance from us become white as silver as they flew in the sunshine, and when they went still further, they looked like shapes of water passing over the green fields. . . .

Saturday, 17th.—A mild warm rain. We sate in the garden all the morning. William dug a little. I transplanted a honey-suckle. The lake was still. The sheep on the island, reflected in the water, like the grey-deer we saw in Gowbarrow Park. We walked after tea by moonlight. I had been in bed in the afternoon, and William had slept in his chair. We walked towards Rydale backwards and forwards below Mr. Olliff's. The village was beautiful in the moonlight. Helm

Crag we observed very distinct. The dead hedge round Benson's field bound together at the top by an interlacing of ash sticks, which made a chain of silver when we faced the moon. A letter from C. and also one from S. H. I saw a robin chasing a scarlet butterfly this morning.

Sunday, 18th.—Again a mild grey morning, with rising vapours. We sate in the orchard. William wrote the poem on *The Robin and the Butterfly.* . . .

Dorothy Wordsworth.

191. EMPLOYED BY NATURE.

I SHALL shortly return to Bergholt where I shall make some laborious studies from nature—and I shall endeavour to get a pure and unaffected representation of the scenes that may employ me with respect to Colour particularly and anything else. . . . There is little or nothing in the exhibition worth looking up to. *There is room enough for a natural painture.*

John Constable.

192. BEES, BIRDS AND OXEN:

TOM MOORE AND W. L. BOWLES

ARTHUR HOULTON told us the following story last night . . . 22nd December, 1838: Four months ago, I was visiting Old Bowles (87 *aet.*) at Bremhill. He was getting rather deaf, and had been to London, where he had met with a new ear trumpet, invented, *on dit*, by Miss Martineau (the Political Œconomist). Bowles was very proud of his treasure, and anxious to display it. He had seen Southey in town: and "Southey told me," he said, "that when I got back to the country I should be able with this trumpet to hear the bees hum, the birds sing, and the cattle low."

He then proposed taking a drive to Moore's to show him the novelty, and tell him what Southey had said. Upon reaching Sloperton, Bowles said to Arthur Houlton, "Now you can stay here in the carriage, whilst I go in." Moore, spying at the window with his glass, came to the door when the carriage drew up, and, seeing a second person remaining behind, called out, "Who's that?" "Oh, it's young Houlton; just come to take a drive with me."

"What, Arthur?" said Tom Moore.

"Yes."

"Oh, come out; I'm very glad to see you." So up they went into the drawing room.

When they got up, Bowles began his account of what he had got to show, and produced the trumpet. "Now," says he, "I want to know how I can hear with it—so just go to your piano, Moore, and let me try." Moore good naturedly sat down, and ran over a few chords, accompanying it with some pretty lines, in his own tiny but most articulate and melodious way.

"Beautiful; very fine; heard quite plain," said Bowles. "But now, I want to try how I can catch conversation. Now go to the other end of the room, Moore, and talk to me."

Moore, who began to be tired of the nonsense, good naturedly went to the other end of the room, and sat down on the window seat, or some place in the opposite corner, just under the bust of Lord Byron. "Now that'll do, Moore. Now, begin." ("I remembered the conversation well," said Arthur.) Moore, mightily puzzled and teased, began—"Well, how's Mrs. Bowles?"

"Very well, very well. That'll do—heard very plain."

"Well—did you drive over in the pony carriage?"

"Yes, yes."

"Well, how did the pony go?"

"Very well. Very well—that'll do. Capital."

Moore descended from his throne, and came out and sat down on a chair opposite to Bowles.

"Now," said Bowles, "I'll tell you what I have done. Southey told me that with this trumpet I should be able to hear the bees hum, the birds sing, and the oxen low. So the other day, I saw a bee flying about, so I got near to him and put my trumpet down; and indeed I heard him quite plain—buzz—I then went through the Barton, and what do you think—the very first thing I heard was—Cock-a-doodle-doo.

I then went out past the cowhouse, and there I heard—the oxen low—! There, what do you think of that?"

Moore, who was splitting with laughter and scarcely able to keep his countenance, replied in a moment, "Why, I'll tell you what, Bowles; if you had told this to anybody else, they would have said that it was a very *Cock and Bull Story*."

193. MAY

Friday, 14th May.—A very cold morning—hail and snow showers all day. We went to Brothers wood, intending to get plants, and to go along the shore of the lake to the foot. We did go a part of the way, but there was no pleasure in stepping along that difficult sauntering road in this ungenial weather. We turned again, and walked backwards and forwards in Brothers wood. William tired himself with seeking an epithet for the cuckoo. I sate a while upon my last summer seat, the mossy stone. William's, unemployed, beside me, and the space between, where Coleridge has so often lain. The oak trees are just putting forth yellow knots of leaves. The ashes with their flowers passing away, and leaves coming out; the blue hyacinth is not quite full blown; gowans are coming out; marsh marigolds in full glory; the little star plant, a star without a flower. We took home a great load of gowans, and planted them about the orchard. After dinner, I worked bread, then came and mended stockings beside William; he fell asleep. After tea I walked to Rydale for letters. It was a strange night. The hills were covered over with a slight covering of hail or snow, just so as to give them a hoary winter look with the black rocks. The woods looked miserable, the coppices green as grass, which looked quite unnatural, and they seemed half shrivelled up, as if they shrank from the air. O, thought I! what a beautiful thing God has made winter to be, by stripping the trees, and letting us see their shapes and forms. What a freedom does it seem to give to the storms! There were several new flowers out, but I had no pleasure in looking at them. I walked as fast as I could back again with my letter from S. H. . . .

Dorothy Wordsworth.

194. AN APRIL MORNING

It was an April morning: fresh and clear
The Rivulet, delighting in its strength,
Ran with a young man's speed; and yet the voice
Of waters which the winter had supplied
Was softened down into a vernal tone.
The spirit of enjoyment and desire,
And hopes and wishes, from all living things
Went circling, like a multitude of sounds.
The budding groves seemed eager to urge on
The steps of June; as if their various hues
Were only hindrances that stood between
Them and their object: but, meanwhile, prevailed
Such an entire contentment in the air,
That every naked ash, and tardy tree
Yet leafless, showed as if the countenance
With which it looked on this delightful day
Were native to the summer.—Up the brook
I roamed in the confusion of my heart,
Alive to all things and forgetting all.
At length I to a sudden turning came
In this continuous glen, where down a rock
The Stream, so ardent in its course before,
Sent forth such sallies of glad sound, that all
Which I till then had heard appeared the voice
Of common pleasure: beast and bird, the lamb,
The shepherd's dog, the linnet and the thrush
Vied with this waterfall, and made a song
Which, while I listened, seemed like the wild growth
Or like some natural produce of the air,
That could not cease to be. Green leaves were here;
But 'twas the foliage of the rocks—the birch,
The yew, the holly, and the bright green thorn,
With hanging islands of resplendent furze:
And on a summit, distant a short space,
By any who should look beyond the dell,
A single mountain-cottage might be seen . . .

—Soon did the spot become my other home,
My dwelling, and my out-of-doors abode....
      William Wordsworth.

195. ALCIPHRON AND LEUCIPPE

An ancient chestnut's blossoms threw
Their heavy odour over two:
Leucippe, it is said, was one,
The other then was Alciphron.
 "Come, come! why should we stand beneath
This hollow tree's unwholesome breath,"
Said Alciphron, "here's not a blade
Of grass or moss, and scanty shade.
Come; it is just the hour to rove
In the lone dingles shepherds love,
There, straight and tall, the hazel twig
Divides the crooked rock-held fig,
O'er the blue pebbles where the rill
In winter runs, and may run still.
Come then, while fresh and calm the air,
And while the shepherds are not there."

    Leucippe

But I would rather go when they
Sit round about and sing and play.
Then why so hurry me? For you
Like play and song and shepherds too.

    Alaciphron

I like the shepherds very well,
And song and play, as you can tell.
But there is play I sadly fear,
And song I would not have you hear.

    Leucippe

What can it be? what can it be?

    Alaciphron

To you may none of them repeat
 The play that you have played with me,
The song that made your bosom beat.

LEUCIPPE

Don't keep your arm about my waist.

ALACIPHRON

Might not you stumble?

LEUCIPPE

Well then, do.
But why are we in all this haste?

ALACIPHRON

To sing.

LEUCIPPE
Alas! and not play too?

W. S. Landor.

196. TO H. C.: SIX YEARS OLD

O THOU! whose fancies from afar are brought;
Who of thy words dost make a mock apparel,
And fittest to unutterable thought
The breeze-like motion and the self-born carol;
Thou faery voyager! that dost float
In such clear water, that thy boat
May rather seem
To brood on air than on an earthly stream;
Suspended in a stream as clear as sky,
Where earth and heaven do make one imagery;
O blessed vision! happy child!
That art so exquisitely wild,
I think of thee with many fears
For what may be thy lot in future years.

I thought of times when Pain might be thy guest,
Lord of thy house and hospitality;
And Grief, uneasy lover! never rest
But when she sate within the touch of thee.
O too industrious folly !
O vain and causeless melancholy!

Nature will either end thee quite;
Or, lengthening out thy season of delight,
Preserve for thee, by individual right,
A young lamb's heart among the full-grown flocks.
What hast thou to do with sorrow,
Or the injuries of to-morrow?
Thou art a dew-drop, which the morn brings forth,
Ill fitted to sustain unkindly shocks,
Or to be trailed along the soiling earth;
A gem that glitters while it lives,
And no forewarning gives;
But, at the touch of wrong, without a strife
Slips in a moment out of life.
William Wordsworth.

197. NATURE AND IMAGINATION

NATURAL objects always did and now do weaken, deaden and obliterate Imagination in me. Wordsworth must know that what he writes valuable is Not to be found in Nature.
William Blake.

198. FROM THE ITALIAN OF MICHAEL ANGELO

i

YES! hope may with my strong desire keep pace,
And I be undeluded, unbetrayed;
For if of our affections none finds grace
In sight of Heaven, then, wherefore hath God made
The world which we inhabit? Better plea
Love cannot have than that in loving thee
Glory to that eternal Peace is paid.
Who such divinity to thee imparts
As hallows and makes pure all gentle hearts.
His hope is treacherous only whose love dies
With beauty, which is varying every hour;
But, in chaste hearts, uninfluenced by the power
Of outward change, there blooms a deathless flower,
That breathes on earth the air of paradise.

ii
No mortal object did these eyes behold
When first they met the placid light of thine,
And my Soul felt her destiny divine,
And hope of endless peace in me grew bold:
Heaven-born, the Soul a heavenward course must hold;
Beyond the visible world she soars to seek
(For what delights the sense is false and weak)
Ideal Form, the universal mould.
The wise man, I affirm, can find no rest
In that which perishes: nor will he lend
His heart to aught which doth on time depend.
'Tis sense, unbridled will, and not true love,
That kills the soul: love betters what is best,
Even here below, but more in heaven above.
       William Wordsworth.

199. THE PROGRESS OF POETS

. . . I thought of Chatterton, the marvellous Boy,
The sleepless Soul that perished in his pride;
Of Him who walked in glory and in joy
Following his plough, along the mountain-side:
By our own spirits are we deified:
We poets in our youth begin in gladness;
But thereof come in the end despondency and madness. . .
       William Wordsworth.

200. OPIUM DREAM

 . . . I know not how, but I am brought
  Into a large and Gothic hall,
 Seated with those I never sought—
  Kings, Caliphs, Kaisers—silent all;
 Pale as the dead; enrobed and tall,
  Majestic, frozen, solemn, still;
 They wake my fears, my wits appal,
  And with both scorn and terror fill.

Now are they seated at a board
  In that cold grandeur—I am there,
But what can mummied kings afford?
  This is their meagre ghostly fare,
And proves what fleshless things they stare!
  Yes! I am seated with the dead:
How great, and yet how mean they are!
  Yes! I can scorn them while they dread?

They're gone!—and in their room I see
  A fairy being, form and dress
Brilliant as light; nor can there be
  On earth that heavenly loveliness,
Nor words can that sweet look express,
  Or tell what living gems adorn
That wond'rous beauty: who can guess
  Where such celestial charms were born?

Yet, as I wonder and admire,
  The grace is gone, the glory dead;
And now it is but mean attire
  Upon a shrivel'd beldame spread;
Laid loathsome on a pauper's bed,
  Where wretchedness and woe are found,
And the faint putrid odour shed
  By all that's foul and base around! . . .
                    George Crabbe.

201. OPIUM JOTTINGS

a dusky light—a purple *flash*
crystalline splendor—light blue—
    Green lightnings—
in that eternal and delirious misery
    wrath fires—
        inward desolations
an horror of great darkness
    great things—on the ocean
        counterfeit infinity—
                S. T. Coleridge.

202. THE DEMONS OF OPIUM

... Then was I cast out from my state;
   Two fiends of darkness led my way;
They wak'd me early, watch'd me late,
   My dread by night, my plague by day!
Oh! I was made their sport, their play,
   Through many a stormy troubled year;
And how they used their passive prey
   Is sad to tell:—but you shall hear.

At first, before they sent me forth,
   Through this unpitying world to run,
They robb'd Sir Eustace of his worth,
   Lands, manors, lordships, every one;
So was that gracious man undone,
   Was spurn'd as vile, was scorn'd as poor,
Whom every former friend would shun,
   And menials drove from every door.

Then those ill-favour'd Ones, whom none
   But my unhappy eyes could view,
Led me, with wild emotion, on,
   And, with resistless terror, drew.
Through lands we fled, o'er seas we flew,
   And halted on a boundless plain;
Where nothing fed, nor breathed, nor grew,
   But silence ruled the still domain.

Upon that boundless plain, below,
   The setting sun's last rays were shed,
And gave a mild and sober glow,
   Where all were still, asleep, or dead;
Vast ruins in their midst were spread,
   Pillars and pediments sublime,
Where the grey moss had form'd a bed,
   And clothed the crumbling spoils of time.

There was I fix'd, I know not how,
    Condemn'd for untold years to stay:
Yet years were not;—one dreadful now
    Endured no change of night or day;
The same mild evening's sleeping ray
    Shone softly solemn and serene,
And all that time I gazed away,
    The setting sun's sad rays were seen.

At length a moment's sleep stole on,—
    Again came my commission'd foes;
Again through sea and land we're gone,
    No peace, no respite, no repose:
Above the dark broad sea we rose,
    We ran through bleak and frozen land;
I had no strength their strength t' oppose,
    An infant in a giant's hand.

They placed me where those streamers play,
    Those nimble beams of brilliant light;
It would the stoutest heart dismay,
    To see, to feel that dreadful sight:
So swift, so pure, so cold, so bright,
    They pierced my frame with icy wound,
And all that half-year's polar night,
    Those dancing streamers wrapp'd me round.

Slowly that darkness pass'd away,
    When down upon the earth I fell,—
Some hurried sleep was mine by day;
    But soon as toll'd the evening bell,
They forced me on, where ever dwell
    Far distant men in cities fair,
Cities of whom no trav'lers tell,
    Nor feet but mine were wanderers there.

Their watchmen stare, and stand aghast,
    As on we hurry through the dark;
The watch-light bunks as we go past,
    The watch-dog shrinks and fears to bark;

The watch-tower's bell sounds shrill; and, hark I
  The free wind blows—we've left the town—
A wide sepulchral ground I mark,
  And on a tombstone place me down.

What monuments of mighty dead!
  What tombs of various kinds are found!
And stones erect their shadows shed
  On humble graves, with wickers bound;
Some risen fresh above the ground,
  Some level with the native clay,
What sleeping millions wait the sound,
  "Arise, ye dead, and come away!"

Alas! they stay not for that call;
  Spare me this woe! ye demons, spare!—
They come! the shrouded shadows all,—
  'Tis more than mortal brain can bear;
Rustling they rise, they sternly glare
  At man upheld by vital breath;
Who, led by wicked fiends, should dare
  To join the shadowy troops of death!

Yes, I have felt all man can feel,
  Till he shall pay his nature's debt;
Ills that no hope has strength to heal,
  No mind the comfort to forget:
Whatever cares the heart can fret,
  The spirits wear, the temper gall,
Woe, want, dread, anguish, all beset
  My sinful soul!—together all!

Those fiends upon a shaking fen
  Fix'd me in dark tempestuous night;
There never trod the foot of men,
  There flock'd the fowl in wint'ry flight;
There danced the moor's deceitful light
  Above the pool where sedges grow;
And when the morning-sun shone bright,
  It shone upon a field of snow.

They hung me on a bough so small,
    The rook could build her nest no higher;
They fix'd me on the trembling ball
    That crowns the steeple's quiv'ring spire;
They set me where the seas retire,
    But drown with their returning tide;
And made me flee the mountain's fire,
    When rolling from its burning side.

I've hung upon the ridgy steep
    Of cliffs, and held the rambling brier;
I've plunged below the billowy deep,
    Where air was sent me to respire;
I've been where hungry wolves retire;
    And (to complete my woes) I've ran
Where Bedlam's crazy crew conspire
    Against the life of reasoning man.

I've furl'd in storms the flapping sail,
    By hanging from the topmost head;
I've served the vilest slaves in jail,
    And pick'd the dunghill's spoil for bread;
I've made the badger's hole my bed,
    I've wander'd with a gipsy crew;
I've dreaded all the guilty dread,
    And done what they would fear to do.

On sand, where ebbs and flows the flood,
    Midway they placed and bade me die;
Propp'd on my staff, I stoutly stood
    When the swift waves came rolling by;
And high they rose, and still more high,
    Till my lips drank the bitter brine;
I sobb'd convulsed, then cast mine eye,
    And saw the tide's re-flowing sign.

And then, my dreams were such as nought
    Could yield but my unhappy case;
I've been of thousand devils caught,
    And thrust into that horrid place,

Where reign dismay, despair, disgrace;
   Furies with iron fangs were there,
To torture that accursed race,
   Doom'd to dismay, disgrace, despair.

Harmless I was; yet hunted down
   For treasons to my soul unfit;
I've been pursued through many a town,
   For crimes that petty knaves commit;
I've been adjudged t' have lost my wit,
   Because I preach'd so loud and well,
And thrown into the dungeon's pit
   For trampling on the pit of hell. . . .
                    George Crabbe.

203. THE SECRET OF THE DEEP

ONE day, leaning out of the cabin window, by the side of an officer who was employed in fishing, the corpse of a man newly sewed in a hammock, started half out of the water, and continued its course, with the current, towards the shore— Nothing could be more horrible: its head and shoulders were visible, turning first to one side, then to the other, with a solemn and awful movement, as if impressed with some dreadful secret of the deep, which, from its watery grave, it came upwards to reveal. Such sights became afterwards frequent, hardly a day passing without ushering the dead to the contemplation of the living, until at length they passed without observation.   *E. D. Clarke.*

204. POETS

IDLY talk they who speak of poets as mere indulgers of fancy, imagination, superstition, etc. They are the bridlers by delight, the purifiers; they that combine all these with reason and order—the true protoplasts—Gods of Love who tame the chaos.   *S. T. Coleridge.*

205. A SCIENTIST AT TINTERN

I AWOKE at midnight: the recollection of indistinct but painful visions passed across my mind; the spectre of horrible images still trembled in my eyes when I raised them to the light which shone through the green windows of my chamber. The moon was high in heaven; the sky was blue and cloudless; the woodbine, that surrounded the casement, was waving its dark foliage to the breeze. How intimately connected together are life, light and motion! I was no longer solitary, no longer terrified; the restless and uneasy feeling which superstition, almost conquered by reason, is capable of awakening in the mind, disappeared before the beautiful, or combined with it to form a sublime energy. You know a moonlight scene is peculiarly delightful to me; I always considered it as beautiful: but so much solitary enthusiasm, so much social feeling, so much of the sublime energy of love, of sorrow, and consolation, have occurred to me beneath the moon-beams on the shore of that sea where Nature first spoke to me in the murmurs of the waves and winds, in the granite caves of Michael, that it is now become sublime. Restless, and filled with vivid imaginations, I was unable to sleep: I arose and stole to the window. The moon had just sunk beneath the ruins of the abbey, and her broken and trembling light shone through the west windows upon the burying ground, beyond which the moving waters of the Wye were dancing and murmuring beneath the light. For a few minutes I was lost and swallowed up in impression. No longer connected with the earth, I seemed to mingle with Nature; I pursued the dazzling of the moon-beams; I raised myself above the stars, and gave imaginary beings to the immeasurable paths of ether. But when I cast my eyes on the remains of mortality—when I considered, that in that deserted spot, where the song of the nightingale and the whispering of the wings of the bat were the only signs of life, thousands of thoughts, an immense mass of pleasureable ideas, had rolled through the minds of a hundred intelligent beings,—I was lost in a deep and intense social feeling. I began to think, to reason, what is existence? What is this eternal series of changes in life, in thought, and sentiment? The globe undergoes no physical revolution, whilst the physical organized beings upon the surface of it are perpetually modifying; the laws by which the physical phenomena of the universe are ruled are always the same: are there no laws by which the moral phenomena are governed? Nothing remains of them but mouldering bones; their thoughts and their names have perished. Shall we, too, sink in the dust? shall we, too, like these beings, in the course of time, be no more? shall that ever modified consciousness be lost in the immensity of being? No, my friend, individuality can never cease to exist; that ideal self which exists in dreams and reveries, that ideal self which never slumbers, is the child of immortality, and these deep intense feelings which man sometimes perceives in the bosom of Nature and Deity, are presentiments of a more sublime and energetic state of existence. *Humphry Davy.*

206. ART AND COLOUR

THE English Artist may be assured that he is doing an injury & injustice to his Country while he studies & imitates the effects of Nature. England will never rival Italy while we servilely copy what the wise Italians, Rafael & Michael Angelo, scorned, nay abhorred, as Vasari tells us.

> Call that the Public Voice which is their Error,
> Like as a Monkey peeping in a Mirror
> Admires all his colours brown & warm
> And never once perceives his ugly form.

What kind of Intellects must he have who sees only the Colours of things & not the Form of Things. *William Blake.*

207. LOVELY IN DECAY

> ... Yon hanging woods, that touched by autumn seem
> As they were blossoming hues of fire and gold,
> The flower-like woods, most lovely in decay,
> The many clouds, the sea, the rock, the sands
> Lie in the silent moonshine. ...   *S. T. Coleridge.*

208. NEVER THINK OF STYLE

ENTER into the mind and heart of your own creatures: think of them long, entirely, solely: never of style, never of self, never of critics, cracked or sound. Like the miles of an open country, and of an ignorant population, when they are correctly mentioned they become smaller. In the loftiest rooms and richest entablatures are suspended the most spider-webs; and the quarry out of which palaces are erected is the nursery of nettle and bramble. *W. S. Landor.*

209. THE SUFFOLK SHORE

    ... Then come his sister and his village-friend,
       And he will now the sweetest moments spend
       Life has to yield;—no! never will he find
       Again on earth such pleasure in his mind:
       He goes through shrubby walks these friends among,
       Love in their looks and honour on the tongue;
       Nay, there's a charm beyond what nature shows,
       The bloom is softer and more sweetly grows;—
       Pierced by no crime and urged by no desire
       For more than true and honest hearts require,
       They feel the calm delight, and thus proceed
       Through the green lane—then linger in the mead—
       Stray o'er the heath in all its purple bloom—
       And pluck the blossom where the wild bees hum;
       Then through the broomy bound with ease they pass
       And press the sandy sheep-walk's slender grass,
       Where dwarfish flowers among the gorse are spread,
       And the lamb browses by the linnet's bed;
       Then 'cross the bounding brook they make their way
       O'er its rough bridge—and there behold the bay!—
       The ocean smiling to the fervid sun,
       The waves that faintly fall and slowly run—
       The ships at distance and the boats at hand;
       And now they walk upon the sea-side sand,

Counting the number and what kind they be,
Ships softly sinking in the sleepy sea;
Now arm in arm, now parted, they behold
The glitt'ring waters on the shingles roll'd;
The timid girls, half dreading their design,
Dip the small foot in the retarded brine,
And search for crimson weeds, which spreading flow,
Or lie like pictures on the sand below;
With all those bright red pebbles that the sun
Through the small waves so softly shines upon;
And those live lucid jellies which the eye
Delights to trace as they swim glitt'ring by:
Pearl-shells and rubied star-fish they admire,
And will arrange above the parlour-fire,—
Tokens of bliss! . . .
George Crabbe.

210. THE DEWY FRESHNESS

CALLING upon Constable, one day, I found him with a palette-knife, on which was some white, mixed with a viscous vehicle, and with which he touched the surface of a beautiful picture he was painting. Upon expressing my surprise, he said "Oh! My dear Hart, I'm giving my picture the dewy freshness." He maintained that the process imparted the dewy freshness of nature, and he contended that the apparent crudeness would readily subside, and that the chemical change which would ensue in a short time, would assume the truthful aspect of nature. *Solomon Hart, R.A.*

211. THE POETESS NATURE

I REMEMBER, if I mistake not, the artist you ailude to—whose works are indeed replete with fine taste and elegant invention, and who might have been a splendid ornament to his country had he met with the encouragement he deserved: I remember seeing him, however, when I was a boy, painting the beautiful trees in Kensington Gardens; and though they stood before his eyes in all the freshness of their verdure, he changed them in his painting to a hot autumnal brown. Not that he was insensible to their natural beauty, but he complained that the materials of his art were inadequate to its representation. I am convinced, however, that he thought more at the time of some splendid artifice in the pictures of Rubens, than of the *true* splendour of the green trees glistening in the sun, whose golden rays checkered their warm velvet shades, and which the mild reflection of the sky served every where to relieve and heighten by its contrast. This is the true Poetical Light in which NATURE, that great and original POETESS, exhibits to us the objects of HER INEXHAUSTIBLE INVENTION. *Henry Richter.*

212. NATURAL TRUTH

(ON a painting by him with a bird in it.) Yes, I saw it. I had sat a long time without a living thing making its appearance. I always sit till I see some living thing; because if any such appears, it is sure to be appropriate to the place. If no living thing shews itself, I put none in my picture.
John Constable.

213. SEA MARSH

   ... When tides were neap, and, in the sultry day,
     Through the tall bounding mud-banks made their way,
     Which on each side rose swelling, and below
     The dark warm flood ran silently and slow:
     There anchoring, Peter chose from man to hide,
     There hang his head, and view the lazy tide
     In its hot slimy channel slowly glide;
     Where the small eels that left the deeper way
     For the warm shore, within the shallows play;
     Where gaping mussels, left upon the mud,
     Slope their slow passage to the fallen flood: —
     Here dull and hopeless he'd lie down and trace
     How sidelong crabs had scrawl'd their crooked race;
     Or sadly listen to the tuneless cry
     Of fishing gull or clanging golden-eye;

What time the sea-birds to the marsh would come,
And the loud bittern, from the bull-rush home,
Gave from the salt-ditch side the bellowing boom.
He nursed the feelings these dull scenes produce,
And loved to stop beside the opening sluice;
Where the small stream, confined in narrow bound,
Ran with a dull, unvaried, sadd'ning sound;
Where all presented to the eye or ear
Oppress'd the soul with misery, grief, and fear. . . .
George Crabbe.

214. THE PAINTER'S EYE

THERE is nothing ugly; I never saw an ugly thing in my life: for let the form of an object be what it may, light, shade, and perspective will always make it beautiful.
John Constable.

215. SONG

HEAR, sweet spirit, hear the spell,
Lest a blacker charm compel!
So shall the midnight breezes swell
With thy deep long-lingering knell.

And at evening evermore,
In a chapel on the shore,
Shall the chaunter, sad and saintly,
Yellow tapers burning faintly,
Doleful masses chaunt for thee,
Miserere Domine!

Hark! the cadence dies away
　　On the quiet moonlight sea:
The boatmen rest their oars and say,
　　Miserere Domine!
S. T. Coleridge.

216. EGYPT

... Egypt! thy pyramid of power is closed....
                                            W. S. Landor.

217. MAJESTIC INTELLECT

... It was a close, warm, breezeless summer night,
Wan, dull, and glaring, with a dripping fog
Long-hung and thick that covered all the sky;
But, undiscouraged, we began to climb
The mountain-side. The mist soon girt us round,
And after ordinary travellers' talk
With our conductor, pensively we sank
Each into commerce with his private thoughts:
Thus did we breast the ascent, and by myself
Was nothing either seen or heard that checked
Those musings or diverted, save that once
The shepherd's lurcher, who, among the crags,
Had to his joy unearthed a hedgehog, teased
His coiled-up prey with barkings turbulent.
This small adventure, for even such it seemed
In that wild place and at the dead of night,
Being over and forgotten, on we wound
In silence as before. With forehead bent
Earthward, as if in opposition set
Against an enemy, I panted up
With eager pace, and no less eager thoughts.
Thus might we wear a midnight hour away,
Ascending at loose distance each from each,
And I, as chanced, the foremost of the band;
When at my feet the ground appeared to brighten,
And with a step or two seemed brighter still;
Nor was time given to ask or learn the cause,
For instantly a light upon the turf
Fell like a flash, and lo! as I looked up,
The Moon hung naked in a firmament
Of azure without cloud, and at my feet

Rested a silent sea of hoary mist.
A hundred hills their dusky backs upheaved
All over this still ocean; and beyond,
Far, far beyond, the solid vapours stretched,
In headlands, tongues, and promontory shapes,
Into the main Atlantic, that appeared
To dwindle, and give up his majesty,
Usurped upon far as the sight could reach.
Not so the ethereal vault; encroachment none
Was there, nor loss; only the inferior stars
Had disappeared, or shed a fainter light
In the clear presence of the full-orbed Moon,
Who, from her sovereign elevation, gazed
Upon the billowy ocean, as it lay
All meek and silent, save that through a rift—
Not distant from the shore whereon we stood,
A fixed, abysmal, gloomy, breathing-place—
Mounted the roar of waters, torrents, streams
Innumerable, roaring with one voice!
Heard over earth and sea, and, in that hour,
For so it seemed, felt by the starry heavens.

When into air had partially dissolved
That vision, given to spirits of the night
And three chance human wanderers, in calm thought
Reflected, it appeared to me the type
Of a majestic intellect, its acts
And its possessions, what it has and craves,
What in itself it is, and would become. . . .
William Wordsworth.

218. NATURE, SCIENCE AND ART

THE contemplation of the laws of the universe is connected with an immediate tranquil exaltation of mind, and pure mental enjoyment. The perception of truth is almost as simple a feeling as the perception of beauty; and the genius of Newton, of Shakespeare, of Michael Angelo, and of Handel are not very remote in character from each other. Imagination, as well as reason, is necessary to perfection in the philosophical mind. A rapidity of combination, a power of perceiving analogies, and of comparing them by facts, is the creative source of discovery. Discrimination and delicacy of sensation, so important in physical research, are other words for taste; and the love of nature is the same passion, as the love of the magnificent, the sublime, and the beautiful.

Humphry Davy.

219. THE EXHIBITION OF NEW SUBSTANCES, OR DISCOVERY OF POTASSIUM AND SODIUM

i

A SMALL piece of pure potash, which had been exposed for a few seconds to the atmosphere ... was placed upon an insulated disc of platina, connected with the negative side of the battery of the power of 250 of 6 and 4, in a state of intense activity; and a platina wire, communicating with the positive side, was brought into contact with the upper surface of the alkali ... a vivid action was soon observed to take place. The potash began to fuse at both its points of electrization. There was a violent effervescence at the upper surface; at the lower, or negative surface, there was no liberation of elastic fluid; but small globules having a high metallic lustre, and being precisely similar in visible character to quicksilver, appeared, some of which burst with explosion and bright flame, as soon as they were formed. . . .

Soda, when acted upon in the same manner as potash, exhibited an analogous result. . . . When the power of 250 was used, with a very high charge for the decomposition of soda, the globules often burnt at the moment of their formation, and sometimes violently exploded and separated into smaller globules, which flew with great velocity through the air in a state of vivid combustion, producing a beautiful effect of continued jets of fire. *Humphry Davy.*

ii

. . . when he saw the minute globules of potassium burst through the crust of potash and take fire as they entered the atmosphere, he could not contain his joy—he actually bounded about the room in extatic delight. *John Davy.*

220. THE LIFE OF NATURE

... O Lady! we receive but what we give,
   And in our life alone does nature live:
    Ours is her wedding-garment, ours her shroud!
      And would we aught behold, of higher worth,
Than that inanimate cold world allowed
To the poor loveless ever-anxious crowd,
   Ah! from the soul itself must issue forth,
A light, a glory, a fair luminous cloud
        Enveloping the Earth—
And from the soul itself must there be sent
   A sweet and potent voice, of its own birth,
Of all sweet sounds the life and element!

O pure of heart! thou need'st not ask of me
What this strong music in the soul may be!
What, and wherein it doth exist,
This light, this glory, this fair luminous mist,
This beautiful and beauty-making power.
   Joy, virtuous Lady! Joy that ne'er was given,
Save to the pure, and in their purest hour,
Life, and Life's effluence, cloud at once and shower,
Joy, Lady! is the spirit and the power,
Which wedding Nature to us gives in dower,
   A new Earth and new Heaven,
Undreamt of by the sensual and the proud—
Joy is the sweet voice, Joy the luminous cloud—
     We in ourselves rejoice!
And thence flows all that charms or ear or sight,
   All melodies the echoes of that voice,
All colours a suffusion from that light. ...
                 S. T. Coleridge.

221. DEATH OF THE HEART

THE Pine Tree blasted at the top was applied by Swift to himself as a prophetic emblem of his own decay. The Chestnut is a fine shady tree, and its wood excellent, were it not that it dies away at the *heart* first. Alas! poor me!

S. T. Coleridge.

222. THE GLOW-WORM

>   . . . I heard,
> After the hour of sunset yester-even,
> Sitting within doors, between light and dark,
> A choir of redbreasts gathered somewhere near
> My threshold,—minstrels from the distant woods
> Sent in on Winter's service, to announce,
> With preparation artful and benign,
> That the rough lord had left the surly North
> On his accustomed journey. The delight,
> Due to this timely notice, unawares
> Smote me, and, listening, I in whispers said,
> "Ye heartsome Choristers, ye and I will be
> Associates, and, unscared by blustering winds,
> Will chant together." Thereafter, as the shades
> Of twilight deepened, going forth, I spied
> A glow-worm underneath a dusky plume
> Or canopy of yet unwithered fern,
> Clear-shining, like a hermit's taper seen
> Through a thick forest. Silence touched me here
> No less than sound had done before; the child
> Of Summer, lingering, shining, by herself,
> The voiceless worm on the unfrequented hills,
> Seemed sent on the same errand with the choir
> Of Winter that had warbled at the door,
> And the whole year breathed tenderness and love. . . .

William Wordsworth.

223. LOVE

         . . . By love subsists
All lasting grandeur, by pervading love;
That gone, we are as dust.—Behold the fields
In balmy spring-time full of rising flowers
And joyous creatures; see that pair, the lamb
And the lamb's mother, and their tender ways
Shall touch thee to the heart; thou callest this love,
And not inaptly so, for love it is,
Far as it carries thee. In some green bower
Rest, and be not alone, but have thou there
The One who is thy choice of all the world:
There linger, listening, gazing, with delight
Impassioned, but delight how pitiable!
Unless this love by a still higher love
Be hallowed, love that breathes not without awe;
Love that adores, but on the knees of prayer,
By heaven inspired; that frees from chains the soul,
Lifted in union with the purest, best,
Of earth-born passions, on the wings of praise
Bearing a tribute to the Almighty's Throne.
This spiritual Love acts not nor can exist
Without Imagination, which, in truth,
Is but another name for absolute power
And clearest insight, amplitude of mind,
And Reason in her most exalted mood. . . .
                              William Wordsworth.

224. SHAKESPEARE

OUR own Shakespeare, himself a nature humanized, a genial understanding directing self-consciously a power and implicit wisdom deeper than consciousness.

                              S. T. Coleridge.

225. MODERATION AND HARLOTRY

THERE are poets among us who mistake in themselves the freckles of the hay-fever for beauty-spots. In another half-century their volumes will be enquired after; but only for the sake of cutting out an illuminated letter from the title-page, or of transplanting the willow at the end, that hangs so prettily over the tomb of Amaryllis. If they wish to be healthy, and vigorous, let them open their bosoms to the breezes of Sunium; for the air of Latium is heavy and overcharged. Above all they must remember two admonitions; first, that sweet things hurt digestion; secondly that great sails are ill adapted to small vessels. What is there lovely in poetry unless there be moderation and composure? Are they not better than the hot, uncontrollable harlotry of a flaunting dishevelled enthusiasm? Whoever has the power of creating, has likewise the inferior power of keeping his creation in order. The best poets are most impressive because their steps are regular; for without regularity there is neither strength nor state.
W. S. Landor.

226. THE DAISY

... That to this mountain-daisy's self were known
The beauty of its star-shaped shadow, thrown
On the smooth surface of this naked stone! ...
William Wordsworth.

227. THE DEMOBILIZED SOLDIER

... My homeward course led up a long ascent,
Where the road's watery surface, to the top
Of that sharp rising, glittered to the moon
And bore the semblance of another stream
Stealing with silent lapse to join the brook
That murmured in the vale. All else was still;

No living thing appeared in earth or air,
And, save the flowing water's peaceful voice,
Sound there was none—but, lo! an uncouth shape,
Shown by a sudden turning of the road,
So near that, slipping back into the shade
Of a thick hawthorn, I could mark him well,
Myself unseen. He was of stature tall,
A span above man's common measure, tall,
Stiff, lank, and upright; a more meagre man
Was never seen before by night or day.
Long were his arms, pallid his hands; his mouth
Looked ghastly in the moonlight: from behind,
A mile-stone propped him; I could also ken
That he was clothed in military garb,
Though faded, yet entire. Companionless,
No dog attending, by no staff sustained,
He stood, and in his very dress appeared
A desolation, a simplicity,
To which the trappings of a gaudy world
Make a strange back-ground. From his lips, ere long,
Issued low muttered sounds, as if of pain
Or some uneasy thought; yet still his form
Kept the same awful steadiness—at his feet
His shadow lay, and moved not. From self-blame
Not wholly free, I watched him thus; at length
Subduing my heart's specious cowardice,
I left the shady nook where I had stood
And hailed him. Slowly from his resting-place
He rose, and with a lean and wasted arm
In measured gesture lifted to his head
Returned my salutation; then resumed
His station as before; and when I asked
His history, the veteran, in reply,
Was neither slow nor eager; but, unmoved,
And with a quiet uncomplaining voice,
A stately air of mild indifference,
He told in few plain words a soldier's tale—
That in the Tropic Islands he had served,
Whence he had landed scarcely three weeks past;

That on his landing he had been dismissed,
And now was travelling towards his native home.
This heard, I said, in pity, "Come with me."
He stooped, and straightway from the ground took up
An oaken staff by me yet unobserved—
A staff which must have dropped from his slack hand
And lay till now neglected in the grass.
Though weak his step and cautious, he appeared
To travel without pain, and I beheld,
With an astonishment but ill suppressed,
His ghostly figure moving at my side;
Nor could I, while we journeyed thus, forbear
To turn from present hardships to the past,
And speak of war, battle, and pestilence,
Sprinkling this talk with questions, better spared,
On what he might himself have seen or felt.
He all the while was in demeanour calm,
Concise in answer; solemn and sublime
He might have seemed, but that in all he said
There was a strange half-absence, as of one
Knowing too well the importance of his theme,
But feeling it no longer. Our discourse
Soon ended, and together on we passed
In silence through a wood gloomy and still.
Up-turning, then, along an open field,
We reached a cottage. At the door I knocked,
And earnestly to charitable care
Commended him as a poor friendless man,
Belated and by sickness overcome.
Assured that now the traveller would repose
In comfort, I entreated that henceforth
He would not linger in the public ways,
But ask for timely furtherance and help
Such as his state required. At this reproof,
With the same ghastly mildness in his look,
He said, "My trust is in the God of Heaven,
And in the eye of him who passes me!" . . .

William Wordsworth.

228. PEDANTRY AGAINST WORDSWORTH

MR. PORSON, it does not appear to me that anything more is necessary, in the first instance, than to interrogate our hearts in what manner they have been affected. If the ear is satisfied; if at one moment a tumult is aroused in the breast, and tranquillized at another, with a perfect consciousness of equal power exerted in both cases; if we rise up from a perusal of the work with a strong excitement to thought, to imagination, to sensibility; above all, if we sat down with some propensities toward evil, and walk away with much stronger toward good, in the midst of a world which we never had entered and of which we never had dreamed before— shall we perversely put on again the *old man* of criticism, and dissemble that we have been conducted by a most beneficent and most potent genius? Nothing proves to me so manifestly in what a pestiferous condition are its lazarettos, as when I observe how little hath been objected against those who have substituted words for things, and how much against those who have reinstated things for words.

Let Wordsworth prove to the world that there may be animation without blood and broken bones, and tenderness remote from the stews. Some will doubt it; for even things the most evident are often but little perceived and strangely estimated. Swift ridiculed the music of Handel and the generalship of Marlborough; Pope the perspicacity and the scholarship of Bentley; Gray the abilities of Shaftesbury and the eloquence of Rousseau. Shakespeare hardly found those who would collect his tragedies; Milton was read from Godliness; Virgil was antiquated and rustic; Cicero, Asiatic. What a rabble has persecuted my friend! An elephant is born to be consumed by ants in the midst of his unapproachable solitudes: Wordsworth is the prey of Jeffrey. Why repine? Let us rather amuse ourselves with allegories, and recollect that God in the creation left His noblest creature at the mercy of a serpent. *W. S. Landor.*

229. PORTRAIT OF A VICAR

... But let applause be dealt in all we may:
Our priest was cheerful, and in season gay;
His frequent visits seldom fail'd to please;
Easy himself, he sought his neighbour's ease.
To a small garden with delight he came,
And gave successive flowers a summer's fame;
These he presented with a grace his own
To his fair friends, and made their beauties known,
Not without moral compliment: how they
"Like flowers were sweet, and must like flowers decay."

   Simple he was, and loved the simple truth,
Yet had some useful cunning from his youth;
A cunning never to dishonour lent,
And rather for defence than conquest meant;
'Twas fear of power, with some desire to rise,
But not enough to make him enemies;
He ever aim'd to please; and to offend
Was ever cautious; for he sought a friend;
Yet for that friendship never much would pay,
Content to bow, be silent, and obey,
And by a soothing suff'ranee find his way.

   Fiddling and fishing were his arts; at times
He alter'd sermons, and he aim'd at rhymes;
And his fair friends, not yet intent on cards,
Oft he amused with riddles and charades.

   Mild were his doctrines, and not one discourse
But gain'd in softness what it lost in force:
Kind his opinions; he would not receive
An ill report, nor evil act believe;
"If true, 'twas wrong; but blemish great or small
Have all mankind; yea, sinners are we all." ...

Habit with him was all the test of truth,
"It must be right: I've done it from my youth."
Questions he answer'd in as brief a way,
"It must be wrong—it was of yesterday."

Though mild benevolence our priest possess'd,
'Twas but by wishes or by words express'd:
Circles in water, as they wider flow,
The less conspicuous in their progress grow;
And when at last they touch upon the shore,
Distinction ceases, and they're viewed no more.
His love, like that last circle, all embraced,
But with effect that never could be traced.

   Now rests our Vicar. They who knew him best
Proclaim his life t'have been entirely rest—
Free from all evils which disturb his mind
Whom studies vex and controversies blind.

   The rich approved—of them in awe he stood;
The poor admired—they all believed him good;
The old and serious of his habits spoke;
The frank and youthful loved his pleasant joke;
Mothers approved a safe contented guest
And daughters one who back'd each small request:
In him his flock found nothing to condemn;
Him secretaries liked—he never troubled them;
No trifles fail'd his yielding mind to please
And all his passions sunk in early ease;
Nor one so old has left this world of sin,
More like the being that he enter'd in.

George Crabbe.

230. MILTON

WILL mortals never know each other's station
Without the herald? O abomination!

> Milton, even Milton, rankt with living men!
> Over the highest Alps of mind he marches,
> And far below him spring the baseless arches
> Of Iris, colouring dimly lake and fen.
>
> W. S. Landor.

231. NATURE

THE love of Nature is ever returned double to us, not only the delighter in our delight, but by linking our sweetest, but of themselves perishable feelings to distinct and vivid images, which we ourselves, at times, and which a thousand casual recollections, recall to our memory. She is the preserver, the treasurer of our joys. Even in sickness and nervous diseases, she has peopled our imagination with lovely forms which have sometimes overpowered the inward pain and brought with them their old sensations. And even when all men have seemed to desert us and the friend of our heart has passed on, with one glance from his "cold disliking eye"—yet even then the blue heaven spreads it out and bends over us, and the little tree still shelters us under its plumage as a second cope, a domestic firmament, and a low creeping gale will sigh in the heath-plant and soothe us by sound of sympathy till the lulled grief lose itself in fixed gaze on the purple heath-bloom, till the present beauty becomes a vision of memory.

S. T. Coleridge.

232. PAINTING IS FEELING

How much I wish I had been with you on your fishing excursion in the New Forest! What river can it be? But the sound of water escaping from mill-dams, etc., willows, old rotten planks, slimy posts and brickwork, I love such things. . . . Still I should paint my own places best; painting is with me but another word for feeling, and I associate "my careless boyhood" with all that lies on the banks of the Stour; those scenes made me a painter, and I am grateful.   *John Constable.*

233. THE CORRUPTION OF POWER

... O brother, brother! are men always men?
  They are full-grown then only when grown up
  Above their fears. Power never yet stood safe;
  Compass it round with friends and kindnesses,
  And not with moats of blood. Remember Thebes:
  The towers of Cadmus toppled, split asunder,
  Crasht: in the shadow of her oleanders
  The pure and placid Dirce still flows by.
  What shatter'd to its base but cruelty,
  (Mother of crimes, all lesser than herself)
  The house of Agamemnon king of kings? ...
                                         W. S. Landor.

234. AUTUMNAL SONG

  Very true, the linnets sing
  Sweetest in the leaves of spring:
  You have found in all these leaves
  That which changes and deceives,
  And, to pine by sun or star,
  Left them, false ones as they are.
  But there be who walk beside
  Autumn's, till they all have died,
  And who lend a patient ear
  To low notes from branches sere.
                                         W. S. Landor.

235. THE SELF-POWER OF IMAGINATION

O, Strange is the self-power of the imagination—when painful sensations have made it their interpreter, or returning gladmeness or convalescence has made its chilled and evanished res and landscapes bud, blossom, and live in scarlet, green, snowy white (like the fire-screen inscribed with the nitrate muriate of cobalt,)—strange is the power to represent the and circumstances, even to the anguish or the triumph of the quasi-credent soul, while the necessary conditions, the only possible causes of such contingencies, are known to be in fact quite hopeless;—yea, when the pure mind would recoil from the eve-lengthened shadow of an approaching hope, as from a crime;—and yet the effect shall have place, and substance, and living energy, and, on a blue islet of ether, in a whole sky of blackest cloudage, shine like a firstling of creation!

S. T. Coleridge.

236. DEATH AND LOVE

WEARIED with the length, of my walk over the mountains, and finding a soft old molehill, covered with grey grass, by the wayside, I laid my head upon it and slept. I cannot tell how long it was before a species of dream or vision came over me.

Two beautiful youths appeared beside me; each was winged; but the wings were hanging down, and seemed ill adapted to flight. One of them, whose voice was the softest I ever heard, looking at me frequently, said to the other:

"He is under my guardianship for the present: do not awaken him with that feather."

Methought, hearing the whisper, I saw something like the feather on an arrow; and then the arrow itself; the whole of it, even to the point; although he carried it in such a manner that it was difficult at first to discover more than a palm's length of it: the rest of the shaft, and the whole of the barb, was behind his ankles.

"This feather never awakens any one," replied he, rather petulantly; "but it brings more of confident security, and more of cherished dreams, than you without me are capable of imparting."

"Be it so!" answered the gentler . . . "none is less inclined to quarrel or dispute than I am. Many whom you have wounded grievously, call upon me for succour. But so little am I disposed to thwart you, it is seldom I venture to do more for them than to whisper a few words of comfort in passing. How many reproaches on these occasions have been cast upon me for indifference and infidelity! Nearly as many, and nearly in the same terms, as upon you!"

"Odd enough that we, o Sleep! should be thought so alike," said Love contemptuously. "Yonder is he who bears a nearer resemblance to you: the dullest have observed it." I fancied I turned my eyes to where he was pointing, and saw at a distance the figure he designated. Meanwhile the contention went on uninterruptedly. Sleep was slow in asserting his power or his benefits. Love recapitulated them; but only that he might assert his own above them. Suddenly he called on me to decide, and to choose my patron. Under the influence, first of the one, then of the other, I sprang from repose to rapture, I alighted from rapture on repose . . . and knew not which was sweetest. Love was very angry with me, and declared he would cross me throughout the whole of my existence. Whatever I might on other occasions have thought of his veracity, I now felt too surely the conviction that he would keep his word. At last, before the close of the altercation, the third Genius had advanced, and stood near us. I cannot tell how I knew him, but I knew him to be the Genius of Death. Breathless as I was at beholding him, I soon became familiar with his features. First they seemed only calm; presently they grew contemplative; and lastly beautiful: those of the Graces themselves are less regular, less harmonious, less composed. Love glanced at him unsteadily, with a countenance in which there was somewhat of anxiety, somewhat of disdain; and cried: "Go away! go away! nothing that thou touchest, lives."

"Say rather, child!" replied the advancing form, and advancing grew loftier and statelier, "say rather that nothing of beautiful or of glorious lives its own true Me until my wing hath passed over it."

Love pouted, and rumpled and bent down with his forefinger the stiff short feathers on his arrow-head; but replied not. Although he frowned worse than ever, and at me, I dreaded him less and less, and scarcely looked towards him. The milder and calmer Genius, preferred, in proportion as I took courage to contemplate him, regarded me with more and more complacency. He held neither flower nor arrow, as the others did; but, throwing back the clusters of dark curls that overshadowed his countenance, he presented to me his hand, openly and benignly. I shrank on looking at him so near, and yet I sighed to love him. He smiled, not without an expression of pity, at perceiving my diffidence, my timidity: for I remembered how soft was the hand of Sleep, how warm and entrancing was Love's. By degrees, I became ashamed of my ingratitude; and turning my face away, I held out my arms, and felt my neck within his. Composure strewed and delayed all the throbbings of my bosom; the coolness of the freshest morning breathed around: the heavens seemed to open above me; while the beautiful cheek of my deliverer rested on my head. I would now have looked for those others; but knowing my intention by my gesture, he said, consolatorily:

"Sleep is on his way to the Earth, where many are calling him; but it is not to these he hastens; for every call only makes him fly farther off. Sedately and gravely as he looks, he is nearly as capricious and volatile as the more arrogant and ferocious one."

"And Love!" said I, "whither is he departed? If not too late, I would propitiate and appease him."

"He who cannot follow me, he who cannot overtake and pass me," said the Genius, "is unworthy of the name, the most glorious in earth or heaven. Look up! Love is yonder, and ready to receive thee."

I looked; the earth was under me: I saw only the clear blue sky, and something brighter above me.

W. S. Landor.

237. LANDSCAPE OF THE HEART

  ... The landscape lies in snow: brown leafless woods
    Stretch to the water's edge, contrasting dark
    With the dell's whiten'd hollows: dark the stream
    Now winding at its full: a mirror'd flood
    Of clearest blackness, so intensely white
    Glare the frozen banks above it, and the vales
    Fringed with their bare brown thickets: oh drear scene!
    How alter'd, yet how meet!—when last I stood
    Upon this beetling clift, the leafy dells
    Laugh'd in their greenness: hawthorns blossom'd thick

And hazels spread their clusters, and the paths
And brakes were gemm'd with flowerets, while the birds
Chirp'd their shrill notes, confus'd with bleating sounds
From the sloped vallies by that river's side;
And the full current, sparkling in the sun,
Wafted some home-bound ship, its streamers spread
To the soft fanning breeze: and when I look'd
Beyond me, that fair stripling youth was seen
Lifting his half-bower'd head among the dells;
The whilst that other rose-cheek'd boy, who track'd
His steps, was busied with the treasury
Of mosses, hare-bells, wild anemonies,
Or honeysuckle. . . .
                      But now I look

   Upon a scene of wintry dreariment,
   Pale, leafless, herbless, cold: on that black stream
   Black from o'erpowering white, the very barks
   And they, the living beings, that propel
   Their sullen sluggish motion, darkling move,
   As if the nether Acheron roll'd on
   Its tide before me, and a ghostly fleet
   Sail'd on its ebon current. Oh most strange
   And most congenial picture! death is there—
   Death is before my vision: death within
   My heart: but as I lift my saddening eyes
   The tops of those tall clifts are tinged with light
   As it were gold: and on my left the sky
   Is one clear space of azure, where the sun,
   A broaden'd orb, in ruddy splendour, hangs
   About to drop beyond the western hills:
   Making the whiten'd banks and woodlands brown,
   The clear black current and the darksome barks
   More desolate from contrast, yet to all
   Yielding a glory and sublime relief
   With mingled gorgeous imagery of light;
   Though solemn still, and chasten'd by the gloom
   And desolation. . . .
                      Charles Abraham Elton.

238. ALL THINGS DIFFER

THE world is wide; no two days are alike, nor even two hours; neither were there ever two leaves of a tree alike since the creation of the world; and the genuine productions of art, like those of nature, are all distinct from each other.

John Constable.

239. TWO PICTURES

i

A MINER, ABOUT TO DESCEND THE SHAFT OF A MINE
IN DERBYSHIRE

WHILE Mr. Ward was pursuing his professional studies at Castleton, he had returned to the light of day, from the dreary subterraneous cavern of the Peak Hole, (that which nothing can be conceived more awfully terrible, or more expressive of the fabled Charon ferrying over the river Styx the departed spirits of the damned to the infernal regions), he was attracted to the side of the overhanging rock by the appearance of a shaft, or descent, to a lead mine, into which he entered. The depth appeared bottomless, as he lowered himself perpendicularly by the bars of wood, or pegs, thrust into the rocks. The silence was only interrupted by the distant clink of a solitary hammer, beating out the lead from its primeval bed of stone. He came at length to an aged venerable-looking man, doomed by hard necessity to pass an unvarying life amid solitary damps and midnight gloom. He said little in reply to the questions that were put to him; offered some few specimens of his trade; and pointed to a lower sphere, in which he said his son was working, To this Mr. Ward descended, and found a man steadily at work, with irons at his feet. He uttered not one word to the interrogatories by which he seemed to feel himself assailed; but fixed, as if wedged into a small nook in which he appeared to have worked out his own form and size, continued to pick out the small bits of lead. Such was the situation of the being here represented. On learning that this unhappy man had been in a state of insanity, some few years before, during which he had stabbed an individual, and that a fixed gloom differing but little from lunacy hung upon him still, it was considered, that his character was not to be lost, as a part of that diversity of Nature's operation, which it is the business of the painter to embrace in all its varieties. Mr. Ward, therefore, got the man to stand for his portrait, and from that drawing the present picture was painted, while the recollection was fresh on the mind of the Artist.

ii
PORTRAITS OF LUKE AND KATE KENNY

Two remarkable characters—Luke, aged 96, and Kate, his wife, 88. They lived as charcoal burners, in the woods of Alderwaslie, Derbyshire, and brought up a family of eight children, without ever having entered a house except for the purchase of necessaries. Their habitation was a moveable hut, in the form of a cone, or sugar-loaf, one side of which was furnished with a bed upon the turf; and the opening was covered by a large board laid upon the outside. In cold weather they usually took a portion of their wood fire within-side the hut: the outside of this tenement was covered with the turf they used in making charcoal. A rainy night had preceded the morning on which the artist went to make his studies from the various articles connected with their mode of life. He found the woman bailing out water with a wooden bowl from the lower ground of the steamy bed-chamber, where it had settled at the foot of the bed in a considerable quantity:— yet, such is the force of habit, that when the old man was standing for his picture in the large dining parlour, he expressed himself miserably uncomfortable from the cold, and at the same time observed, how much more warm and comfortable he was in his snug little habitation, than in these great and comfortless rooms. Luke was the first portrait. When his wife came to sit for her likeness, and saw the representation of her husband, she burst into tears, exclaiming, "Ah! poor old soul, there he is, for all the world, with his round back! he was once as straight as an arrow; but he is *welly* done." Their favourite spot in the woods was the shade of an immense yew-tree, under which one of their children lies buried.

After toiling for years in this miserable employment of charcoal burning, they accumulated a sum of ten pounds. Some wretched miscreant, having ascertained this circumstance, broke in upon their retirement, dragged them from their bed, and after treating them with great cruelty, robbed them of their treasure. The man survived his loss but a short time.

James Ward, R. A.

240. MURDER

ONCE at a dinner-table, Landseer told Professor Owen that, in early life, he was fond of making drawings of any tragical event, and that in 1824 he had made a series of designs of the particulars of the murder of Weare, at Elstree, by the brothers Thurtell. Upon the Professor expressing surprise, that he should have been interested in that dreadful murder, he exclaimed, "Oh, but I like murders."

Solomon Hart, R.A.

241. CONSTABLE'S ABSTRACTED ART

I AM much interested with your account of the pictures at Petworth. I remember most of Turner's early works; amongst them was one of singular intricacy and beauty; it was a canal with numerous boats making thousands of beautiful shapes, and I think the most complete work of genius I ever saw. . . .

Your mention of a solemn twilight by Gainsborough has awakened all my sympathy; do pray make me a sketch of it of some kind or other, if it is only a slight splash.

As to meeting you in these grand scenes, dear Leslie, remember the Great were not made for me, nor I for the Great; things are better as they are. My limited and abstracted art is to be found under every hedge and in every lane, and therefore nobody thinks it worth picking up; but I have my admirers, each of whom I consider an host.

John Constable.

242. VISIONARIES: JAKOB BOEHME AND FENELON

LET us imagine a poor pilgrim benighted in a wilderness or desert, and pursuing his way in the starless dark with a lantern in his hand. Chance or his happy genius leads him to an Oasis or Natural Garden, such as in the creations of my youthful fancy I supposed Enos the Child of Cain to have found. And here, hungry and thirsty, the way-wearied man rests at a fountain; and the taper of his lantern throws its light on an over-shadowing tree, a boss of snow-white blossoms, through which the green and glowing fruits peeped, and the ripe golden fruitage glowed. Deep, vivid, and faithful are the impressions, which the lovely Imagery comprised within the scanty circle of light, makes and leaves on his memory! But scarcely has he eaten of the fruits and drunk of the fountain, ere scared by the roar and howl from the desert he hurries forward: and as he passes with hasty steps through grove and glade, shadows and imperfect beholdings and vivid fragments of things distinctly seen blend with the past and present shapings of his brain. Fancy modifies sight. His dreams transfer their forms to real objects; and these lend a substance and an *outness* to his dreams. Apparitions greet him; and when at a distance from this enchanted land, and on a different track, the dawn of day discloses to him a caravan, a troop of his fellow-men, his memory, which is itself half fancy, is interpolated afresh by every attempt to recall, connect, and *piece out* his recollections. His narration is received as a madman's tale. He shrinks from the rude laugh and the contemptuous sneer, and retires into himself. Yet the craving for sympathy, strong in proportion to the intensity of his convictions, impels him to unbosom himself to abstract auditors; and the poor Quietest becomes a Penman, and, all too poorly stocked for the writer's trade, he borrows his phrases and figures from the only writings to which he has had access, the sacred books of his religion. And thus I shadow out the enthusiastic Mystic of the first sort; at the head of which stands the illuminated Teutonic theosopher and shoemaker, honest Jacob Behmen. . . .

To delineate a Mystic of the second and higher order, we need only endow our pilgrim with equal gifts of nature, but these developed and displayed by all the aids and arts of education and favourable fortune. *He* is on the way to the Mecca of his ancestral and national faith, with a well-guarded and numerous procession of merchants and fellow-pilgrims on the established track. At the close of the day the caravan has halted: the full moon rises on the desert: and he strays forth alone, out of sight but to no unsafe distance; and chance leads *him* too, to the same oasis or Islet of Verdure on the Sea of Sand. He wanders at lesiure in its maze of beauty and sweetness, and thrids his way through the odorous and flowering thickets into open spots of greenery, and discovers statues and memorial characters, grottos, and refreshing caves. But the moonshine, the imaginative poesy of nature, spreads its soft shadowy charm over all, conceals distances, and magnifies heights, and modifies relations: and fills up vacuities with its own whiteness, counterfeiting substance; and where the dense shadows lie, makes solidity imitate hollowness; and gives to all objects a tender visionary hue and softening. Interpret the moonlight and the shadows as the peculiar genius and, sensibility of the individual's own spirit: and here you have the other sort: a Mystic, an Enthusiast of a nobler breed—a: Fenelon. But the residentiary, or the frequent visitor of the favoured spot, who has scanned its beauties by steady day-light, and mastered its true proportions and lineaments, he will discover that both pilgrims have indeed been there. *He* will know, that the delightful dream, which the latter tells, is a dream of truth; and that even in the bewildered tale of the former there is truth mingled with the dream.

S. T. Coleridge.

243. WORK WITHOUT HOPE

Lines Composed 21St February, 1825

ALL Nature seems at work. Slugs leave their lair—
The bees are stirring—birds are on the wing—
And Winter slumbering in the open air,
Wears on his smiling face a dream of Spring!

And I the while, the sole unbusy thing,
  Nor honey make, nor pair, nor build, nor sing.

   Yet well I ken the banks where amaranths blow,
  Have traced the fount whence streams of nectar flow.
  Bloom, O ye amaranths! bloom for whom ye may
  For me ye bloom not I Glide, rich streams, away!
  With lips unbrightened, wreathless brow, I stroll:
  And would you learn the spells that drowse my soul?
  Work without Hope draws nectar in a sieve,
  And Hope without an object cannot live.
                                     S. T. Coleridge.

244. THE ELDER BUSHES

I NEVER saw the Elder Bushes so filled with blossom—they are quite beautifull—& some of their blossom forshortened as they curve over the round head of the tree itself are quite elegant—it is a favourite of mine & always was—but 'tis melancholy.   *John Constable.*

245. SONG

  THOUGH veiled in spires of myrtle-wreath,
  Love is a sword which cuts its sheath,
  And through the clefts itself has made,
  We spy the flashes of the blade!

  But through the clefts itself has made,
  We likewise see Love's flashing blade
  By rust consumed, or snapt in twain;
  And only hilt and stump remain.
                                     S. T. Coleridge.

246. AYE! AND WHAT THEN?

IF a man could pass through Paradise in a dream, and have a flower presented to him as a pledge that his soul had really been there, and if he found that flower in his hand when he awoke—Aye! and what then?   *S. T. Coleridge.*

PART III: THE SENSUAL VALLEY

> . . . *even minds possessing much of the power of understanding, may be little disposed to undergo the labour of it, when amidst the ease of the deepest indolence they can revel in the activity of a more animating employment. Imagination may be indulged till it usurp an entire ascendancy over the mind, and then every subject presented to that mind will be taken under the action of imagination, instead of understanding; imagination will throw its colours where the intellectual faculty ought to draw its lines; will accumulate metaphors where reason ought to deduce arguments; images will take the place of thoughts, and scenes of disquisitions. The whole mind may become at length something like a hemisphere of cloud-scenery, filled with an ever-moving train of changing melting forms, of every colour, mingled with rainbows, meteors, and an occasional gleam of pure sunlight, all vanishing away, the mental like this natural imagery, when its hour is up, without leaving anything behind but the wish to recover the vision.*
>
> John Foster.

247. THE ACCURSED

THAT Power whicn strikes the luminaries of me world with sudden darkness and extinction, by awakening them to too exquisite a perception of its influences, dooms to a slow and poisonous decay those meaner spirits that dare to abjure its dominion. Their destiny is more abject and inglorious as their delinquency is more contemptible and pernicious. They, who deluded by no generous error, instigated by no sacred thirst of doubtful knowledge, duped by no illustrious superstition, loving nothing on this earth, and cherishing no hopes beyond, yet keep aloof from sympathies with their kind, rejoicing neither in human joy nor mourning with human grief; these, and such as they, have their apportioned curse. They languish, because none feel with them their common nature. They are morally dead. They are neither friends, nor lovers, nor fathers, nor citizens of the world, nor benefactors of their country. Among those who attempt to exist without human sympathy, the pure and tender-hearted perish through the intensity and passion of their search after its communities, when the vacancy of their spirit suddenly makes itself felt. All else, selfish, blind, and torpid, are those unforeseeing multitudes who constitute, together with their own, the lasting misery and loneliness of the world. Those who love not their fellow-beings live unfruitful lives, and prepare for their old age a miserable grave.

> "The good die first,
> And those whose hearts are dry as summer dust,
> Burn to the socket!"

P. B. Shelley.

248. LOVE UNSEEN

... Oh Love I no habitant of earth thou art—
An unseen seraph, we believe in thee,
A faith whose martyrs are the broken heart,
But never yet hath seen, nor e'er shall see
The naked eye, thy form, as it should be;

> The mind hath made thee, as it peopled heaven,
> Even with its own desiring phantasy,
> And to a thought such shape and image given,
> As haunts the unquenched soul—parched—wearied—wrung—
>   and riven.
>
> Of its own beauty is the mind diseased,
> And fevers into false creation:—where,
> Where are the forms the sculptor's soul hath seized?
> In him alone. Can Nature show so fair?
> Where are the charms and virtues which we dare
> Conceive in boyhood and pursue as men,
> The unreached Paradise of our despair,
> Which o'er-informs the pencil and the pen,
> And overpowers the page where it would bloom again?
>
> Lord Byron.

249. MASSACRE IN A CAVE

26th August, 1814.—At seven this morning we were in the Sound which divides the Isle of Rum from that of Eigg. The latter, although hilly and rocky, and traversed by a remarkably high and barren ridge, called Scoor-Rigg, has, in point of soil, a much more promising appearance. Southward of both lies the Isle of Muich, or Muck, a low and fertile island, and though the least, yet probably the most valuable of the three. We manned the boat and rowed along the shore of Egg in quest of a cavern, which had been the memorable scene of a horrid feudal vengeance. We had rounded more than half the island, admiring the entrance of many a bold natural cave, which its rocks exhibited, without finding that which we sought, until we procured a guide. Nor, indeed, was it surprising that it should have escaped the search of strangers, as there are no outward indications more than might distinguish the entrance of a fox-earth. This noted cave has a very narrow opening, through which one can hardly creep on his knees and hands. It rises steep and lofty within, and runs into the bowels of the rock to the depth of 255 measured feet; the height at the entrance may be about three feet, but rises within to eighteen or twenty, and the breadth may vary in the same proportion. The rude and stony bottom of this cave is strewed with the bones of men, women, and children, the sad relics of the ancient inhabitants of the island, 200 in number, who were slain on the following occasion:—The Mac-Donalds of the Isle of Egg, a people dependent on Clan-Ranald, had done some injury to the Laird of Mac-Leod. The tradition of the isle says, that it was by a personal attack on the chieftain, in which his back was broken But that of the other isles bears, more probably, that the injury was offered to two or three of the Mac-Leods, who, landing upon Eigg, and using some freedom with the young women, were seized by the islanders, bound hand and foot, and turned adrift in a boat, which the winds and waves safely conducted to Skye. To avenge the offence given, Mac-Leod sailed with such a body of men as rendered resistance hopeless. The natives, fearing his vengeance, concealed themselves in this cavern, and, after a strict search, the Mac-Leods went on board their galleys, after doing what mischief they could, concluding the inhabitants had left the isle, and betaken themselves to the Long Island, or some of Clan-Ranald's other possessions. But next morning they espied from the vessels a man upon the island, and immediately landing again, they traced his retreat by the marks of his footsteps, a light snow being unhappily on the ground. Mac-Leod then surrounded the cavern, summoned the subterranean garrison, and demanded that the individuals who had offended him should be delivered up to him. This was peremptorily refused. The chieftain then caused his people to divert the course of a rill of water, which, falling over the entrance of the cave, would have prevented his purposed vengeance. He then kindled at the entrance of the cavern a huge fire, composed of turf and fern, and maintained it with unrelenting assiduity, until all within were destroyed by suffocation. The date of this dreadful deed must have been recent, if one may judge from the fresh appearance of those relics. I brought off, in spite of the prejudice of our sailors, a skull from among the numerous specimens of mortality which the cavern afforded. Before re-embarking we visited another cave, opening to the sea, but of a character entirely different, being a large open vault, as high as that of a cathedral, and running back a great way into the rock at the same height. The height and width of the opening gives ample light to the whole. Here, after 1745, when the Catholic priests were scarcely tolerated, the priest of Eigg used to perform the Roman Catholic service, most of the islanders being of that persuasion. A huge ledge of rocks rising about half-way up one side of the vault, served for altar and pulpit; and the appearance of a priest and Highland congregation in such an extraordinary place of worship, might have engaged the pencil of Salvator.

Sir Walter Scott.

250. THE NEST OF LOVE

... When hearts have once mingled
  Love first leaves the well-built nest;
    The weak one is singled
  To endure what it once possessed.
    O Love! who bewailest
  The frailty of all things here,
    Why choose you the frailest
  For your cradle, your home, and your bier?

    Its passions will rock thee
  As the storms rock the ravens on high;
    Bright reason will mock thee,
  Like the sun from a wintry sky.
    From thy nest every rafter
  Will rot, and thine eagle home
    Leave thee naked to laughter,
  When leaves fall and cold winds come.

P. B. Shelley.

251. THE OUTLAW OF LOCH LENE

FROM THE IRISH

O, MANY a day have I made good ale in the glen,
That came not of stream or malt;—like the brewing of men.
My bed was the ground; my roof, the greenwood above,
And the wealth that I sought one far kind glance from my love.

Alas! on that night when the horses I drove from the field,
That I was not near from terror my angel to shield.
She stretched forth her arms,—her mantle she flung to the wind,
And swam o'er Loch Lene, her outlawed lover to find.

O would that a freezing sleet-wing'd tempest did sweep,
And I and my love were alone, far off on the deep;
I'd ask not a ship, or a bark, or pinnace, to save,—
With her hand round my waist, I'd fear not the wind or the wave.

'Tis down by the lake where the wild tree fringes its sides,
The maid of my heart, my fair one of Heaven resides;—
I think as at even she wanders its mazes along,
The birds go to sleep by the sweet wild twist of her song.

J. J. Callanan.

252. A SPRING MORNING

THE Spring comes in with all her hues and smells,
In freshness breathing over hills and dells,
O'er woods where May her gorgeous drapery flings,
And meads washed fragrant by their laughing springs.
Fresh are new-opened flowers, untouched and free
From the bold rifling of the amorous bee.
The happy time of singing birds is come,
And love's long pilgrimage now finds a home;
Among the mossy oaks now coos the dove,
And the hoarse crow finds softer notes for love.
The foxes play around their dens and bark
In joy's excess, in woodland shadows dark.
The flowers join lips below, the leaves above,
And every sound that meets the air is love.

John Clare.

253. THE WANDERING KNIGHT'S SONG

My ornaments are arms,
My pastime is in war,
My bed is cold upon the wold,
My lamp yon star:

>   My journeyings are long,
>   My slumbers short and broken;
>   From hill to hill I wander still,
>   Kissing thy token.
>
>   I ride from land to land,
>   I sail from sea to sea;
>   Some day more kind I fate may find,
>   Some night kiss thee.
>   *J. G. Lockhart,* from the Spanish.

254. ETERNAL POETRY

I find that I cannot exist without poetry—without eternal poetry—half the day will not do—the whole of it—I began with a little, but habit has made me a Leviathan. I had become all of a Tremble from not having written any thing of late—the Sonnet over leaf did me some good. I slept the better last night for it—this Morning, however, I am nearly as bad again. Just now I opened Spenser, and the first Lines I saw were these:—

> "The noble Heart that harbors virtuous thought,
>   And is with Child of glorious great intent,
>   Can never rest, until it forth have brought
>   Th' eternal Brood of Glory excellent—"
>   *John Keats.*

255. THE TRUTH OF IMAGINATION

O I wish I was as certain of the end of all your troubles as that of your momentary start about the authenticity of the Imagination. I am certain of nothing but of the holiness of the Heart's affections and the truth of Imagination—What the imagination seizes as Beauty must be truth—whether it existed before or not—for I have the same Idea of all our Passions as of Love, they are all in their sublime, creative of essential Beauty. . . . The Imagination may be compared to Adam's dream—he awoke and found it truth.   *John Keats.*

256. DINNER WITH WORDSWORTH, KEATS AND LAMB

1817.—On December 28th the immortal dinner came off in my painting-room, with Jerusalem towering up behind us as a background. Wordsworth was in fine cue, and we had a glorious set-to—on Homer, Shakespeare, Milton and Virgil. Lamb got exceedingly merry and exquisitely witty; and his fun in the midst of Wordsworth's solemn intonations of oratory was like the sarcasm and wit of the fool in the intervals of Lear's passion. He made a speech and voted me absent, and made them drink my health. "Now," said Lamb, "you old lake poet, you rascally poet, why do you call Voltaire dull?" We all defended Wordsworth, and affirmed there was a state of mind when Voltaire would be dull. "Well," said Lamb, "here's (to) Voltaire—the Messiah of the French nation, and a very proper one too."

He then, in a strain of humour beyond description, abused me for putting Newton's head into my picture; "a fellow," said he, "who believed nothing unless it was as clear as the three sides of a triangle." And then he and Keats agreed he had destroyed all the poetry of the rainbow by reducing it to the prismatic colours. . . .

By this time other friends joined, amongst them poor Ritchie who was going to penetrate by Fezzan to Timbuctoo. I introduced him to all as "a gentleman going to Africa." Lamb seemed to take no notice; but all of a sudden he roared out: "Which is the gentleman we are going to lose?" We then drank the victim's health, in which Ritchie joined. . . .

It was indeed an immortal evening. Wordsworth's fine intonation as he quoted Milton and Virgil, Keats' eager inspired look, Lamb's quaint sparkle of lambent humour, so speeded the stream of conversation, that in my life I never passed a more delightful time. . . . It was a night worthy of the Elizabethan age, and my solemn Jerusalem flashing up by the flame of the fire, with Christ hanging over us like a vision, all made up a picture which will long glow upon

> "that inward eye
> Which is the bliss of solitude."

Keats made Ritchie promise he would carry his *Endymion* to the great desert of Sahara and fling it in the midst.

Benjamin Robert Haydon.

257. TWO ARTISTS
i. The Setting Of Nature

LET us exult in the confidence that we belong to that class of our fellow-men, who by the elixir you describe, "the true enjoyment of nature," retain the heart of youth, though the eye grow dim, the hand tremble, and the head fade grey . . . though the mind may be a diamond it will require a fresh setting if the body be as lead, and its very hardness and durability will help to destroy the setting.

Francis Danby, A.R.A.

ii. A Romantic Death

In 1844 we lost the aged Nicholson, one of the founders of the Society of Painters in Watercolours, whose last effort, when dying at the age of 91, was to have himself lifted up, to brighten a dark cloud in a picture of a shipwreck.

Harriet Martineau.

258. THE WITCH'S NIPPLES

June 18 [1816].—My leg much worse. Shelley and party here. Mrs. S called me her brother (younger). Began my ghost-story after tea. Twelve o'clock, really began to talk ghostly. Lord Byron repeated some verses of Coleridge's *Christabel*, of the witch's breast; when silence ensued, and Shelley, suddenly shrieking and putting his hands to his head, ran out of the room with a candle. Threw water in his face, and after gave him ether. He was looking at Mrs. S, and suddenly thought of a woman he had heard of who had eyes instead of nipples, which taking hold of his mind, horrified him.

John William Polidori.

259. LINES INSCRIBED UPON A CUP FORMED FROM A SKULL

Start not—nor deem my spirit fled;
   In me behold the only skull,
From which, unlike a living head,
   Whatever flows is never dull.

I lived, I loved, I quaffed, like thee:
   I died: let earth my bones resign;
Fill up—thou canst not injure me;
   The worm hath fouler lips than thine.

Better to hold the sparkling grape,
   Than nurse the earth-worm's slimy brood;
And circle in the goblet's shape
   The drink of Gods, than reptiles' food.

Where once my wit, perchance, hath shone,
   In aid of others' let me shine;
And when, alas! our brains are gone,
   What nobler substitute than wine?

Quaff while thou canst: another race,
   When thou and thine, like me, are sped,
May rescue thee from earth's embrace,
   And rhyme and revel with the dead.

Why not? since through life's little day
   Our heads such sad effects produce;
Redeem'd from worms and wasting clay,
   This chance is theirs, to be of use.

Lord Byron.

260. THE WILD POSTURES OF FUSELI

THAT some of Fuseli's postures appear strained, I am very free to confess; yet we should be careful how we condemn . . . it is to be observed that this great genius generally selects his subjects from the traditions of early barbarous times, when men freely obeyed the fierce impulses of their nature, when their passions were undisguised and naked as their forms.

Is it to be supposed, that the strong-tossing, white arms of Chriemhild, the future wife of Attila the Hun (the Etzel of the Nibelunglay) were tied down by the shoulder-straps of Mrs. Bell's corsets?

Thomas Griffiths Wainewright.

261. TEMPTED BY NAPOLEON

1811 *May 6th.* —Last evening, Rigo, a French artist, member of the Egyptian expedition . . . spent the evening with me.

I was curious to get out every anecdote about Buonaparte from one who had seen him repeatedly, indeed had always been with him during the Egyptian expedition.

Rigo said the night before the battle of Aboukir, he lay on the ground in the same tent with Buonaparte. About midnight Buonaparte told Berthier and the rest of his generals who were with him to go to sleep in their cloaks till daybreak. Rigo said . . . that this night when all the rest were buried in sleep he could not avoid watching him. In a little time he observed Napoleon take the compasses and a chart of Aboukir and the Mediterranean and measure, and then take a ruler and draw lines. He then arose, went to the door of his tent and looked towards the horizon; then returned to his tent, and looked at his watch; after a moment he took a knife, and cut the table in all ways like a boy. He then rested his head on his hand, looked again at his watch for some time, went again to the door of his tent, and again returned to his seat. . . . Buonaparte then looked all round to see if all slept. Rigo shut his eyes a moment like the rest. In a short time Napoleon called them all up, ordered his horse, and asked how long before daybreak. They told him an hour. The army were under arms. He rode round, spoke to the colonels and soldiers, told them in his energetic manner that at a mile from them there existed a Turkish army which he expected by ten o'clock should exist no longer.

1814 *June* 12*th.*—. . . Went to Gerard the painter's, and was much affected at the portraits I saw there.

Buonaparte ten years ago: A horrid yellow for complexion; the tip of his nose tinged with red; his eyes fixed and stern, with a liquorish wateriness; his lips red dirt; his mouth cool, collected and resolute. All the other heads in the room looked like children beside him, Wilkie said, and so they did. I never was so horribly touched by a human expression.

1815 *June* 24*th* (after the news of Waterloo).—How this victory pursues one's imagination! I read the *Gazette* four times without stopping.

25*th.*—Read the *Gazette* again, till I know it actually by heart. Dined with (Leigh) Hunt. I give myself great credit for not worrying him to death at this news; he was quiet for some time, but knowing it must come by and by and putting on an air of indifference, he said: "Terrible battle this, Haydon." "A glorious one, Hunt." "Oh, yes, certainly," and to it we went.

Yet Hunt took a just and liberal view of the question. As for Hazlitt, it is not to be believed how the destruction of Napoleon affected him; he. seemed prostrated in mind and body: he walked about unwashed, unshaved, hardly sober by day, and always intoxicated by night, literally, without exaggeration, for weeks; until at length wakening as it were from his stupor, he at once left off all stimulating liquors, and never touched them after.

Hazlitt's principle was, that crimes, want of honour, want of faith, or want of every virtue on earth, were nothing on the part of an individual raised from the middle classes to the throne, if they forwarded the victory of the popular principle while he remained there. I used to maintain that the basis of such a victory should be the very reverse of the vices, and cruelties, and weaknesses of decayed dynasties, and that in proportion as a man elevated as Napoleon was in such a cause deviated from the abstract virtue required he injured the cause itself and excused the very dynasties he wished to supplant and surpass.

1821 *July* 12.—. . . Wilkie drank tea with me to-night, and brought me news Napoleon was dead! Good God! I remember in 1806, as we were walking to the Academy, just after the battle of Jena, we were both groaning at the slowness of our means of acquiring fame in comparison with his. He is now dead in captivity, and we have gone quietly on, *"parvis componere magna,"* rising in daily respect, and have no cause to lament our silent progress. Ah, Napoleon, what an opportunity you lost! His death affects me to deep musing. I remember his rise in 1796, his glory, and his fall. Posterity can never estimate the sensations of those living at the time.

1845 *April* 14*th.*—Higginson lunched with me. He sailed with Napoleon in the *Bellerophon*. He said his influence on the men was fascinating, and he really feared they would have let him go if an enemy's ship had hove in sight. He used to borrow sixpences of the men, pinch the ears of the officers, and bewitch them without the least familiarity, in a manner that was unaccountable. Even Sir George (Cockburn) was affected by the end of the voyage. Higginson said, when he was caught watching you, he put on an expression of silliness to disguise his thoughts. (So too said Madame de Staël.)

1846 *June* 22*nd* (*written a few minutes before Haydon cut his throat*).

Last Thoughts of B. R. Haydon, half-past ten.

No man should use certain evil for probable good, however great the object. Evil is the prerogative of the Deity.

I create good, I create, I the Lord do these things. Wellington never used evil if the good was not certain. Napoleon had no such scruples, and I fear the glitter of his genius rather dazzled me; but had I been encouraged nothing but good would have come from me, because when encouraged I paid everybody. God forgive the evil for the sake of the good. Amen.

262. THE SPARROW ON THE GRAVEL

You perhaps at one time thought there was such a thing as Worldly Happiness to be arrived at, at certain periods of time marked out—you have of necessity from your disposition been thus led away—I scarcely remember counting upon any Happiness—I look not for it if it be not in the present hour—nothing startles me beyond the Moment. The setting Sun will always set me to rights—or if a Sparrow come before my Window I take part in its existence and pick about the Gravel.

John Keats.

263. DEFIANCE

. . . I have not loved the world, nor the world me;
    I have not flatter'd its rank breath, nor bow'd
    To its idolatries a patient knee,
    Nor coin'd my cheek to smiles, nor cried aloud
    In worship of an echo; in the crowd
    They could not deem me one of such; I stood
    Among them, but not of them; in a shroud
    Of thoughts which were not their thoughts, and still could,
Had I not filed my mind, which thus itself subdued.

    I have not loved the world, nor the world me,—
    But let us part fair foes; I do believe,
    Though I have found them not, that there may be
    Words which are things, hopes which will not deceive,
    And virtues which are merciful, nor weave
    Snares for the failing; I would also deem
    O'er others' grief that some sincerely grieve;
    That two, or one, are almost what they seem,
That goodness is no name, and happiness no dream. . . .

Lord Byron.

264. THE ALLEGORY OF A MAN

A Man's life of any worth is a continual allegory, and very few eyes can see the Mystery of his life—a life like the scriptures, figurative—which such people can no more make out

than they can the hebrew Bible. Lord Byron cuts a figure—
but he is not figurative—Shakespeare led a life of Allegory:
his works are the comments on it.   *John Keats.*

265. THE WANDERER'S DREAM

HE dreamed that he stood on the summit of a precipice, whose
downward height no eye could have measured, but for the
fearful waves of a fiery ocean that lashed and blazed and roared
at its bottom, sending its burning spray far up, so as to drench
the dreamer with its sulphurous rain. The whole glowing
ocean below was alive—every billow bore an agonizing soul,
that rose like a wreck or a putrid corse on the waves of earth's
oceans—uttered a shriek as it burst against that adamantine
precipice—sunk—and rose again to repeat the tremendous
experiment I Every billow of fire was thus instinct with
immortal and agonizing existence,—each was freighted with
a soul, that rose on the burning wave in torturing hope, burst
on the rock in despair, added its eternal shriek to the roar
of that fiery ocean, and sunk to rise again—in vain, and—for
ever!

Suddenly the Wanderer felt himself flung half-way down
the precipice. He stood, in his dream, tottering on a crag
midway down the precipice—he looked upward, but the upper
air (for there was no heaven) showed only blackness unshadowed
and impenetrable—but blacker than that blackness, he could
distinguish a gigantic outstretched arm that held him as in
sport on the ridge of that infernal precipice, while another,
that seemed in its motions to hold fearful and invisible con-
junction with the arm that grasped him, as if both belonged
to some being too vast and horrible even for the imagery of a
dream to shape, pointed up to a dial-plate fixed on the top of
that precipice, and which the flashes of that ocean of fire made
fearfully conspicuous. He saw the mysterious single hand
revolve—he saw it reach the appointed period of 150 years—
(for in this mystic plate centuries were marked, not hours) he
shrieked in his dream, and, with that strong impulse often
felt in sleep, burst from the arm that held him, to arrest the
motion of the hand.

In the effort he fell, and falling grasped at aught that might save him. His fall seemed perpendicular—there was naught to save him—the rock was as smooth as ice—the ocean of fire broke at its foot! Suddenly a group of figures appeared, ascending as he fell. He grasped at them successively . . . to each he seemed in his slumber to cling in order to break his fall—all ascended the precipice. He caught at each in his downward flight, but all forsook him and ascended.

His last despairing reverted glance was fixed on the clock of eternity—the upraised black arm seemed to push forward the hand—it arrived at its period—he fell—he sunk—he blazed—he shrieked! The burning waves boomed over his sinking head, and the clock of eternity rung out its awful chime—"Room for the soul of the Wanderer!"—and the waves of the burning ocean answered, as they lashed the adamantine rock—"There is room for more!"

Charles Robert Maturin.

266. THE WIFE AND CHILDREN OF KEATS

THE roaring of the wind is my wife and the Stars through the window pane are my Children. The mighty abstract Idea I have of Beauty in all things stifles the more divided and minute domestic happiness—an amiable wife and sweet Children I contemplate as a part of that Beauty, but I must have a thousand of those beautiful particles to fill up my heart. I feel more and more every day, as my imagination strengthens, that I do not live in this world alone but in a thousand worlds. No sooner am I alone than shapes of epic greatness are stationed around me, and serve my Spirit the office which is equivalent to a King's body guard—then "Tragedy with scepter'd pall, comes sweeping by." According to my state of mind I am with Achilles shouting in the Trenches, or with Theocritus in the Vales of Sicily. Or I throw my whole being into Troilus, and repeating those lines, "I wander, like a lost Soul upon the Stygian Banks staying for waftage," I melt into the air with a voluptuousness so delicate that I am content to be alone.

John Keats.

267. CYBELE DRAWN BY LIONS

... Forth from a rugged arch, in the dusk below,
    Came mother Cybele! alone—alone—
    In sombre chariot; dark foldings thrown
    About her majesty, and front death-pale,
    With turrets crown'd. Four maned lions hale
    The sluggish wheels; solemn their toothed maws,
    Their surly eyes brow-hidden, heavy paws
    Uplifted drowsily, and nervy tails
    Cowering their tawny brushes. Silent sails
    This shadowy queen athwart, and faints away
    In another gloomy arch....
John Keats.

268. OZYMANDIAS

I MET a traveller from an antique land
Who said: Two vast and trunkless legs of stone
Stand in the desert... Near them, on the sand,
Half sunk, a shattered visage lies, whose frown,
And wrinkled lip, and sneer of cold command,
Tell that its sculptor well those passions read
Which yet survive, stamped on these lifeless things,
The hand that mocked them, and the heart that fed:
And on the pedestal these words appear:
"My name is Ozymandias, kind of kings:
Look on my works, ye Mighty, and despair!"
Nothing beside remains. Round the decay
Of that colossal wreck, boundless and bare,
The lone and level sands stretch far away.
P. B. Shelley.

269. OZYMANDIAS STARTS FOR ENGLAND

AFTER having taken a cursory view of Luxor and Carnak, to which my curiosity led me on my landing, I crossed the Nile to the west, and proceeding straight to the Memnonium, I had to pass before the two colossal figures in the plain. I need not say, that I was struck with wonder. They are mutilated indeed, but their enormous size strikes the mind with admiration. The next object which met my view was the Memnonium. It stands elevated above the plain, which is annually inundated by the Nile. . . . The groups of columns of that temple, and the views of the numerous tombs excavated in the high rock behind it, present a strange appearance to the eye. On my approaching these ruins, I was surprised at the sight of the great colossus of Memnon, or Sesostris, or Ozymandias, or Phamenoph, or perhaps some other king of Egypt; for such are the various opinions of its origin, and so many names have been given to it that at last it has no name at all. I can but say, that it must have been one of the most venerated statues of the Egyptians; for it would have required more labour to have conveyed such a mass of granite from Assouan to Thebes, than to transport the obelisk, commonly known under the appellation of Pompey's Pillar, to Alexandria.

As I entered these ruins, my first thought was to examine the colossal bust I had to take away. I found it near the remains of its body and chair, with its face upwards, and apparently smiling on me, at the thought of being taken to England. I must say, that my expectations were exceeded by its beauty, but not by its size. . . .

All the implements brought from Cairo to the Memnonium consisted of fourteen poles, eight of which were employed in making a sort of car to lay the bust on, four ropes of palm leaves, and four rollers, without tackle of any sort. . . . I examined the road by which I was to take the bust to the Nile. As it appeared that the season of the inundation was advancing very fast, all the lands which extend from the Memnonium to the water side would have been covered in one month's time; and the way at the foot of the mountain was very uneven, and in some parts ran over the ground to which the water reached, so that, unless the bust was drawn over those places before the inundation commenced, it would become impossible to affect it after, till next summer. . . . I arranged my men in a row, and agreed to give them thirty paras a day, which is equal to fourpence halfpenny English money, with which they were much pleased, as it was more by one-half than they were accustomed to receive for their daily labour in the fields. The carpenter had made the car, and the first operation was to endeavour to place the bust on it. The Fellahs of Gournou, who were familiar with Caphany, as they named the colossus, were persuaded that it could never be moved from the spot where it lay; and when they saw it moved they all set up a shout. Though it was the effect of their own efforts, it was the devil, they said, that did it; and as they saw me taking notes, they concluded it was done by means of a charm. The mode I adopted to place it on the car was very simple, for work of no other description could be executed by these people, as their utmost sagacity reaches only to pulling a rope, or sitting on the extremity of a lever as a counterpoise. By means of four levers I raised the bust, so as to leave a vacancy under it, to introduce the car; and after it was slowly lodged on this, I had the car raised in the front, with the bust on it, so as to get one of the rollers underneath. I then had the same operation performed at the back, and the colossus was ready to be pulled up. I caused it to be well secured on the car, and the ropes so placed that the power might be divided. I stationed men at each side of the car, to assist occasionally, if the colossus should be inclined to turn to either side. In this manner I kept it safe from falling. Lastly, I placed men in the front, distributing them equally at the four ropes, while others were ready to change alternately. Thus I succeeded in getting it removed the distance of several yards from its original place.

According to my instructions, I sent an Arab to Cairo with the intelligence that the bust had begun its journey towards England.... *G. Belzoni.*

270. EVE'S SWEET PIPPIN

O BLUSH not so, O blush not so
Or I shall think ye knowing;
And if ye smile, the blushing while,
Then Maidenheads are going.

There's a blush for won't, and a blush for shan't
    And a blush for having done it,
There's a blush for thought, and a blush for naught
    And a blush for just begun it.

O sigh not so, O sigh not so
    For it sounds of Eve's sweet pippin.
By those loosen'd Lips, you have tasted the pips
    And fought in an amorous nipping.

Will ye play once more, at nice cut core
    For it only will last our youth out,
And we have the prime of the kissing time
    We have not one sweet tooth out.

There's a sigh for yes, and a sigh for no,
    And a sigh for "I can't bear it" —
O what can be done, shall we stay or run?
    O cut the sweet apple and share it.
                  Song quoted by John Keats.

271. A MEMORY OF KEATS

SUCH was the romantic poet of Endymion, who for the phantom of his waking dreams, gave up the study of that science, which might have nursed and fortified a mind, so soon chilled to death by the icy finger of criticism. Erato was the mistress of John Keats; but while he wooed, he perished: like the Rosicrucian, who, to save the life of his lady, took the oath of celibacy, and thus lost her love for ever. Even in the lecture-room of Saint Thomas's, I have seen Keats in a deep poetic dream: his mind was on Parnassus with the Muses. And here is a quaint fragment which he one evening scribbled in our presence, while the precepts of Sir Astley Cooper fell unheeded on his ear:—

"Whenne Alexandre the Conqueroure was wayfayringe in ye londe of Inde, there mette hym a damoselle of marveillouse beautie slepynge uponne the herbys and flowrys. He colde ne loke uponne her withouten grete plesance, and he was welle nighe loste in wondrement. Her forme was everyche whytte lyke ye fayrest carvynge of Quene Cythere, onlie thatte yt was swellyd and blushyd wyth warmthe and lyffe wythalle.

"Her forhed was as whytte as ys the snowe whyche ye talle hed of a Norwegian pyne stelythe from ye northerne wynde. One of her fayre hondes was yplaced thereonne, and thus whytte wyth whytte was ymyngld as ye gode Arthure saythe, lyke whytest lylys yspredde on whyttest snowe; and her bryghte eyne whenne she them oped, sparklyd lyke Hesperus through an evenynge cloude.

"They were yclosyd yn slepe, save that two slauntynge raies shotte to her mouthe, and were theyre bathyd yn swetenesse, as whenne bye chaunce ye moone fyndeth a banke of violettes and droppethe thereonne ye sylverie dewe.

"The authoure was goynge onne withouthen descrybynge ye ladye's breste, whenne lo, a genyus appearyd—' Guthberte,' sayeth he, 'an thou canst not descrybe ye ladye's breste, and fynde a simile thereunto, I forbyde thee to proceede yn thy romaunt.' Thys, I kennd fulle welle, far surpassyd my feble powres, and forthwythe I was fayne to droppe my quille."

W. C. Dendy.

272. SONNET

    Two flowers I love, the March-flower and the rose,
        The lovely rose that is to Venus dear,
        The March-flower that of her the name doth bear,
        Who will not leave my spirit in repose:
    Three birds I love; one, moist with May-dew, goes
        To dry his feathers in the sunshine clear;
        One for his mate laments throughout the year,
        And for his child the other wails his woes:
    And Bourgeil's pine I love, where Venus hung,
        For a proud trophy on the darksome bough,
        Ne'er since releas'd, my youthful liberty:
    And Phoebus' tree love I, the laurel tree,
        Of whose fair leaves, my mistress, when I sung,
        Bound with her locks a garland for my brow.

H. F. Cary
(translation from *Ronsard*).

273. FLOWERS OF THE SEA

CALL us not weeds, we are flowers of the sea,
And lovely and bright and gay-tinted are we,
And quite independent of sunshine or showers;
Then call us not weeds, we are Ocean's gay flowers.

Not nursed like the plants of a summer parterre,
Where gales are but sighs of an evening air,
Our exquisite, fragile, and delicate forms
Are nursed by the Ocean and rocked by the storms.

274. THE SWEET MONTH OF APRIL

APRIL, sweet month, the daintiest of all,
    Fair thee befal:
  April, fond hope of fruits that lie
  In buds of swathing cotton wrapt,
    There closely lapt,
  Nursing their tender infancy.

April, that dost thy yellow, green, and blue,
    All round thee strew,
  When, as thou go'st, the grassy floor
  Is with a million flowers depeint,
    Whose colours quaint
  Have diaper'd the meadows o'er.

April, at whose glad coming Zephyrs rise
    With whisper'd sighs,
  Then on their light wing brush away,
  And hang amid the woodlands fresh
    Their aery mesh
  To tangle Flora on her way.

April, it is thy hand that doth unlock,
    From plain and rock,

> Odours and hues, a balmy store,
> That breathing lie on Nature's breast,
>   So richly blest,
> That earth or heaven can ask no more.
>
> April, thy blooms, amid the tresses laid
>   Of my sweet maid,
> Adown her neck and bosom flow;
> And in a wild profusion there,
>   Her shining hair
> With them hath blent a golden glow.
>
> April, the dimpled smiles, the playful grace,
>   That in the face
> Of Cytherea haunt, are thine;
> And thine the breath, that from their skies
>   The deities
> Inhale, an offering at thy shrine.
>
> 'Tis thou that dost with summons blithe and soft,
>   High up aloft,
> From banishment these heralds bring,
> These swallows that along the air
>   Scud, swift, and bear
> Glad tidings of the merry spring.
>
> April, the hawthorn and the eglantine,
>   Purple woodbine,
> Streak'd pink, and lily-cup, and rose,
> And thyme, and marjoram, are spreading,
>   Where thou art treading,
> And their sweet eyes for thee unclose.
>
> The little nightingale sits singing aye
>   On leafy spray,
> And in her fitful strain doth run
> A thousand and a thousand changes,
>   With voice that ranges
> Through every sweet division.

April, it is when thou dost come again,
    That love is fain
With gentlest breath the fires to wake,
That cover'd up and slumbering lay,
    Through many a day,
When winter's chill our veins did slake.

Sweet month, thou seest at this jocund prime
    Of the spring-time,
The hives pour out their lusty young,
And hear'st the yellow bees that ply,
    With laden thigh,
Murmuring the flowery wilds among.

May shall with pomp his wavy wealth unfold,
    His fruits of gold,
His fertilizing dews, that swell
In manna on each spike and stem,
    And, like a gem,
Red honey in the waxen cell.

Who will may praise him; but my voice shall be,
    Sweet month, for thee;
Thou that to her dost owe thy name,
Who saw the sea-wave's foamy tide
    Swell and divide,
Whence forth to life and light she came.
                    H. F. Carey
            (translation from *Remy Belleau*).

275. MORNING

THE morning now right earlily in dew
Bathed her sweet naked limbs of fairest hue,
While like a veil all careless thrown aback
On her white shoulders hung her hair so black;
And when the sun a minute earlier rose
The lovely morning sought her cloudy clothes,

But finding none she hasting shrank away;
For night abashed had startled into day.
The sun reigned absolute in cloudless sky
And wooed morn's timid beauty to comply,
And scarlet as the dress she earlier wore
Her white face turned that was so fair before;
While fear in every limb diffused its charms
As soft she sighed and melted in his arms.

John Clare.

276. MAY

Come out o' door, 'tis Spring! 'tis Mây I
The trees be green, the viel's be gây;
The weather's warm, the winter blast,
Wi' all his train o' clouds, is past;
The zun da rise while vo'ke da sleep,
An' tiake a higher daely zweep,
Wi' cloudless fiace a-flingèn down
His sparklèn light upon the groun'.

The âir's a-streamèn soft,—come drow
The winder oben; let it blow
In droo the house, wher vire an 'door
A-shut kept out the cuold avore.
Come, let the vew dull embers die,
An' come below the oben sky;
An' wear your best, var fear the groun'
In colours gay mid shiame your gown:
An' goo an' rig wi' I a mile
Ar two up auver geät an' stile,
Droo zunny parricks that da leäd,
Wi' crooked hedges, to the meäd,
Wher elems high, in stiately ranks,
Da rise vrom yoller cowslip-banks,
An' birds da twitter vrom the spray
O' bushes deck'd wi' snow-white Mây;
An' gil'cups, wi' the diaisy bed,
Be under ev'ry step ya tread.

We'll wine' up roun' the hill, an' look
All down the thickly-timber'd nook,
Out wher the squier's house da show
His grey-wall'd peaks up droo the row
O' shiady elems, where the rook
Da build her nest; an' where the brook
Da creep along the meäds, and lie
To catch the brightness o' the sky;
An' cows, in water to ther knees,
Da stan' a-whiskèn off the vlees.

Mother o' blossoms, an' ov all
That's fair a-vield vrom spring till fall,
The gookoo auver white-wiav'd seas
Da come to zing in thy green trees,
An' buttervlees, in giddy flight,
Da gleäm the muost by thy gay light.
Oh! when at laste my fleshly eyes
Shall shut upon the viel's and skies,
Mid rammer's zunny daes be gone,
An' winter's clouds be comen on:
Nar mid I dra', upon the eth,
O' thy sweet air my liatest breath;
Alassen I mid want to stây
Behine' var thee, O flow'ry Mây!

William Barnes.

277. A DIRGE

  Rough wind, that moanest loud
    Grief too sad for song;
  Wild wind, when sullen cloud
    Knells all the night long;
Sad storm, whose tears are vain,
Bare woods, whose branches strain,
Deep caves and dreary main,—
    Wail, for the world's wrong!

P. B. Shelley.

278. THE OPIUM EATER

UNDER the connecting feeling of tropical heat and vertical sunlights, I brought together all creatures, birds, beasts, reptiles, all trees and plants, usages and appearances, that are found in all tropical regions, and assembled them together in China or Hindostan. From kindred feelings I soon brought Egypt and her gods under the same law. I was stared at, hooted at, grinned at, chattered at, by monkeys, by paroquets, by cockatoos. I ran into pagodas, and was fixed for centuries at the summit, or in secret rooms; I was the idol; I was the priest; I was worshipped; I was sacrificed. I fled from the wrath of Brama through all the forests of Asia; Vishnu hated me; Seeva lay in wait for me. I came suddenly upon Isis and Osiris: I had done a deed, they said, which the ibis and the crocodile trembled at. Thousands of years I lived and was buried in stone coffins, with mummies and sphinxes, in narrow chambers at the heart of eternal pyramids. I was kissed, with cancerous kisses, by crocodiles, and was laid confounded with all unutterable abortions, amongst reeds and Nilotic mud. . . .

The cursed crocodile became to me the object of more horror than all the rest. I was compelled to live with him; and (as was always the case in my dreams) for centuries. Sometimes I escaped and found myself in Chinese houses. All the feet of the tables, sofas, etc., soon became instinct with life: the abominable head of the crocodile, and his leering eyes, looked out at me, multiplied into ten thousand repetitions; and I stood loathing and fascinated. So often did this hideous reptile haunt my dreams, that many times the very same dream was broken up in the very same way: I heard gentle voices speaking to me (I hear everything when I am sleeping), and instantly I awoke; it was broad noon, and my children were standing, hand in hand, at my bedside, come to show me their coloured shoes, or new frocks, or to let me see them dressed for going out.
Thomas de Quincey.

279. FRAGMENT

I WENT into the deserts of dim sleep—
  That world which, like an unknown wilderness,
Bounds this with its recesses wide and deep—
                                    P. B. Shelley.

280. A VISION OF YOUNG DEATH

SWEET funeral bells from some incalculable distance, wailing over the dead that die before the dawn, awakened me as I slept in a boat moored to some familiar shore. The morning twilight even then was breaking; and, by the dusky revelations which it spread, I saw a girl, adorned with a garland of white roses about her head for some great festival, running along the solitary strand in extremity of haste. Her running was the running of panic; and often she looked back as to some dreadful enemy in the rear. But when I leaped ashore, and followed on her steps to warn her of a peril in front, alas! from me she fled as from another peril, and vainly I shouted to her of quicksands that lay ahead. Faster and faster she ran; round a promontory of rocks she wheeled out of sight; in an instant I also wheeled round it, but only to see the treacherous sands gathering above her head. Already her person was buried; only her fair young head and the diadem of white roses around it were still visible to the pitying heaven; and, last of all, was visible one white marble arm. I saw by the early twilight this fair young head, as it was sinking down to darkness—saw this marble arm, as it rose above her head and her treacherous grave, tossing, faltering, rising, clutching, as at some false deceiving hand stretched out from the clouds— saw this marble arm uttering her dying hope, and then uttering her dying despair. The head, the diadem, the arm—these all had sunk; at last over these also the cruel quicksand had closed; and no memorial of the fair young girl remained on earth, except my own solitary tears, and the funeral bells from the desert seas, that, rising again more softly, sang a requiem over the grave of the buried child, and over her blighted dawn.   *Thomas de Quincey.*

281. EVENING PRIMROSE

W&#xsmall;HEN once the sun sinks in the west,
And dew-drops pearl the evening's breast,
Almost as pale as moonbeams are,
Or its companionable star,
The evening primrose opes anew
Its delicate blossoms to the dew;
And shunning, hermit-like, the light,
Wastes its fair bloom upon the night;
Who, blindfold to its fond caresses,
Knows not the beauty he possesses,
Thus it blooms on till night is by;
When day looks out with open eye,
'Bashed at the gaze it cannot shun,
It faints, and withers, and is done.

John Clare.

282. DEATH AND A CHILD

ON the day after my sister's death, whilst the sweet temple of her brain was yet unviolated by human scrutiny, I formed my own scheme for seeing her once more. Not for the world would I have made this known, nor have suffered a witness to accompany me. I had never heard of feelings that take the name of "sentimental," nor dreamed of such a possibility. But grief, even in a child, hates the light, and shrinks from human eyes. The house was large enough to have two staircases; and by one of these I knew that about mid-day, when all would be quiet (for the servants dined at one o'clock), I could steal up into her chamber. I imagine that it was about an hour after high noon when I reached the chamber door; it was locked but the key was not taken away. Entering, I closed the door so softly, that, although it opened upon a hall which ascended through all the storeys, no echo ran along the silent walls. Then, turning round, I sought my sister's face. But the bed had been moved, and the back was now turned towards myself. Nothing met my eyes but one large window, wide open, through which the sun of midsummer at mid-day was showering down torrents of splendour. The weather was dry, the sky was cloudless, the blue depths seemed the express types of infinity; and it was not possible for eye to behold, or for heart to conceive, any symbols more pathetic of life and the glory of life.

From the gorgeous sunlight I turned round to the corpse. There lay the sweetest childish figure; there the angel face; and, as people usually fancy, it was said in the house that no features had suffered any change. Had they not? The forehead, indeed—the serene and noble forehead—*that* might be the same; but the frozen eyelids, the darkness that seemed to steal from beneath them, the marble lips, the stiffening hands, laid palm to palm, as if repeating the supplications of closing anguish—could these be mistaken for life? Had it been so, wherefore did I not spring to those heavenly lips with tears and never-ending kisses? But so it was *not*. I stood checked for a moment; awe, not fear, fell upon me; and, whilst I stood, a solemn wind began to blow—the saddest that ear ever heard. It was a wind that might have swept the fields of mortality for a thousand centuries. Many times since, upon summer days, when the sun is about the hottest, I have remarked the same wind arising and uttering the same hollow, solemn, Memnonian, but saintly swell: it is in this world the one great audible symbol of eternity. And three times in my life have I happened to hear the same sound in the same circumstances—viz., when standing between an open window and a dead body on a summer day.

Instantly, when my ear caught this vast Æolian intonation, when my eye filled with the golden fulness of life, the pomps of the heavens above, or the glory of the flowers below, and turning when it settled upon the frost which overspread my sister's face, instantly a trance fell upon me. A vault seemed to open in the zenith of the far blue sky, a shaft which ran up for ever. I, in spirit, rose as if on billows that also ran up the shaft for ever; and the billows seemed to pursue the throne of God; but *that* also ran before us and fled away continually. The flight and the pursuit seemed to go on for ever and ever. Frost gathering frost, some Sarsar wind of death, seemed to repel me; some mighty relation between God and death dimly struggled to evolve itself from the dreadful antagonism between them; shadowy meanings even yet continue to exercise and torment, in dreams, the deciphering oracle within me. I slept —for how long I cannot say; slowly I recovered my self-possession; and, when I woke, found myself standing, as before, close to my sister's bed.

I have reason to believe that a *very* long interval had elapsed during this wandering or suspension of my perfect mind. When I returned to myself, there was a foot (or I fancied so) on the stairs. I was alarmed, for if anybody had detected me, means would have been taken to prevent my coming again. Hastily, therefore, I kissed the lips that I should kiss no more, and slunk, like a guilty thing, with stealthy steps from the room. Thus perished the vision, loveliest amongst all the shows which earth has revealed to me; thus mutilated was the parting which should have lasted for ever; tainted thus with fear was that farewell sacred to love and grief, to perfect love and to grief that could not be healed.

O Ahasuerus, everlasting Jew! fable or not a fable, thou, when first starting on thy endless pilgrimage of woe—thou, when first flying through the gates of Jerusalem, and vainly yearning to leave the pursuing curse behind thee—couldst not more certainly in the words of Christ have read thy doom of endless sorrow, than I when passing for ever from my sister's room.

On the day following this which I have recorded, came a body of medical men to examine the brain, and the particular nature of the complaint; for in some of its symptoms it had shown perplexing anomalies. An hour after the strangers had withdrawn, I crept again to the room; but the door was now locked, the key had been taken away—and I was shut out for ever. *Thomas de Quincey.*

283. A DREAM OF LOVE

THE fifth canto of Dante pleases me more and more—it is that one in which he meets with Paolo and Francesca. I had passed many days in rather a low state of mind, and in the midst of them I dreamt of being in that region of Hell. The dream was one of the most delightful enjoyments I ever had in my life. I floated about the whirling atmosphere as it is described with a beautiful figure to whose lips mine were joined, as it seemed for an age—and in the midst of all this cold and darkness I was warm—even flowery tree tops sprung up and we rested on them sometimes with the lightness of a cloud, till the wind blew us away again. I tried a Sonnet upon it—there are fourteen lines but nothing of what I felt in it—O that I could dream it every night—

> As Hermes once took to his feathers light
> When lulled Argus, baffled, swoon'd and slept,
> So on a delphic reed my idle spright
> So play'd, so charm'd, so conquer'd, so bereft
> The dragon world of all its hundred eyes
> And seeing it asleep so fled away:—
> Not to pure Ida with its snow clad cold skies,
> Nor unto Tempe where Jove grieved that day,
> But to that second circle of sad hell,
> Where in the gust, the whirlwind and the flaw
> Of rain and hailstones lovers need not tell
> Their sorrows. Pale were the sweet lips I saw,
> Pale were the lips I kiss'd and fair the form
> I floated with about that melancholy storm.
>
> John Keats.

284, THE SEA OF DEATH

> ... Methought I saw
> Life swiftly treading over endless space;
> And, at her footprint, but a bygone pace,
> The ocean-past, which, with increasing wave,
> Swallow'd her steps like a pursuing grave.
> Sad were my thoughts that anchor'd silently
> On the dead waters of that passionless sea,
> Unstirr'd by any touch of living breath:
> Silence hung over it, and drowsy Death,

Like a gorged sea-bird, slept with folded wings
On crowded carcases—sad passive things
That wore the thin grey surface, like a veil
Over the calmness of their features pale.

And there were spring-faced cherubs that did sleep
Like water-lilies on that motionless deep,
How beautiful! with bright unruffled hair
On sleek unfretted brows, and eyes that were
Buried in marble tombs, a pale eclipse!
And smile-bedimpled cheeks, and pleasant lips,
Meekly apart, as if the soul intense
Spake out in dreams of its own innocence:
And so they lay in loveliness, and kept
The birth-night of their peace, that Life e'en wept
With very envy of their happy fronts;
For there were neighbour brows scarr'd by the brunts
Of strife and sorrowing—where care had set
His crooked autograph, and marr'd the jet
Of glossy locks with hollow eyes forlorn,
And lips that curl'd in bitterness and scorn—
Wretched,—as they had breathed of this world's pain,
And so bequeath'd it to the world again
Through the beholder's heart in heavy sighs.

So lay they garmented in torpid light,
Under the pall of a transparent night,
Like solemn apparitions lull'd sublime
To everlasting rest,—and with them Time
Slept, as he sleeps upon the silent face
Of a dark dial in a sunless place.

Thomas Hood.

285. THE QUESTION

I

I Dreamed that, as I wandered by the way,
   Bare Winter suddenly was changed to Spring,
And gentle odours led my steps astray,
   Mixed with a sound of waters murmuring

Along a shelving bank of turf, which lay
   Under a copse, and hardly dared to fling
Its green arms round the bosom of the stream,
But kissed it and then fled, as thou mightest in dream.

II

There grew pied wind-flowers and violets,
   Daisies, those pearled Arcturi of the earth,
The constellated flower that never sets;
   Faint oxlips; tender bluebells, at whose birth
The sod scarce heaved; and that tall flower that wets—
   Like a child, half in tenderness and mirth—
Its mother's face with Heaven's collected tears,
When the low wind, its playmate's voice, it hears.

III

And in the warm hedge grew lush eglantine,
   Green cowbind and the moonlight-coloured may,
And cherry-blossoms, and white cups, whose wine
   Was the bright dew, yet drained not by the day;
And wild roses, and ivy serpentine,
   With its dark buds and leaves, wandering astray;
And flowers azure, black, and streaked with gold,
Fairer than any wakened eyes behold.

IV

And nearer to the river's trembling edge
   There grew broad flag-flowers, purple pranked with white,
And starry river buds among the sedge,
   And floating water-lilies, broad and bright,
Which lit the oak that overhung the hedge
   With moonlight beams of their own watery light;
And bulrushes, and reeds of such deep green
As soothed the dazzled eye with sober sheen.

V

Methought that of these visionary flowers
   I made a nosegay, bound in such a way
That the same hues, which in their natural bowers
   Were mingled or opposed, the like array

>   Kept these imprisoned children of the Hours
>   Within my hand, — and then, elate and gay,
>   I hastened to the spot whence I had come,
>   That I might there present it! — Oh! to whom?
>
>   *P. B. Shelley.*

286. THE FATAL VISION

>   ... Some say, when nights are dry and clear,
>   And the death-dews sleep on the morass,
>   Sweet whispers are heard by the traveller,
>   Which make night day:
>   And a silver shape like his early love doth pass
>   Upborne by her wild and glittering hair,
>   And when he awakes on the fragrant grass,
>   He finds night day. . . .
>
>   *P. B. Shelley.*

287. SOLITUDE

OH, burden of solitude, that cleavest to man through every stage of his being! in his birth, which *has* been — in his life, which *is* — in his death, which *shall* be — mighty and essential solitude! that wast, and art, and art to be; thou broodest, like the Spirit of God moving upon the surface of the deeps, over every heart that sleeps in the nurseries of Christendom. Like the vast laboratory of the air, which, seeming to be nothing, or less than the shadow of a shade, hides within itself the principle of all things, solitude for the meditating child is the Agrippa's mirror of the unseen universe. Deep is the solitude of millions who, with hearts welling forth love, have none to love them. Deep is the solitude of those who, under secret griefs, have none to pity them. Deep is the solitude of those who, fighting with doubts or darkness, have none to counsel them. But deeper than the deepest of these solitudes is that which broods over childhood under the passion of sorrow — bringing before it, at intervals, the final solitude which watches for it, and is waiting for it within the gates of death. Oh, mighty and essential solitude, that wast, and art, and art to be! thy kingdom is made perfect in the grave; but even over those that keep watch outside the grave, like myself, an infant of six years old, thou stretchest out a sceptre of fascination.

Thomas de Quincey.

288. AXIOMS OF POETRY

i

IN Poetry I have a few Axioms, and you will see how far I am from their Centre. 1st. I think Poetry should surprise by a fine excess and not by Singularity—it should strike the Reader as a wording of his own highest thoughts, and appear almost a Remembrance—2nd. Its touches of Beauty should never be half way, thereby making the reader breathless instead of content: the rise, the progress, the setting of imagery should nice the sun come natural to him—shine over him and set soberly although in magnificence leaving him in the Luxury of twilight—but it is easier to think what Poetry should be than to write it—and this leads me on to another axiom. That if Poetry comes not as naturally as the Leaves to a tree it had better not come at all.

ii

As to the poetical Character itself (I mean that sort of which, if I am any thing, I am a Member; that sort distinguished from the wordsworthian or egotistical sublime; which is a thing per se and stands alone) it is not itself—it has no self—it is every thing and nothing—It has no character—it enjoys light and shade; it lives in gusto, be it foul or fair, high or low, rich or poor, mean or elevated—It has as much delight in conceiving an Iago as an Imogen. What shocks the virtuous philosopher, delights the camelion Poet. It does no harm from its relish of the dark side of things any more than from its taste for the bright one; because they both end in speculation. A Poet is the most unpoetical of any thing in existence; because he has no Identity—he is continually in for and fining some other Body—The Sun, the Moon, the sea and Men and Women who are creatures of impulse are poetical and have about them

an unchangeable attribute—the poet has none; no identity—
he is certainly the most unpoetical of all God's Creatures.
John Keats.

289. THE DESERTER'S MEDITATION

If sadly thinking, with spirits sinking,
   Could, more than drinking, my cares compose,
A cure from sorrow from sighs I'd borrow,
   And hope to-morrow would end my woes.

But as in wailing there's nought availing,
   And Death unfailing will strike the blow,
Then for that reason, and for a season,
   Let us be merry before we go!

To joy a stranger, a wayworn ranger,
   In every danger my course I've run;
Now hope all ending, and death befriending,
   His last aid lending, my cares are done;

No more a rover, or hapless lover—
   My griefs are over—my glass runs low;
Then for that reason, and for a season,
   Let us be merry before we go!   *J. P. Curran.*

290. THE WORLD OUTSIDE THE WORLD

... Scanty the hour and few the steps beyond the bourn of care,
Beyond the sweet and bitter world,—beyond it unaware!
Scanty the hour and few the steps, because a longer stay
Would bar return, and make a man forget his mortal way. . . .
John Keats.

291. THE FISH, THE MAN, AND THE SPIRIT

TO FISH

You strange, astonish'd-looking, angle-faced,
   Dreary-mouth'd, gaping wretches of the sea,
   Gulping salt water everlastingly,
Cold-blooded, though with red your blood be graced,

And mute, though dwellers in the roaring waste;
    And you, all shapes beside, that fishy be,—
    Some round, some flat, some long, all devilry,
Legless, unloving, infamously chaste:—

O scaly, slippery, wet, swift, staring wights,
    What is't ye do? What life lead? eh, dull goggles?
How do ye vary your vile days and nights?
    How pass your Sundays? Are ye still but joggles
In ceaseless wash? Still nought but gapes, and bites,
    And drinks, and stares, diversified with boggles?

A FISH ANSWERS

Amazing monster! that, for aught I know,
    With the first sight of thee didst make our race
    For ever stare! O flat and shocking face,
Grimly divided from the breast below!
Thou that on dry land horribly dost go
    With a split body and most ridiculous pace,
    Prong after prong, disgracer of all grace,
Long-useless-finned, hair'd, upright, unwet, slow!

O breather of unbreathable, sword-sharp air,
    How canst exist? How bear thyself, thou dry
And dreary sloth? What particle canst share
    Of the only blessed life, the watery?
I sometimes see of ye an actual *pair*
    Go by! link'd fin by fin! most odiously.

THE FISH TURNS INTO A MAN, AND THEN INTO A SPIRIT, AND AGAIN SPEAKS

Indulge thy smiling scorn, if smiling still,
    O man! and loathe, but with a sort of love;
    For difference must its use by difference prove,
And, in sweet clang, the spheres with music fill.
One of the spirits am I, that at his will
    Lives in whate'er has life—fish, eagle, dove—
    No hate, no pride, beneath nought, nor above,
A visitor of the rounds of God's sweet skill.

Man's life is warm, glad, sad, 'twixt loves and graves,
   Boundless in hope, honour'd with pangs austere,
  Heaven-gazing; and his angel-wings he craves:—
    The fish is swift, small-needing, vague yet clear,
  A cold, sweet, silver life, wrapp'd in round waves,
    Quicken'd with touches of transporting fear.
Leigh Hunt.

292. THE STOAT, THE FIELDMOUSE, AND THE MAN

I GO among the Fields and catch a glimpse of a Stoat or a fieldmouse peeping out of the withered grass—the creature hath a purpose and its eyes are bright with it. I go amongst the buildings of a city and I see a Man hurrying along—to what? the Creature has a purpose and his eyes are bright with it.
John Keats.

293. THE MATERIALS OF IMAGINATION

I KNOW no one but you who can be fully sensible of the turmoil and anxiety, the sacrifice of all what is called comfort, the readiness to measure time by what is done and to die in six hours could plans be brought to conclusions—the looking upon the Sun, the Moon, the Stars, the Earth and its contents, as materials to form greater things—that is to say ethereal things—but here I am talking like a Madman,—greater things than our Creator himself made. John Keats.

294. TO SUFFER WOES WHICH HOPE THINKS INFINITE

DEMOGORGON

... Thou, Earth, calm empire of a happy soul,
  Sphere of divinest shapes and harmonies,
  Beautiful orb! gathering as thou dost roll
    The love which paves thy path along the skies:

THE EARTH

I hear: I am as a drop of dew that dies.

Demogorgon

Thou, Moon, which gazest on the nightly Earth
  With wonder, as it gazes upon thee;
Whilst each to men, and beasts, and the swift birth
  Of birds, is beauty, love, calm, harmony:

The Moon

I hear: I am a leaf shaken by thee!

Demogorgon

Ye Kings of suns and stars, Daemons and Gods,
  Aetherial dominations, who possess
Elysian, windless, fortunate abodes
  Beyond Heaven's constellated wilderness:

A Voice from Above

Our great Republic hears, we are blest, and bless.

Demoorgon

Ye happy Dead, whom beams of brightest verse
  Are clouds to hide, not colours to portray,
Whether your nature is that universe
  Which once ye saw and suffered—

A Voice from Beneath

              Or as they
Whom we have left, we change and pass away.

Demogorgon

Ye elemental Genii, who have homes
  From man's high mind even to the central stone
Of sullen lead: from heaven's star-fretted domes
  To the dull weed some sea-worm battens on:

A Confused Voice

We hear: thy words waken Oblivion.

Demogorgon

Spirits, whose homes are flesh: ye beasts and birds,
  Ye worms, and fish; ye living leaves and buds;

> Lightning and wind; and ye untameable herds,
>   Meteors and mists, which throng air's solitudes:—
>
> A VOICE
>
> Thy voice to us is wind among still woods.
>
> DEMOGORGON
>
> Man, who wert once a despot and a slave;
>   A dupe and a deceiver; a decay;
> A traveller from the cradle to the grave
>   Through the dim night of this immortal day:—
>
> ALL
>
> Speak: thy strong words may never pass away.
>
> DEMOGORGON
>
> This is the day, which down the void abysm
> At the Earth-born's spell yawns for Heaven's despotism,
>   And Conquest is dragged captive through the deep:
> Love, from its awful throne of patient power
> In the wise heart, from the last giddy hour
>   Of dread endurance, from the slippery, steep,
> And narrow verge of crag-like agony, springs
> And folds over the world its healing wings.
>
> Gentleness, Virtue, Wisdom, and Endurance,
> These are the seals of that most firm assurance
>   Which bars the pit over Destruction's strength;
> And if, with infirm hand, Eternity,
> Mother of many acts and hours, should free
>   The serpent that would clasp her with his length;
> These are the spells by which to reassume
> An empire o'er the disentangled doom.
>
> To suffer woes which Hope thinks infinite;
> To forgive wrongs darker than death or night;
>   To defy Power, which seems omnipotent;
> To love, and bear; to hope till Hope creates
> From its own wreck the thing it contemplates;

Neither to change, nor falter, nor repent;
This, like thy glory, Titan, is to be
Good, great and joyous, beautiful and free;
This is alone Life, Joy, Empire, and Victory.
P. B. Shelley.

295. DEATH AND LOVELINESS

I HAVE two luxuries to brood over in my walks, your Loveliness and the hour of my death. O that I could have possession of them both in the same minute. J. Keats.

296. FRAGMENT: THE VINE-SHROUD

FLOURISHING vine, whose kindling clusters glow
  Beneath the autumnal sun, none taste of thee;
For thou dost shroud a ruin, and below
  The rotting bones of dead antiquity.

P. B. Shelley.

297. AFTER THE DEATH OF JOHN KEATS

March 29th, 1821.—Keats too is gone! He died at Rome, the 23rd February, aged twenty-five: A genius more purely poetical never existed!

In fireside conversation he was weak and inconsistent, but he was in his glory in the fields. The humming of a bee, the sight of a flower, the glitter of the sun, seemed to make his nature tremble. . . . He began life full of hopes, fiery impetuous and ungovernable, expecting the world to fall at once beneath his powers. Poor fellow! his genius had no sooner begun to bud than hatred and malice spat their poison on its leaves, and sensitive and young it shrivelled beneath their effusions. Unable to bear the sneers of ignorance or the attacks of envy, not having strength of mind enough to buckle himself together like a porcupine and present nothing but his prickles to his enemies, he began to despond and flew to dissipation as a relief, which after a temporary elevation of spirits plunged him into deeper despondency than ever. For six weeks he was scarcely sober, and—to show what a man does to gratify his appetites when once they get the better of him—once covered his tongue and throat as far as he could reach with cayenne pepper in order to appreciate the "delicious coldness of claret in all its glory"—his own expression. . . . The last time I ever saw him was at Hampstead lying in a white bed with a book, hectic and on his back, irritable at his weakness and wounded at the way he had been used. He seemed to be going out of life with a contempt for this world and no hopes for the other.

Benjamin Robert Haydon.

PART IV THE FINISH

"What's o'clock?" —
"It wants a quarter to twelve,
And to-morrow's doomsday."
T. L. Beddoes.

298. THE PLANTS DECAY

... Swift Summer into the Autumn flowed,
   And frost in the mist of the morning rode,
   Though the noonday sun looked clear and bright,
   Mocking the spoil of the secret night.

   The rose-leaves, like flakes of crimson snow,
   Paved the turf and the moss below.
   The lines were drooping, and white, and wan,
   Like the head and the skin of a dying man.

   And Indian plants, of scent and hue
   The sweetest that ever were fed on dew,
   Leaf by leaf, day after day,
   Were massed into the common clay.

   And the leaves, brown, yellow, and gray, and red,
   And white with the whiteness of what is dead,
   Like troops of ghosts on the dry wind passed;
   Their whistling noise made the birds aghast.

   And the gusty winds waked the winged seeds,
   Out of their birthplace of ugly weeds,
   Till they clung round many a sweet flower's stem,
   Which rotted into the earth with them....
                                    P. B. Shelley.

299. THE BIRTH OF FRANKENSTEIN

MANY and long were the conversations between Lord Byron and Shelley, to which I was a devout but nearly silent listener. During one of these, various philosophical doctrines were discussed, and among others the nature of the principle of life, and whether there was any probability of its ever being discovered and communicated. They talked of the experiments of Dr. Darwin, (I speak not of what the Doctor really did, or said that he did, but, as more to my purpose, of what was then spoken of as having been done by him,) who preserved a piece of vermicelli in a glass case, till by some extraordinary means it began to move with voluntary motion. Not thus, after all, would life be given. Perhaps a corpse would be re-animated; galvanism had given token of such things: perhaps the component parts of a creature might be manufactured, brought together, and endued with vital warmth.

Night waned upon this talk; and even the witching hour had gone by, before we retired to rest. When I placed my head on the pillow, I did not sleep, nor could I be said to think. My imagination, unbidden, possessed and guided me, gifting the successive images that arose in my mind with a vividness far beyond the usual bounds of reverie. I saw—with shut eyes, but acute mental vision—I saw the pale student of unhallowed arts kneeling beside the thing he had put together. I saw the hideous phantasm of a man stretched out, and then, on the working of some powerful engine, show signs of life, and stir with an uneasy, half vital motion. Frightful must it be; for supremely frightful would be the effect of any human endeavour to mock the stupendous mechanism of the Creator of the world. His success would terrify the artist; he would rush away from his odious handywork, horror-stricken. He would hope that, left to itself, the slight spark of life which he had communicated would fade; that this thing, which had received such imperfect animation, would subside into dead matter; and he might sleep in the belief that the silence of the grave would quench for ever the transient existence of the hideous corpse which he had looked upon as the cradle of life. He sleeps; but he is awakened; he opens his eyes; behold the horrid thing stands at his bedside, opening his curtains, and looking on him with yellow, watery, but speculative eyes.

I opened mine in terror. The idea so possessed my mind that a thrill of fear ran through me, and I wished to exchange the ghastly image of my fancy for the realities around. I see them still; the very room, the dark *parquet*, the closed shutters, with the moonlight struggling through, and the sense I had that the glassy lake and white high Alps were beyond. I could not so easily get rid of my hideous phantom; still it haunted me. I must try to think of something else. I recurred to my ghost story,—my tiresome unlucky ghost story! O! if I could only contrive one that would frighten my reader as I myself had been frightened that night!

Swift as light and as cheering was the idea that broke in upon me. "I have found it! What terrified me will terrify others; and I need only describe the spectre which haunted my midnight pillow." On the morrow I announced that I had *thought of a story*. I began that day with the words, *It was on a dreary night of November*, making only a transcript of the grim terrors of my waking dream.

Mary Shelley.

300. DEATH'S JEST BOOK

... In it Despair has married wildest mirth
And to their wedding-banquet all the earth
Is bade to bring its enmities and loves,
Triumphs and horrors: you shall see the doves
Billing with quiet joy and all the while
Their nest's the scull of some old king of Nile. . . .

T. L. Beddoes.

301. THE DAISY AND THE FLOOD

.. How thou art like the daisy in Noah's meadow,
On which the foremost drop of rain fell warm
And soft at evening; so the little flower
Wrapped up its leaves, and shut the treacherous water
Close to the golden welcome of its breast,—
Delighting in the touch of that which led
The shower of oceans, in whose billowy drops
Tritons and lions of the sea were warring. . . .

T. L. Beddoes.

302. THE LAST MAN

'TWAS in the year two thousand and one,
A pleasant morning of May,
I sat on the gallows-tree all alone,
A chaunting a merry lay,—
To think how the pest had spared my life,
To sing with the larks that day!

When up the heath came a jolly knave,
Like a scarecrow, all in rags:
It made me crow to see his old duds
All abroad in the wind, like flags:—
So up he came to the timbers' foot
And pitch'd down his greasy bags.—

Good Lord I how blythe the old beggar was!
At pulling out his scraps,—
The very sight of his broken orts
Made a work in his wrinkled chaps:
"Come down," says he, "you Newgate bird,
And have a taste of my snaps!"—

Then down a rope, like a tar from the mast,
I slided, and by him stood;
But I wished myself on the gallows again
When I smelt that beggar's food,
A foul beef-bone and a mouldy crust;
"Oh!" quoth he, "the heavens are good!"

Then after this grace he cast him down:
Says I, "You'll get sweeter air
A pace or two off, on the windward side,"
For the felons' bones lay there.
But he only laugh'd at the empty skulls,
And offar'd them part of his fare.

"I never harm'd *them*, and they won't harm me:
Let the proud and the rich be cravens!"
I did not like that strange beggar man,
He look'd so up at the heavens.
Anon he shook out his empty old poke;
"There's the crumbs," saith he, "for the ravens!"

It made me angry to see his face,
It had such a jesting look;
But while I made up my mind to speak,
A small case-bottle he took:
Quoth he, "though I gather the green water-cress,
My drink is not of the brook!"

Full manners-like he tender'd the dram;
Oh, it came of a dainty cask!
But, whenever it came to his turn to pull,
"Your leave, good sir, I must ask;
But I always wipe the brim with my sleeve,
When a hangman sups at my flask!"

And then he laugh'd so loudly and long,
The churl was quite out of breath;
I thought the very Old One was come
To mock me before my death,
And wish'd I had buried the dead men's bones
That were lying about the heath!

But the beggar gave me a jolly clap—
"Come, let us pledge each other,
For all the wide world is dead beside,
And we are brother and brother—
I've a yearning for thee in my heart,
As if we had come of one mother.

"I've a yearning for thee in my heart
That almost makes me weep,
For as I pass'd from town to town
The folks were all stone-asleep,—
But when I saw thee sitting aloft,
It made me both laugh and leap!"

Now a curse (I thought) be on his love,
And a curse upon his mirth,—
An' if it were not for that beggar man
I'd be the King of the earth,—
But I promis'd myself an hour should come
To make him rue his birth—

So down we sat and bous'd again
Till the sun was in mid-sky,
When, just when the gentle west-wind came,
We hearken'd a dismal cry;
"Up, up, on the tree," quoth the beggar man,
"Till these horrible dogs go by!"

And, lo! from the forest's far-off skirts,
They came all yelling for gore,
A hundred hounds pursuing at once,
And a panting hart before,
Till he sunk down at the gallows' foot,
And there his haunches they tore!

His haunches they tore, without a horn
To tell when the chase was done;
And there was not a single scarlet coat
To flaunt it in the sun!—
I turn'd, and look'd at the beggar man,
And his tears dropt one by one!

And with curses sore he chid at the hounds,
Till the last dropt out of sight,
Anon, saith he, "Let's down again,
And ramble for our delight,
For the world's all free, and we may choose
A right cozie barn for to-night!"

With that, he set up his staff on end,
And it fell with the point due West;
So we far'd that way to a city great,
Where the folks had died of the pest—
It was fine to enter in house and hall
Wherever it liked me best;

For the porters all were stiff and cold,
And could not lift their heads;
And when we came where their masters lay,
The rats leapt out of the beds;
The grandest palaces in the land
Were as free as the workhouse sheds.

But the beggar man made a mumping face,
And knocked at every gate:
It made me curse to hear how he whined,
So our fellowship turned to hate,
And I bade him walk the world by himself,
For I scorn'd so humble a mate!

So *he* turn'd right and I turn'd left,
As if we had never met;
And I chose a fair stone house for myself,
For the city was all to let;
And for three brave holidays drank my fill
Of the choicest that I could get.

And because my jerkin was coarse and worn,
I got me a properer vest;
It was purple velvet stitch'd o'er with gold,
And a shining star at the breast!—
'Twas enough to fetch old Joan from her grave
To see me so purely drest!

But Joan was dead and under the mould,
And every buxom lass;
In vain I watch'd, at the window pane
For a Christian soul to pass!
But sheep and kine wander'd up the street,
And browz'd on the new-come grass.—

When lo! I spied the old beggar man,
And lustily he did sing!—
His rags were lapp'd in a scarlet cloak,
And a crown he had like a King;
So he stept right up before my gate
And danc'd me a saucy fling!

Heaven mend us all!—but within my mind,
I had killed him then and there;
To see him lording so braggart-like
That was born to his beggar's fare,
And how he had stolen the royal crown
His betters were meant to wear.

But God forbid that a thief should die
Without his share of the laws!
So I nimbly whipt my tackle out,
And soon tied up his claws,—
I was judge myself, and jury, and all,
And solemnly tried the cause.

But the beggar man would not plead, but cried
Like a babe without its corals,
For he knew how hard it is apt to go
When the law and a thief have quarrels,—
There was not a Christian soul alive
To speak a word for his morals.

Oh, how gaily I doff'd my costly gear,
And put on my work-day clothes;
I was tired of such a long Sunday life,—
And never was one of the sloths;
But the beggar man grumbled a weary deal,
And made many crooked mouths.

So I haul'd him off to the gallows' foot,
And bunded him in his bags;
'Twas a weary job to heave him up,
For a doom'd man always lags;
But by ten of the clock he was off his legs
In the wind, and airing his rags!

So there he hung, and there I stood,
The LAST MAN left alive,
To have my own will of all the earth:
Quoth I, now I shall thrive!
But when was ever honey made
With one bee in a hive?

My conscience began to gnaw my heart,
Before the day was done,
For other men's lives had all gone out,
Like candles in the sun!—
But it seem'd as if I had broke, at last,
A thousand necks in one!

So I went and cut his body down
To bury it decentlie;—
God send there were any good soul alive
To do the like by me!
But the wild dogs came with terrible speed,
And bay'd me up the tree!

My sight was like a drunkard's sight,
And my head began to swim,
To see their jaws all white with foam,
Like the ravenous ocean-brim;—
But when the wild dogs trotted away
Their jaws were bloody and grim!

Their jaws were bioody and grim, good Lord!
But the beggar man, where was he?—
There was nought of him, but some ribbons of rags
Below the gallows' tree!—
I know the Devil, when I am dead,
Will send his hounds for me!—

I've buried my babies one by one,
And dug the deep hole for Joan,
And cover'd the faces of kith and kin,
And felt the old churchyard stone
Go cold to my heart full many a time,
But I never felt so lone!

For the lion and Adam were company,
And the tiger him beguiled;
But the simple kine are foes to my life,
And the household brutes are wild.
If the veriest cur would lick my hand,
I could love it like a child!

And the beggar man's ghost besets my dream,
At night, to make me madder,—
And my wretched conscience within my breast,
Is like a stinging adder;—
I sigh when I pass the gallows' foot,
And look at the rope and ladder!

For hanging looks sweet,—but, alas! in vain,
My desperate fancy begs,—
I must turn my cup of sorrows quite up,
And drink it to the dregs,—
For there is not another man alive
In the world to pull my legs!

Thomas Hood.

303. VOLTAIRE, COBBETT, AND GASTRONOMY

... Take back the lute! I make no claim
To inspiration or to fame;
The hopes and fears that bards should cherish,
I care not when they fade and perish;
I read political economy,
Voltaire and Cobbett, and gastronomy,
And, when I would indite a story
Of woman's faith or warrior's glory,
I always wear a night-cap sable,
And put my elbows on the table,
And hammer out the tedious toil
By dint of Walker, and lamp-oil.
I never feel poetic mania,
I gnaw no laurel with Urania,
I court no critic's tender mercies,
I count the feet in all my verses,
And own myself a screaming gander
Among the shrill swans of Mæander.

W. M. Praed

304. THE CITIZEN AND THE VULTURE

IF you dissect a vulture that has just been feeding on carrion, you must expect that your olfactory nerves will be somewhat offended with the rank effluvia from his craw; just as they would be were you to dissect a citizen after the Lord Mayor's dinner. If, on the contrary, the vulture be empty at the time you commence the operation, there will be no offensive smell, but a strong scent of musk. *Charles Waterton.*

305. EUGENE ARAM, OR THE STORMS OF THE BLACK DEEPS OF SLUMBER

FOR the more imaginative part of the version I must refer back to one of those unaccountable visions, which come upon us like frightful monsters thrown up by storms from the great black deeps of slumber. A lifeless body, in love and relationship the nearest and dearest, was imposed upon my back, with an overwhelming sense of obligation—not of filial piety merely, but some awful responsibility, equally vague and intense, and involving, as it seemed, inexpiable sin, horrors unutterable, torments intolerable,—to bury my dead, like Abraham, out of my sight. In vain I attempted, again and again, to obey the mysterious mandate—by some dreadful process the burthen was replaced with a more stupendous weight of injunction, and an appalling conviction of the impossibility of its fulfilment. My mental anguish was indescribable;—the mighty agony of souls tortured on the supernatural racks of sleep are not to be penned—and if in sketching those that belong to blood-guiltiness I have been at all successful, I owe it mainly to the uninvoked inspiration of that terrible dream.
Thomas Hood.

306. THE WATER LADY

ALAS, the moon should ever beam
To show what man should never see!—
I saw a maiden on a stream,
And fair was she!

I staid awhile, to see her throw
Her tresses back, that all beset
The fair horizon of her brow
With clouds of jet.

I staid a little while to view
Her cheek, that wore in place of red
The bloom of water, tender blue,
Daintily spread.

I staid to watch, a little space,
Her parted lips if she would sing,
The waters closed above her face
With many a ring.

And still I staid a little more,
Alas! she never comes again!
I throw my flowers from the shore,
And watch in vain.
Thomas Hood.

307. DEATH

FLOWERS shall hang upon the palls,
Brighter than patterns upon shawls,
And blossoms shall be on the coffin hid,
Sadder than tears on grief's eyelid,
Garlands shall hide pale corpses' faces
When beauty shall rot in charnel places,
Spring flowers shall come in tears and sorrow
For the maiden goes down to her grave to-morrow....
John Clare.

308. VAMPIRES

As there was a free entrance and exit to the vampire in the loft where I slept, I had many a fine opportunity of paying attention to this nocturnal surgeon. He does not always live on blood. When the moon shone bright, and the fruit of the banana-tree was ripe, I could see him approach and eat it. He would also bring into the loft, from the forest, a green round fruit, something like the wild guava, and about the size of a nutmeg. There was something also, in the blossom of the sawarri nut-tree, which was grateful to him; for on coming up Waratilla creek, in a moonlight night, I saw several vampires fluttering round the top of the sawarri-tree, and every now and then the blossoms, which they had broken off, fell into the water. They certainly did not drop off naturally, for on examining several of them, they appeared quite fresh and blooming. So I concluded the vampires pulled them from the tree, either to get at the incipient fruit, or to catch the insects which often take up their abode in flowers. . . . It has been remarked before, that there are two species of vampire in Guiana, a larger and a smaller. The larger sucks men and other animals; the smaller seems to confine himself chiefly to birds. I learnt from a gentleman, high up in the river Demerara, that he was completely unsuccessful with his fowls, on account of the small vampire. He showed me some that had been sucked the night before, and they were scarcely able to walk.

Some years ago I went up the river Paumaron with a Scotch gentleman, by name Tarbet. We hung our hammocks in the thatched loft of a planter's house. Next morning I heard this gentleman muttering in his hammock, and now and then letting fall an imprecation or two, just about the time he ought to have been saying his morning prayers. "What is the matter, Sir," said I, softly; "is anything amiss?" "What's the matter!" answered he, surlily; why, the vampires have been sucking me to death." As soon as there was light enough, I went to his hammock, and saw it much stained with olood. "There," said he, thrusting his foot out of the hammock, "see how these infernal imps have been drawing my life's blood." On examining his foot, I found the vampire had tapped his great toe: there was a wound somewhat less than that made by a leech; the blood was still oozing from it; I conjectured he might have lost from ten to twelve ounces of blood. Whilst examining it I think I put him into a worse humour by remarking, that an European surgeon would not have been so generous as to have blooded him without making a charge. He looked up in my face, but did not say a word: I saw he was of opinion that I had better have spared this piece of ill-timed levity. . . .

I had often wished to have been once sucked by the vampire, in order that I might have it in my power to say it had really happened to me. There can be no pain in the operation, for the patient is always asleep when the vampire is sucking him; and as for the loss of a few ounces of blood, that would be a trifle in the long run. Many a night have I slept with my foot out of the hammock to tempt this winged surgeon, expecting that he would be there; but it was all in vain; the vampire never sucked me, and I could never account for his not doing so, for we were inhabitants of the same lofts for months together.
Charles Waterton.

309. THE GARDENS OF HEAVEN

I HAVE a fondness for the earth, and rather a Phrygian mood of regarding it. I feel a yearning to see the glades and the nooks receding like vistas into the gardens of Heaven.
Edward Calvert.

310. SHOREHAM

  AND now the trembling light
  Glimmers behind the little hills and corn,
  Ling'ring as loth to part; yet part thou must
  And though than open day far pleasing more
  (Ere yet the fields and pearlèd cups of flowers
    Twinkle in the parting light;)
  Thee night shall hide, sweet visionary gleam
  That softly lookest through the rising dew;
    Till all like silver bright,
    The faithful witness, pure and white,
    Shall look o'er yonder grassy hill,
    At this village, safe and still.
    All is safe and all is still,
    Save what noise the watch-dog makes
    Or the shrill cock the silence breaks.

>   Now and then—
>   And now and then—
>   Hark! Once again,
>   The wether's bell
>   To us doth tell
>   Some little stirring in the fold.
>   Methinks the ling'ring dying ray
>   Of twilight time, doth seem more fair,
>   And lights the soul up more than day
>   When wide-spread sultry sunshines are:
>   Yet all is right and all most fair,
>   For thou, dear God, has formed all;
>   Thou deckest every little flower,
>   Thou girdest every planet ball,
>   And mark'st when sparrows fall.
>   *Samuel Palmer.*

311. ART, VISION AND THIS CREATION

I HAVE begun to take off a pretty view of part of the village, and have no doubt but the drawing of choice portions and aspects of external objects is one of the varieties of study requisite to build up an artist, who should be a magnet to all kinds of knowledge; though, at the same time, I can't help seeing that the general characteristics of Nature's beauty not only differ from, but are, in some respects, opposed to those of Imaginative Art; and *that*, even in those scenes and appearances where she is loveliest, and most universally pleasing.

Nature, with mild reposing breadths of lawn and hill, shadowy glades and meadows, is sprinkled and showered with a thousand pretty eyes, and buds, and spires, and blossoms gemm'd with dew, and is clad in living green. Nor must be forgotten the motley clouding, the fine meshes, the aerial tissues, that dapple the skies of spring; nor the rolling volumes and piled mountains of light; nor the purple sunset blazon'd with gold and the translucent amber. Universal nature wears a lovely gentleness of mild attraction; but the leafy lightness, the thousand repetitions of little forms, which are part of its own genuine perfection (and who would wish them but what they are?), seem hard to be reconciled with the unwinning severity, the awfulness, the ponderous globosity of Art.

Milton, by one epithet, draws an oak of the largest girth I ever saw, "Pine and *monumental* oak": I have just been trying to draw a large one in Lullingstone; but the poet's tree is huger than any in the park: there, the moss, and rifts, and barky furrows, and the mouldering grey (tho' that adds majesty to the lords of forests) mostly catch the eye, before the grasp and grapple of the roots, the muscular belly and shoulders, the twisted sinews. . . . I must be called mad to say it but I do believe his stanzas will be read in Heaven: and to be yet more mad—to foam at the mouth, I will declare my conviction that the *St. George* of Donatello, the *Night* of Michelangelo, and *The Last Supper* of Da Vinci are as casts and copies, of which, when their artists had obtained of God to conceive the Idea, an eternal mould was placed above the tenth sphere, beyond changes and decay.

Terrestrial spring showers blossoms and odours in profusion, which, at some moments, "Breathe on earth the air of Paradise": indeed sometimes, when the spirits are in Heav'n, earth itself, as in emulation, blooms again into Eden; rivalling those golden fruits which the poet of Eden sheds upon his landscape, having stolen [them] from that country where they grow without peril of frost, or drought, or blight—"But not in this soil."

Still, the perfection of nature is not the perfection of severest art: they are two things. The former we may liken to an easy, charming colloquy of intellectual friends; the latter is "Imperial Tragedy." *That* is graceful humanity; *this* is Plato's Vision; who, somewhere in untracked regions, prhnigenous Unity, above all things holds his head and bears his forehead among the stars, tremendous to the gods!

If the *Night* could get up and walk, and were to take a swim to the white cliffs, and after the fashion of Shakespeare's tragicomic mixtures, were amusing herself with a huge bit of broken tobacco-pipe, I think about half a dozen whiffs would blow down the strongest beech and oak at Windsor, and the pipe-ashes chance to make a big bonfire of the forest!

General nature is wisely and beneficently adapted to refresh the senses and soothe the spirits of general *observers*. We find hundreds in raptures when they get into the fields, who have not the least relish for grand art. General nature is simple and lovely; but, compared with the loftier vision, it is the shrill music of the "Little herd grooms, Keeping their beasts in the budded brooms; And crowing in pipes made of green corn," to the sound of the chant and great organ, pealing through dusky aisles and reverberating in the dome; or the trombone, and drums, and cymbak of the banner'd march. Everywhere curious, articulate, perfect and inimitable of structure, like her own entomology, Nature does yet leave a space for the soul to climb above her steepest summits. As, in her own dominion, she swells from the herring to leviathan, from the hodmandod to the elephant, so, diyine Art piles mountains on her hills, and continents upon those mountains.

However, creation sometimes pours into the spiritual eye the radiance of Heaven: the green mountains that glimmer in a summer gloaming from the dusky yet bloomy east; the moon opening her golden eye, or walking in brightness among innumerable islands of light, not only thrill the optic nerve, but shed a mild, a grateful, an unearthly lustre into the inmost spirits, and seem the interchanging twilight of that peaceful country, where there is no sorrow and no night.

After all, I doubt not but there must be the study of this creation, as well as art and vision; tho' I cannot think it other than the veil of Heaven, through which her divine features are dimly smiling; the setting of the table before the feast; the symphony before the tune; the prologue of the drama; a dream, and antepast, and proscenium of eternity.

Samuel Palmer.

312. STONE-PIT

THE passing traveller with wonder sees
A deep and ancient stone-pit full of trees;
So deep and very deep the place has been,
The church might stand within and not be seen.

The passing stranger oft with wonder stops
And thinks he e'en could walk upon their tops,
And often stoops to see the busy crow,
And stands above and sees the eggs below;
And while the wild horse gives its head a toss,
The squirrel dances up and runs across.
The boy that stands and kills the black-nosed bee
Dares down as soon as magpies' nests are found,
And wonders when he climbs the highest tree
To find it reaches scarce above the ground.

John Clare.

313. BUTTERFLIES AND SNOW

WHEN Messrs. Hawes and Fellowes ascended Mont Blanc in July, 1827, they observed a butterfly near the summit. Mr. C. Shewell saw two crimson moths at nearly the same elevation.

New Monthly Magazine.

314. ENCHANTED TWILIGHT

HEAD and shoulders will I shove in mine own secular interest, and beg the favour that if in your ivory researches, you meet with 3 or 4 morsels of very fine ivory, size and proportion not very particular so they be from about 1 inch by 1½ inch up to about 3 inches by 2 inches, you would buy them for me. Some thoughts have concocted and condensed in my mind of what I have seen walking about in midsummer eves and I should not care if I got a few of the subjects on ivory now, to study upon with fresh recollections of similar appearances next midsummer, if God spare me; I prefer doing them very small, for they are not things by themselves, but wings, terraces, or outbuildings to the great edifice of the divine human form — otherwise snares. But I have beheld, as in the spirit, such nooks, caught such glimpses of the perfumed and enchanted twilight of natural midsummer (as well as at some other times of day other scenes), as, passed thro' the intense purifying, separating, transmitting heat of the soul's infabulous alchymy, would divinely consist with the severe and stately port of the human, as with the moon thron'd among constellations, and varieties of lesser glories, the regal pomp and glistening brilliance and solemn attendance of her starry train.

Samuel Palmer.

315. DEWDROPS

THE dewdrops on every blade of grass are so much like silver drops that I am obliged to stoop down as I walk to see if they are pearls, and those sprinkled on the ivy-woven beds of primroses underneath the hazels, whitethorns, and maples are so like gold beads that I stooped down to feel if they were hard, but they melted from my finger. And where the dew lies on the primrose, the violet and whitethorn leaves, they are emerald and beryl, yet nothing more than the dews of the morning on the budding leaves; nay, the road grasses are covered with gold and silver beads, and the further we go the brighter they seem to shine, like solid gold and silver. It is nothing more than the sun's light and shade upon them in the dewy morning; every thorn-point and, every bramble-spear has its trembling ornament; till the wind gets a little brisker, and then all is shaken off, and all the shining jewellery passes away into a common spring morning full of budding leaves, primroses, violets, vernal speedwell, bluebell, and orchis, and commonplace objects. *John Clare.*

316. THE POET'S PORTION

... He has th' enjoyment of a flower's birth
Before its budding—ere the first red streaks,
And Winter cannot rob him of their cheeks.

Look—if his dawn be not as other men's!
Twenty bright flushes—ere another kens
The first of sunlight is abroad—he sees
Its golden 'lection of the topmost trees,
And opes the splendid fissures of the morn.

> When do his fruits delay, when doth his corn
> Linger for harvesting? Before the leaf
> Is commonly abroad, in his pil'd sheaf
> The flagging poppies lose their ancient flame. . . .
>
> Oh! blest to see the flower in its seed,
> Before its leafy presence; for indeed
> Leaves are but wings on which the summer flies,
> And each thing perishable fades and dies,
> Escap'd in thought; but his rich thinkings be
> Like overflows of immortality:
> So that what there is steep'd, shall perish never,
> But live and bloom, and be a joy for ever.
> Thomas Hood.

317. POETRY IS PLEASURE

OF Coleridge I cannot speak but with reverence. His towering intellect! his gigantic power! To use an author quoted by himself, "J'ai trouvé souvent que la plupart des sectes ont raison dans une bonne partie de ce qu'elles avancent, mais non pas en ce qu'elles nient;" and, to employ his own language, he has imprisoned his own conceptions by the barrier he has erected against those of others. It is lamentable to think that such a mind should be buried in metaphysics, and, like the Nyctanthis, waste its perfume upon the night alone. In reading that man's poetry I tremble like one who stands upon a volcano, conscious, from the very darkness bursting from the crater, of the fire and the light that are weltering below.

What is Poetry? Poetry! That Proteus-like idea, with as many appellations as the nine-titled Corcyra! Give me, I demanded of a scholar some time ago, give me a definition of Poetry. "Très volontiers"—and he proceeded to his library, brought me a Dr. Johnson, and overwhelmed me with a definition. Shade of the immortal Shakespeare! I imagined to myself the scowl of your spiritual eye upon the profanity of that scurrilous Ursa Major. Think of poetry, dear B——, think of poetry, and then think of—Dr. Samuel Johnson!

Think of all that is airy and fairy-like, and then of all that is hideous and unwieldy: think of his huge bulk, the Elephant! and then—and then think of the Tempest—the Midsummer Night's Dream—Prospero— Oberon—and Titania!

A poem, in my opinion, is opposed to a work of science by having, for its *immediate* object, pleasure, not truth: to romance, by having for its object an *indefinite* instead of a *definite* pleasure, being a poem only so far as this object is attained: romance presenting perceptible images with definite, poetry with indefinite sensations, to which end music is an *essential*, since the comprehension of sweet sound is our most indefinite conception. Music, when combined with a pleasurable idea, is poetry: music without the idea is simply music: the idea without the music is prose from its very defmiteness.

What was meant by the invective against "him who had no music in his soul"? *Edgar Allan Poe.*

318. THE FLOWER

... The wild flower 'neath the shepherd's feet
Looks up and gives him joy. ...
John Clare.

319. LOVE SCORNED BY PRIDE

I WISH I was a happy bird,
And thou a true and timid dove:
O I would fly the land of grief,
And rest me in the land of love.

O I would rest where I love best;
Where I love best I may not be:
A hawk doth on that rose-tree sit,
And drives young love to fear and flee.

O would I were the goldfinch gay!
My richer suit had tempted strong.
O would I were the nightingale!
Then thou hadst listened to my song.
John Clare.

320. CURIOUSNESS IN BEAUTY

I LONG to see some first-rate distances, and hope you have brought a line or two of some of the quaint, rocky, or wooded summits of the Rhine. I believe in my very heart (but the heart's a great liar tho' it's the truest part about us), that all the very finest original pictures, and the topping things in nature, have a certain quaintness by which they partly affect us; not the quaintness of bungling—the queer doing of a common thought, but a curiousness in their beauty, a salt on their tails, by which the imagination catches hold on them, while the sublime eagles and big birds of the French Academy fly up far beyond the sphere of our affections. One of the very deepest sayings I have met with in Lord Bacon seems to me to be, "There is no excellent beauty that hath not some strangeness in the proportion." The Sleeping Mercury in the British Museum has this hard-to-be-defined but most delicious quality to perfection. So have the best antique gems, and bas-reliefs, and statues; so have *not* the Elgin marbles, graceful as they are: but it is continually flashing out in nature; and in nothing more than in the beamings of beautiful countenances. But I begin now to be quite humbled, and to speak of all things as modestly as an impudent man can speak.

Samuel Palmer.

321. TO ——

THE bowers whereat, in dreams, I see
   The wantonest singing birds,
Are lips—and all thy melody
   Of lip-begotten words—

Thine eyes, in Heaven of heart enshrined,
   Then desolately fall,
Oh God! on my funereal mind
   Like starlight on a pall—

Thy heart— *thy* heart!—I wake and sigh,
  And sleep to dream till day
Of the truth that gold can never buy—
  Of the baubles that it may.
                              Edgar Allan Poe.

322. SUNSET

... Now to his restless sea-bed wends
  The slow sun, gazing at our mirth,
And on his lustrous breath he sends,
  Wistful, a warm farewell to earth....
                              George Darley.

323. WHITE AN' BLUE

My Love is o 'comely height an' straïght,
An' comely in all her ways an' gait;
In feäce she do show the rwose's hue,
An' her lids on her eyes be white on blue.

When Elemley clubmen walk'd in Maÿ,
An 'vo'k come in clusters, ev'ry waÿ,
As soon as the zun dried up the dew,
An' clouds in the sky wer white on blue,

She come by the down, wi' trippen walk,
By deäsies, an' sheenèn banks o' chalk,
An' brooks, where the crowvoot flow'rs did strew
The sky-tinted water, white on blue.

She nodded her head as plaÿ'd the band;
She dapp'd wi' her voot as she did stand;
She danced in a reel, a-weärèn new
A skirt wi' a jacket, white wi' blue.

I singled her out vrom thin an 'stout,
Vrom slender an' stout I chose her out;
An' what, in evenèn, could I do,
But gi'e her my breast-knot, white an' blue?
                              William Barnes.

324. MY LOVE'S GUARDIAN ANGEL

As in the cool-aïr'd road I come by,
        —in the night,
Under the moon-climb'd height o' the sky,
        —in the night,
There by the lime's broad lim's I did staÿ,
While in the air dark sheädes were at play
Up on the windor-glass, that did keep
Lew vrom the wind my true-love asleep,
        —in the night.

While in the grey-wall'd height o' the tow'r,
        —in the night,
Sounded the midnight bell wi' the hour,
        —in the night,
There come a bright-heair'd angel that shed
Light vrom her white robe's zilvery thread,
Wi' her vore-vinger held up to meäke
Silence around lest sleepers mid weäke,
        —in the night.

"Oh! then," I whisper'd, "do I behold
        —in the night,
Linda, my true-love, here in the cwold,
        —in the night?"
"No," she did answer, "you do misteäke:
She is asleep, 'tis I be aweäke,
I be her angel brightly a-drest
Watchèn her slumber while she do rest,
        —in the night."

"Zee how the clear win's, brisk in the bough,
        —in the night,
While they do pass, don't smite on her brow,
        —in the night;

> Zee how the cloud-sheädes naïseless do zweep
> Over the house-top where she's asleep.
> You, too, goo on, though times mid be near,
> When you, wi' me, mid speak to her ear
>   —in the night."
>
> William Barnes.

325. THE MOONLIT NIGHT

> . . . The air so still, the sky so mild, like slumbers of the cradled child,
> The moon looks over fields of love, among the ivy sleeps the dove. . . .
>
> John Clare.

326. A DREAM WITHIN A DREAM

> . . . I stand amid the roar
> Of a surf-tormented shore,
> And I hold within my hand
> Grains of the golden sand—
> How few! yet how they creep
> Through my fingers to the deep,
> While I weep—while I weep!
> O God! can I not grasp
> Them with a tighter clasp?
> O God I can I not save
> *One* from the pitiless wave?
> Is *all* that we see or seem
> But a dream within a dream?
>
> Edgar Allan Poe.

327. THE SYMBOLISM OF LANDSCAPE

I THINK we can bear barrenness better in a foreground than a distance—for landscape should be the symbol of prospects brightening in futurity. Samuel Palmer.

328. THE PRIMACY OF IMAGINATION

LORD BACON says, it is the office of poetry to "suit the shows of things to the desires of the mind." We seem to aim at suiting the desires of the mind to the shows of things. Does not the former imply a much more profound and inclusive study of "the shows of things"—"nature," as we call it, itself? What was it but his ideal of Helen which obliged the Greek to study all the most beautiful women he could find?

When I was setting out for Italy I expected to see Claude's magical combinations—miles apart I found the disjointed members, some of them most lovely, which he had "suited to the desires of his mind"; there were the beauties, but the Beautiful—the ideal Helen was his own. And the sense of this ideal is so lost and forgotten by the materialistic eye, that Claude himself is considered rather as an accomplished master of aerial perspective, or what not, than as the genius, equally tender and sublime, who reopened upon canvas the vistas of Eden.

But is not all this gaseous rhodomontade about the Ideal, exploded by the fact, that every artist worthy of the name, finds it almost impossible to render one tithe of its beauty, when he sits down either to copy or to imitate the simplest object? I think not; and it seems to me that in the present state of our faculties, any system which is without its paradoxes, is by the same token as suspicious as an exact correspondence of several witnesses in a trial at the Old Bailey.

Samuel Palmer.

329. POEMS TRANSLATED FROM THE CHINESE

i

THE affairs of the world are all hurry and trouble without end:
Why, then, with bitter anxiety waste the heart's springs?
Search for some pleasant spot to pour out a cup of wine,
Steal a leisure hour to sing the stanzas of an ode!

The fine flower unblown exhales no sweets,
The fair gem unpolished exhibits no radiance:
Were it not that once the cold penetrated its stem,
How could the plum-blossom emit such fragrance?

ii

To the front of yon old peaked hill, the sovereign of verdure returns,
At the base of yon old peaked hill the rain is gently falling:
The peach and pear blossoms successively open and blend their hues,
The white and the yellow bird fly hither and thither:
I recollect how last year, at the monastery that overlooks the sea,
On this very day I watched the spring displaying its brightness.
No tidings have since reached me of my distant brethren:
I sit solitary in this lonely mountain, and brood over my thoughts.

iii

I THROW on my clothes, and wait for the Moon,
—I wait for the Moon, which rises late:
She breaks at length from behind yon hilly summit,
And first illumines the tops of the trees:
How ruffled is the surface of yon golden waves!
The silver stream of the sky* displays a vague and unequal light:
Thus lingering until the stars of Orion have set,
I return to sleep, and dream all over again.

iv

By the side of the *Hoongting* bridge, to the east of the bridge *Haelo*,
There grows thickly the Epidendrum, making a grove of its own:
Its fragrant breath fills the lonely valley,
And a single sprig hath flown hither, to replenish this precious vase.

* The Milky Way.

The solitary flower finds a companion in its own shadow,
Blown by the gentle breeze that pervades my empty hall:
My sleeves are scented with its morning and evening sweets,
I know of none whose delight in it can equal mine.

v

THEIR slender shadows fill the enclosure, and a scattered perfume pervades the flower-beds, planted in triple rows: their deeper and lighter tints reflect a yellow light, and the leaves shine varied from beneath the drops of dew: each hungry flowret inhales the passing breeze, as it sheds around its incomparable lustre. The gazer sympathizes with the languishing blossoms, bending their heads all faint and delicate: the mournful view awakes in his mind thoughts suitable to autumn. Say not that it is a sight to satiate the eyes of the indifferent beholder—know that such flowers as these once inspired the poet Taou-yuen-ming, as he indulged his genius amidst verses and wine.

vi

THE last month of the winter was for the most part clear and mild,
And now at length approach the well-timed showers:
The wide-spread mist has involved yon mountain dwelling,
Its dews are slowly filling each rocky hollow:
The vernal winds obscure the clouded sun,
It is the season for all things in nature to germinate:
Let us convey an exhortation to the husbandman,
That he delay not the business of his western fields.

The green foliage of the willows has not yet shaded the path,
But the peach-blossoms already cover the grove:
Every inanimate thing seems to feel the influence of the season,
Shall I, then, be unmindful of the purposes of heaven?
Like some who lean on their tables, and grow unprofitably old,
Who exert not their strength in the proper time?
—The rain falls in drops before my rude door-way,
As I stroll about, or sit, immersed in such meditations.

                             vii
SEE how the gently falling rain
    Its vernal influence sweetly showers,
As through the calm and tepid eve
    It silently bedews the flowers:

Cloudy and dark th' horizon spreads,
    —Save where some boat its light is burning:
But soon the landscape's tints shall glow
    All radiant, with the morn returning.
                        John Francis Davis.

330. IN THE SPRING

MY love is the maid ov all maïdens,
    Though all mid be comely,
Her skin's lik' the jessamy blossom
    A spread in the Spring.

Her smile is so sweet as a beäby's
    Young smile on his mother,
Her eyes be as bright as the dew drop
    A-shed in the Spring.

O grey-leafy pinks o' the geärden,
    Now bear her sweet blossoms;
Now deck wi' a rwose bud, O briar,
    Her head in the Spring.

O light-rollèn wind, blow me hither
    The vaïce ov her talkèn,
O bring vrom her veet the light doust
    She do tread in the Spring.

O zun, meäke the gil'cups all glitter
    In goold all around her,
An' meäke o' the deäisys' white flowers
    A bed in the Spring.

O whissle, gay birds, up bezide her,
  In drong-waÿ an' woodlands,
O zing, swingèn lark, now the clouds
  Be a-vled in the Spring!

William Barnes,

331. TO MY EGERIA

O PLACID nun!
That lov'st, immured within thy sparry cell,
Whose moist roof makes the crystal floor a well,
To count the drip-falls one by one,
Thy echoing beads and bell,
Which rings thee to perpetual orisons
And keeps thy grotto awful with the knell.

Thy breathless prayer
Comes not from thy still lips, but stedfast eyes
In far-world thought fixt on the distant skies;
Eve's solemn winds hymn for thee there,
Sweet Dawn thy matin sighs:
With tranquil breast that heaved not her soft hair
On simple mosses so much beauty lies! . . .

Hither betimes,
With leaf-light step upon the frosted dews,
Wanders that Queen of Song the poet woos,
Like Nymph to Nun, in Celtic climes
Turned Sylph from sylvan Muse;
O, if thy Sister hear, into his rhymes
Thou, with her spirit wild, thy calm infuse.

George Darley.

332. THE CONDENSING POWER OF ART

I CAN hardly contain myself, when I think of the condensing power of art—when I mentally contemplate the rough, unsightly back of an old panel, not half the size of one of the leaves of a small Pembroke table, and know that on the other side, is Raphael's vision of Ezekiel. *Samuel Palmer,*

333. THE ENCHANTED SPRING

O'ER golden sands my waters flow,
With pearls my road is paven white;
Upon my banks sweet flowers blow,
And amber rocks direct me right.

Look in my mother-spring: how deep
Her dark-green waters, yet how clear!
For joy the pale-eyed stars do weep
To see themselves so beauteous here.

Her pebbles all to emeralds turn,
Her mosses fine as Nereid's hair;
Bright leaps the crystal from her urn,
As pure as dew, and twice as rare.

Taste of the wave, 'twill charm thy blood,
And make thy cheek out-bloom the rose,
'Twill calm thy heart and clear thy mood,
Come! sip it freshly as it flows.
George Darley.

334. THE PHENIX

. . . O blest unfabled Incense Tree
That burns in glorious Araby,
With red scent chalicing the air
Till earth-life grow Elysian there!

Half buried to her flaming breast
In this bright tree she makes her nest,
Hundred-sunned Phenix! when she must
Crumble at length to hoary dust!

Her gorgeous death-bed! her rich pyre
Burnt up with aromatic fire!
Her urn, sight high from spoiler men!
Her birthplace when self-born again!

The mountainless green wilds among
Here ends she her unechoing song!
With amber tears and odorous sighs
Mourned by the desert where she dies!

Laid like the young fawn mossily
In sun-green vales of Araby,
I woke, hard by the Phenix tree
That with shadeless boughs flamed over me;
And upward called by a dumb cry
With moonbroad orbs of wonder, I
Beheld the immortal Bird on high
Glassing the great sun in her eye;
Steadfast she gazed upon his fire,
Still her destroyer and her sire!
As if to his her soul of flame
Had flown already, whence it came;
Like those that sit and glare so still,
Intense with their death struggle, till
We touch, and curdle at their chill! —
But breathing yet while she doth burn,
The deathless Daughter of the sun!
Slowly to crimson embers turn
The beauties of the brightsome one;
O'er the broad nest her silver wings
Shook down their wasteful glitterings;
Her brinded neck high-arched in air,
Like a small rainbow faded there;
But brighter glowed her plumy crown
Mouldering to golden ashes down:
With fume of sweet woods, to the skies
Pure as a Saint's adoring sighs,
Warm as a prayer in Paradise,
Her life-breath rose in sacrifice!

The while with shrill triumphant tone
Sounding aloud, aloft, alone,
Ceaseless her joyful deathwail she
Sang to departing Araby!

　　　　Deep melancholy wonder drew
　　　　Tears from my heartspring at that view;
　　　　Like, cresset shedding its last flare
　　　　Upon some wistful mariner,
　　　　The Bird, fast blending with the sky,
　　　　Turned on me her dead-gazing eye
　　　　Once—and as surge to shallow spray
　　　　Sank down to vapoury dust away!

　　　　O, fast her amber blood doth flow
　　　　From the heart-wounded Incense Tree,
　　　　Fast as earth's deep-embosomed woe
　　　　In silent rivulets to the sea!

　　　　Beauty may weep her fair first-born
　　　　Perchance in as resplendent tears,
　　　　Such golden dewdrops bow the corn
　　　　When the stern sickleman appears;

　　　　But oh! such perfume to a bower
　　　　Never allured sweet-seeeking bee,
　　　　As to sip fast that nectarous shower
　　　　A thirstier minstrel drew in me! . . .
　　　　　　　　　　　　George Darley.

335. DECLIVITIES OF HEAVEN

　　. . . Where green Earth from azure sky
　　　　Seems but one blue step to be;
　　　　Where the sun his wheel of gold
　　　　Burnishes deeply in her mould,
　　　　And her shining walks uneven
　　　　Seem declivities of Heaven. . . .
　　　　　　　　　　　　George Darley.

336. FRAGMENT

　　　　　　Or I will burst
Damnation's iron egg, my tomb, and come
Half damned, ere they make lightning of my soul,

And creep into thy carcase as thou deepest
  Between two crimson fevers.
                              T. L. Beddoes.

337. TOM TATTERS' BIRTHDAY ODE

COME all you jolly dogs, in the Grapes, and King's Head, and
    Green Man, and Bell Taps,
And shy up your hats—if you haven't hats, your paper and
    woollen caps,
Shout with me and cry Eureka! by the sweet Parnassian
    river,
While Echo, in Warner's Wood replies, Huzza! the young
    Squire for ever!
And Vulcan, Mars, and Hector of Troy, and Jupiter and his
    wife,
And Phoebus, from his forked hill, coming down to take a
    knife,
And Mercury, and piping Pan, to the tune of "Old King Cole,"
And Venus the Queen of Love, to eat an ox that was roasted
    whole.

         *   *   *   *   *   *   *

Sir Mark, God bless him! loves good old times, when beards
    wag, and every thing goes merry,
There'll be drinking out of grace-cups, and a Boar's head
    chewing rosemary,
Maid Marian, and a Morris dance, and acting of quaint
    Moralities,
Doctor Ballamy, and a Hobby horse, and many other Old
    Formalities.

         *   *   *   *   *   *   *

But there won't be any Psalm-singing saints, to make us sad
    of a Monday,
But Bacchus will preach to us out of a barrel, instead of that
    methodist Bundy,

We'll drink to the King in good strong ale, like souls that are true and loyal,
And a fig for Mrs. Hanway, camomile, sage, and penny-royal;
And a fig for Master Gregory, that takes tipsy folks into custody,
He was a wise man to-morrow, and will be a wiser man yesterday.

* * * * * * *

Come fill a bumper up, my boys, and toss off every drop of it!
Here's young Squire Ringwood's health, and may he live as long as Jason,
Before Atropos cuts his thread, and Dick Tablet, the bungling mason,
Chips him a marble tea-table, and a marble tea-urn a-top of it?
Quoth Tom in Tatters.
Thomas Hood.

338. I DWELL ON TRIFLES

... I dwell on trifles like a child,
I feel as ill becomes a man,
And still my thoughts like weedlings wild
Grow up to blossom where they can....

John Clare.

339. THE VISION OF A MANIAC ARTIST

I DETERMINED . . . to compaer objects to go forward to seek the means. I had hitherto stood still, expecting breezes as they were wafted on the breeze of ideality, to hitch upon my receptivities, but soon discovered how vague such a monotonous, yet unconcentrated study became. I therefore stirred the feet of my resolution and prospered.

My soles became parched and thirsted for the cool clenching of a humid soil,—my breath lost its elasticity: it had a demure vent, less an expansion than an outcreeping. My brain sank into an autumnal tint, and my eyes neither sparkled with intelligence nor leaped with joy. I felt a twilight without its charm; a suppression of vitality without repose, and there was a quaker-like retention of all my bounding energies. Nature lost her florid bloom; she seemed probably formed, but devoid of Grace. The atmosphere lost its radiance and assumed a rigid expression: it no longer beamed with light, or seemed an azure veil to a Temple beyond; the mountains were clad in severity and sterility,—the trees were constrained, yielding to no breeze with exquisite subtlety. . . . The inhabitants of this dry region were reserved and rigid in demeanour . . . being shrivelled into the semblance of anatomical preparations. . . . They were clad in quaint garbs, meanly fashioned, through which their anatomized forms were detected, presenting walking lectures each on the same subject.

"These are not fit food," thought my best self, "for my poetical and pictorial powers, unless I borrow a satire from one and a caricature from the other." As I arrived at this conclusion, my soles regained their tension, and I sailed along the earth with willingness. A land of milk and honey soon melted in my sight and squeezed the juice of comfort into my expectant mouth. The landscape appeared, after the last or rather the first I encountered, a parody of exuberance, a bloated fertility. One felt inclined to lie on the ground and roll over and over to distil its verdure and aroma—to inhale at every pore the multiform sweets glowing in an intense sunlight. Shouts of laughter assailed my ear—revelry seemed bursting through the gleaming air to reach some aerial fount of enjoyment,—invisible flocks of Gomus-born companions appeared tripping on the blue sward of ether to some ever flowing rill of nectar distilled from a tender cloud by a pressing rainbow . . . forms as different to the dry ones I had just left . . . bounded before my distended vision.—"Hillocks of flesh and mountains of roses," redundant vigour, overcharged voluptuousness, exuberant gorgeousness, and uncontrollable anticry were melted into harmonious masses by the fire of unrepressed passion. Here and there a tender bud timidly peeped forth into the genial region, but with an almost instantaneous fertility leapt into a glowing existence: tenderness imbibed the taint of lasciviousness; vigour became a bully, and hate a demon. . . .

Outward I pressed, and onward pressed the spirit of beauty that tipped all around, but the scene gradually lost its vigorous charm, conception seemed thwarted in its stretch as it had accommodated itself to the boundless imagery I had just witnessed—all about me faded into a fainter lustre: it was still beautiful, but the Graces seemed to have taken possession of this delicate territory. The air became sultry and ennervating, and Nature seemed coquetting with Sense: groups of amorous beauties were disposed on the margins of chrystal streams, in shady bowers, under marble porticoes of wondrous beauty, in all the variety of Love's calendar when loosened from civilized decorum. . . .

My steps imperceptibly accelerated, and my manner became wild and incoherent as the sky pledged its lustre for a terrible veil of black which it cast over the whole arch, save where a lurid gleam spoke like a prophet in a dark age, and struck me as a lamp held out to Horror's step as it advanced giant-like over a half-world. The air became sullen and moaned aloud between fits of moody madness, it felt black as it clammily clang to my quivering cheek, it seared my eyesight, and crept through my brain like a nest of young scorpions gambolling in a lightning flash. Lugubrious sounds rode on the funereal atmosphere, and the gloomy thunder rolled its kettledrums in an agony of rage as it tried to rend asunder the black marble sky, to insult the tranquil azure which reposed peacefully above it. An incensed mineral pit blazed forth its blue and red flames to light a band of frolicsome imps in their mazy dances. Further on was the glare of a torch made of human fat and brains, stuck in a female skull with the scalp fresh reeking from the knife, and the hair floating about to catch the drippings of this choice light ere it soiled the prudish earth. Gazing on a human being, stretched on a complicated frame of tortures, was a man-monster of huge proportions, a lazar-house metempsychosed into a pestilential demon, looking like a living dreadful death—an ultimate agony embodied. Dissolution seemed at work in various parts of his putrid form, his ghastly lineaments were in parts parchment-like stretched over bone—in others leaping with its bosom-worms which sparkled with a thousand jewelled lights from the precious torch. As he rose from his seat, my eye fell on it.—Oh! it was dainty indeed I A blackened, strangled child formed the cushion, the ligaments in places had given way, the peritoneum had played the dastard and let its young prisoners loose from their dungeon: the legs of this choice seat were human bones, fringed with tattered membranes. A beast, fourth dragon, fourth seal, fourth alligator, and fourth buffalo, uttered a fearful yell, as Corruption dropped an atom from the demon, form into the torch, and a hell-hound concert was struck up by metallic voices, which belched forth from underground, dying groans and living shrieks of agony being by particular desire of Despair and his brother Dismay, who were crouched in a gloomy corner, the former tortured by little poignant flames which stole in and out of his pores—the latter crumbling in abjectness and writhing.

In one corner was the den of Famine, where each ate the other and imagined him afresh to gnaw his entrails again. A brother had just consumed his elder all but an arm which he brandished in a threatening manner. One moving skeleton was attacking his own bones, another was rattling his fellow to death—the death of an all but ossified statue. Murder stalked across the scene dropping pools of blood and clotted membranes, while a poor haggard witch was washing her hands in a mixture of gore and flame.

I had hitherto been rivetted to this disgusting scene, had experienced a sort of pleasure in all its atrocities, when my purer self tapped my outward depravity, and my sense grew healthy perceptibly. . . . All had vanished, when I found my nobler nature—my choice monitorial self more commingled with my inferior perceptive self, than had before been the case,. Aspiration touched my brain, and Purity smiled on my lips as the darkness vanished and with it its fiendish legions. Nature cast her purple on her imperial form, the diadem of chaste beauty gleamed on her front, and her offspring walked abroad in simple majesty. I was surrounded with a galaxy of brightness. Unequivocal beauty beamed comfort around. Magnanimity shone in the sun as a leo-born mortal bears traces of his origin. Piety mildly glided by in modest meditation. Charity in her eternal walk of beneficence unostentatiouslypassed. . . . All in fact was in blossom, and universal radiance buoyantly leaped in the sunny air. Olympus glowing touched the golden orb, Parnassus clad in cool grey, lay on the bright horizon, Castalia's fount, Lethe's stream, the verdant Arcadia,—all lay expanded before my enraptured eyes.

From *Arnold's Magazine of the Fine Arts*, January 1834.

340. ROMANCE

ROMANCE, who loves to nod and sing,
With drowsy head and folded wing,
Among the green leaves as they shake
Far down within some shadowy lake,
To me a painted paroquet
Hath been—a most familiar bird—
Taught me my alphabet to say—
To lisp my very earliest word
While in the wild wood I did lie,
A child—with a most knowing eye.

Of late, eternal Condor years
So shake the very Heaven on high
With tumult as they thunder by,
I have no time for idle cares
Through gazing on the unquiet sky.
And when an hour with calmer wings
Its down upon my spirit flings—
That little time with lyre and rhyme
To while away—forbidden things I
My heart would feel to be a crime
Unless it trembled with the strings.

Edgar Allan Poe.

341. DREAM OF DYING

. . . then I was dead;
And in my grave beside my corpse I sat,
In vain attempting to return: meantime
There came the untimely spectres of two babes,

And played in my abandoned body's ruins;
They went away; and one by one, by snakes
My limbs were swallowed; and, at last, I sat
With only one, blue-eyed, curled round my ribs,
Eating the last remainder of my heart,
And hissing to himself....

T. L. Beddoes.

342. THE CITY IN THE SEA

Lo! Death has reared himself a throne
In a strange city lying alone
Far down within the dim West,
Where the good and the bad and the worst and the best
Have gone to their eternal rest.
There shrines and palaces and towers
(Time-eaten towers that tremble not!)
Resemble nothing that is ours.
Around, by lifting winds forgot,
Resignedly beneath the sky
The melancholy waters lie.

No rays from the holy heaven come down
On the long night-time of that town;
But light from out the lurid sea
Streams up the turrets silently—
Gleams up the pinnacles far and free—
Up domes—up spires—up kingly halls—
Up fanes—up Babylon-like walls—
Up shadowy long-forgotten bowers
Of sculptured ivy and stone flowers—
Up many and many a marvellous shrine
Whose wreathéd friezes intertwine
The viol, the violet, and the vine.
Resignedly beneath the sky
The melancholy waters lie.
So blend the turrets and shadows there
That all seem pendulous in air,
While from a proud tower in the town
Death looks gigantically down.

There open fanes and gaping graves
Yawn level with the luminous waves
But not the riches there that lie
In each idol's diamond eye—
Not the gaily-jewelled dead
Tempt the waters from their bed;
For no ripples curl, alas!
Along that wilderness of glass—
No swellings tell that winds may be
Upon some far-off happier sea—
No heavings hint that winds have been
On seas less hideously serene.

But lo, a stir is in the air!
The wave—there is a movement there,
As if the towers had thrust aside,
In slightly sinking, the dull tide—
As if their tops had feebly given
A void within filmy Heaven.
The waves have now a redder glow—
The hours are breathing faint and low—
And when, amid no earthly moans,
Down, down that town shall settle hence,
Hell, rising from a thousand thrones,
Shall do it reverence.
Edgar Allan Poe.

343. NATURE MYSTIFIED

WHEN Bernini's bust of Charles I was being conveyed in a barge. on the Thames, from a strange bird there descended a drop of blood on the bust, *which could never be effaced*.

This is nothing but a fact in nature *mystified*, and (like the growth of the Christian flowering thorn of Glastonbury, from the *walking-staff* of Joseph of Arimathea) is too glaring to be misconstrued. *W. C. Dendy.*

344. THE SOUL'S DEPARTURE

Oh let me die at dawn,
  The stir of living men
Would call my waning spirit back
  Unto its home again.

But at the early light
  Existence seems afar,
Back in the depths of parted time
  As fading planets are.

Let me go forth alone,
  Before the sun uprise,
And meet the springing of the morn
  In its own distant skies.

Yes! let me die at dawn,
  The stir of living men
Would call my waning spirit back
  Unto its home again.

James Smetham.

345. THE ICEBERG

At twelve o'clock we went below, and had just got through dinner, when the cook put his head down the scuttle and told us to come on deck and see the finest sight that we had ever seen.

"Where away, cook?" asked the first man who was up.

"On the larboard bow." And there lay, floating in the ocean, several miles off, an immense irregular mass, its top and points covered with snow, its centre of a deep blue indigo colour. . . . As far as the eye could reach, the sea in every direction was of a deep blue colour, the waves running high and fresh, and sparkling in the light; and in the midst lay this immense mountain island, its cavities and valleys thrown into the shade, and its points and pinnacles glittering in the sun.

All hands were soon on deck, looking at it, and admiring in various ways its beauty and grandeur. But no description can give any idea of the strangeness, splendour, and, really, the sublimity of the sight. Its great size—for it must have been from two to three miles in circumference, and several hundred feet in height; its slow motion, as its base rose and sank in the water, and its high points nodded against the clouds; the dashing of the waves upon it, which, breaking high with foam, lined its base with a white crust; and the thundering sound of the cracking of the mass, and the breaking and tumbling down of huge pieces, together with its nearness and approach, which added a slight element of fear—all combined to give it the character of true sublimity.

The main body of the mass was, as I have said, of an indigo colour, its base crusted with frozen foam; and as it grew thin and transparent towards the edges and top, its colour shaded off from a deep blue to the whiteness of snow. It seemed to be drifting slowly towards the north, so that we kept away and avoided it. It was in sight all the afternoon; and when we got to the leeward of it, the wind died away so that we lay-to quite near it for the greater part of the night. Unfortunately there was no moon; but it was a clear night, and we could plainly mark the long, regular heaving of the stupendous mass, as its edges moved slowly against the stars. *R. H. Dana.*

346. THE LURE

... He who the Siren's hair would win
Is mostly strangled in the tide....
George Darley.

347. THE HAUNTED HOUSE

... The beds were all untouch'd by hand or tool;
No footstep marked the damp and mossy gravel,
Each walk as green as is the mantled pool,
For want of human travel.

The vine unpruned, and the neglected peach,
Droop'd from the wall with which they used to grapple;
And on the canker'd tree, in easy reach,
Rotted the golden apple.

But awfully the truant shunn'd the ground,
The vagrant kept aloof, and daring Poacher;
In spite of gaps that thro' the fences round
Invited the encroacher.

For over all there hung a cloud of fear,
A sense of mystery the spirit daunted,
And said, as plain as whisper in the ear,
The place is haunted.

The pear and quince lay squander'd on the grass;
The mould was purple with unheeded showers
Of bloomy plums — a Wilderness it was
Of fruits, and weeds, and flowers.

The marigold amidst the nettles blew,
The gourd embraced the rose bush in its ramble,
The thistle and the stock together grew,
The holly-hock and bramble.

The bear-bine with the lilac interlaced,
The sturdy bur-dock choked its slender neighbour
The spicy pink. All tokens were effaced
Of human care and labour. . . .

The window jingled in its crumbled frame,
And thro' its many gaps of destitution
Dolorous moans and hollow sighings came,
Like those of dissolution.

The woodlouse dropped, and rolled into a ball,
Touch'd by some impulse occult or mechanic:
And nameless beetles ran along the wall
In universal panic.

The subtle spider, that from overhead
Hung like a spy on human guilt and error,
Suddenly turn'd and up its slender thread
Ran with a nimble terror.

The very stains and fractures on the wall,
Assuming features solemn and terrific,
Hinted some tragedy of that old hall,
Lock'd up in hieroglyphic.

Some tale that might, perchance, have solved the doubt,
Wherefore amongst those flags so dull and livid,
The banner of the BLOODY HAND shone out
So ominously vivid.

Some key to that inscrutable appeal,
Which made the very frame of Nature quiver
And every thrilling nerve and fibre feel
So ague-like a shiver.

For over all there hung a cloud of fear,
A sense of mystery the spirit daunted;
And said, as plain as whisper in the ear,
The place is haunted.

If but a rat had linger'd in the house,
To lure the thought into a social channel!
But not a rat remain'd, or tiny mouse,
To squeak behind the panel.

Huge drops roll'd down the walls, as if they wept;
And where the cricket used to chirp so shrilly,
The toad was squatting and the lizard crept
On that damp hearth and chilly.

For years no cheerful blaze had sparkled there,
Or glanced on coat of buff or knightly metal;
The slug was crawling on the vacant chair,—
The snail upon the settle.

The floor was redolent of mould and dust,
The fungus in the rotten seams had quicken'd;
While on the oaken table coats of dust
Perennially had thicken'd.

No mark of leathern jack or metal can,
No cup—no horn—no hospitable token,—
All social ties between that board and man
Had long been broken.

There was so foul a rumour in the air,
The shadow of a presence so atrocious;
No human creature could have feasted there,
Even the most ferocious.

For over all there hung a cloud of fear,
A sense of mystery the spirit daunted,
And said, as plain as whisper in the ear,
The place is haunted....

Prophetic hints that filled the soul with dread,
But thro' one gloomy entrance pointing mostly,
The while some secret inspiration said,
That chamber is the ghostly!

Across the door no gossamer festoon
Swung pendulous—no web—no dusty fringes,
No silky chrysalis or white cocoon
About its nooks and hinges.

The spider shunn'd the interdicted room,
The moth, the beetle, and the fly were banish'd,
And where the sunbeam fell athwart the gloom
The very midge had vanish'd.

One lonely ray that glanced upon a bed,
As if with awful aim direct and certain,
To show the BLOODY HAND in burning red
Embroider'd on the curtain.

And yet no gory stain was on the quilt—
The pillow in its place had slowly rotted;
The floor alone retain'd the trace of guilt,
Those boards obscurely spotted.

Obscurely spotted to the door, and thence
With mazy doubles to the grated casement—
Oh what a tale they told of fear intense,
Of horror and amazement!

What human creature in the dead of night
Had coursed like hunted hare that cruel distance?
Had sought the door, the window in his flight,
Striving for dear existence?

What shrieking spirit in that bloody room
Its mortal frame had violently quitted?—
Across the sunbeam, with a sudden gloom,
A ghostly shadow flitted.

Across the sunbeam, and along the wall,
But painted on the air so very dimly,
It hardly veil'd the tapestry at all,
Or portrait frowning grimly.

O'er all there hung the shadow of a fear,
A sense of mystery the spirit daunted,
And said, as plain as whisper in the ear,
The place is haunted!

Thomas Hood.

348. THE MERMAIDENS' VESPER-HYMN

TROOP home to silent grots and caves!
Troop home I and mimic as you go
The mournful winding of the waves
Which to their dark abysses flow!

At this sweet hour, all things beside
In amorous pairs to covert creep;
The swans that brush the evening tide
Homeward in snowy couples keep;

In his green den the murmuring seal
Close by his sleek companion lies;
While singly we to bedward steal,
And close in fruitless sleep our eyes.

In bowers of love men take their rest,
In loveless bowers we sigh alone!
With bosom-friends are others blest,—
But we have none! but we have none!
                              George Darley.

349. UNDER THE LIME TREE

UNDER the lime tree on the daisied ground
   Two that I know of made this bed.
There you may see heaped and scattered round
   Grass and blossoms broken and shed
     All in a thicket down in the dale;
Tandaradei—sweetly sang the nightingale.

Ere I set foot in the meadow already
   Some one was waiting for somebody;
There was a meeting—Oh! gracious lady,
   There is no pleasure again for me,
     Thousands of kisses there he took.
Tandaradei—see my lips, how red they look.

Leaf and blossom he had pulled and piled
   For a couch, a green one, soft and high;
And many a one hath gazed and smiled
   Passing the bower and pressed grass by;
     And the roses crushed hath seen,
Tandaradei—where I laid my head between;

In this love passage if any one had been there,
    How sad and shamed should I be;
But what were we adoing alone among the green there
    No soul shall ever know except my love and me,
        And the little nightingale,
Tandaradei—she, I wot, will tell no tale.

> *T. L. Beddoes* (from the German of
> *Walther von der Vogelweide*).

350. TO POETS

You, the choice minions of the proud-lipped Nine
Who warble at the great Apollo's knee,
Why do you laugh at these rude lays of mine?
I seek not of your brotherhood to be!—
I do not play the public swan, nor try
To curve my proud neck on your vocal streams;
In my own little isle retreated, I
Lose myself in my waters and my dreams.
Forgetful of the world,—forgotten too!—
The cygnet of my own secluded wave,
I sing, whilst, dashing up their silver dew
For joy, the petty billows try to rave:
There is a still applause in solitude
Fitting alike my merits and my mood.

> *George Darley.*

351. THREE SONNETS

i

Hast thou not seen an aged rifted tower,
Meet habitation for the Ghost of Time,
Where fearful ravage makes decay sublime,
And destitution wears the face of power?
Yet is the fabric deck'd with many a flower
Of fragrance wild, and many-dappled hue,
Gold streak'd with iron-brown, and nodding blue,
Making each ruinous chink a fairy bower.

E'en such a thing methinks I fain would be,
Should Heaven appoint me to a lengthened age:
So old in look, that Young and Old may see
The record of my closing pilgrimage:
Yet, to the last, a rugged wrinkled thing
To which young sweetness may delight to cling.

ii

How shall a man fore-doom'd to lone estate,
Untimely old, irreverently grey,
Much like a patch of dusky snow in May,
Dead sleeping in a hollow, all too late—
How shall so poor a thing congratulate
The blest completion of a patient wooing,
Or how commend a younger man for doing
What ne'er to do hath been his fault or fate?
There is a fable, that I once did read,
Of a bad angel that was someway good,
And therefore on the brink of Heaven he stood,
Looking each way, and no way could proceed;
Till at the last he purged away his sin
By loving all the joy he saw within.

iii

THE dark green Summer, with its massive hues,
Fades into Autumn's tincture manifold.
A gorgeous garniture of fire and gold
The high slope of the ferny hill indues.
The mists of morn in slumbering layers diffuse
O'er glimmering rock, smooth lake, and spiked array
Of hedge-row thorns, a unity of grey.
All things appear their tangible form to lose
In ghostly vastness. But anon the gloom
Melts, as the Sun puts off his muddy veil;
And now the birds their twittering songs resume,
All Summer silent in the leafy dale.
In Spring they piped of love on every tree,
But now they sing the song of memory.

Hartley Coleridge.

352. HIS OWN EPITAPH

HERE lies one who spat more blood and made more puns than any other man. *Thomas Hood.*

353. FLOWERS IN THE ALPS

ABOUT me lay the grey concave blocks of the Jura limestone—slippery with wet. Large black and white snails had come out everywhere to enjoy the rain. In the crevices of the rocks the lily of the valley grew profusely—accompanied by the wild strawberry and cowslip. I found a root of the star gentian, and kissed it as the harbinger of the Alps. The sunlight on the mossy ground burned russet as I returned, and died away in rose upon the piny hills. *John Ruskin.*

354. THE SKY A-CLEARÈN

The drevèn scud that auvercast
The zummer sky is all a-past,
An' softer âir, a-blowèn droo
The quiv'ren boughs, da shiake the vew
Laste rain draps off the leaves lik' dew;
   An' piaviers now a-gettèn dry,
   Da steam below the zunny sky
     That's now so vast a-clearèn.

The shiades that wer a-lost below
The starmy cloud, agen da show
Ther mockèn shiapes below the light;
An 'house-walls be a-lookèn white,
An' vo'ke da stir oonce muore in zight,
   An' busy birds upon the wing
   Da whiver roun' the boughs an' zing,
     To zee the sky a-clearèn.

Below the hill's an ash; below
The ash, white elder-flow'rs da blow;
Below the elder is a bed
O' robinhoods o' blushèn red;
An' there, wi' nunches all a-spread,
   The hây-miakers, wi' each a cup
   O' drink, da smile to zee hold up
      The râin, an' sky a-clearèn. . . .
William Barnes.

355. MORNING, NOON, SUNSET, AND SUNRISE

STAND upon the peak of some isolated mountain at daybreak, when the night mists first rise from off the plains, and watch their white and lake-like fields, as they float in level bays and winding gulfs about the islanded summits of the lower hills, untouched yet by more than dawn, colder and more quiet than a windless sea under the moon of midnight; watch when the first sunbeam is sent upon the silver channels, how the foam of their undulating surface parts and passes away, and down under their depths the glittering city and green pasture lie like Atlantis, between the white paths of winding rivers; the flakes of light falling every moment faster and broader among the starry spires, as the wreathed surges break and vanish above them, and the confused crests and ridges of the dark hills shorten their grey shadows upon the plain. Has Claude given this? Wait a little longer, and you shall see those scattered mists rallying in the ravines, and floating up towards you, along the winding valleys, till they crouch in quiet masses, iridescent with the morning light, upon the broad breasts of the higher hills, whose leagues of massy undulation will melt back and back into that robe of material light until they fade away, lost in its lustre, to appear again above, in the serene heaven, like a wild, bright, impossible dream, foundationless and inaccessible, their very bases vanishing in the unsubstantial and mocking blue of the deep lake below. Has Claude given this? Wait yet a little longer, and you shall see those mists gather themselves into white towers,

and stand like fortresses along the promontories, massy and
motionless, only piled with every instant higher and higher
into the sky, and casting longer shadows athwart the rocks;
and out of the pale blue of the horizon you will see forming
and advancing a troop of narrow, dark, pointed vapours, which
will cover the sky inch by inch, with their grey net-work, and
take the light off the landscape with an eclipse which will stop
the singing of the birds and the motion of the leaves, together;
and then you will see horizontal bars of black shadow forming
under them, and lurid wreathes create themselves, you know
not how, along the shoulders of the hills; you never see them
form, but when you look back to a place which was clear an
instant ago, there is a cloud on it, hanging by the precipices,
as a hawk pauses over his prey. Has Claude given this? And
then you will hear the sudden rush of the awakened wind,
and you will see those watch-towers of vapour swept away
from their foundations, and waving curtains of opaque rain
let down to the valleys, swinging from the burdened clouds
in black bending fringes, or pacing in pale columns along the
lake level, grazing its surface into foam as they go. And then,
as the sun sinks, you shall see the storm drift for an instant
from off the hills, leaving their broad sides smoking, and
loaded yet with snow-white, torn, steam-like rags of capri-
cious vapour, now gone, now gathered again; while the
smouldering sun, seeming not far away, but burning like a
red-hot ball beside you, and as if you could reach it, plunges
through the rushing wind and rolling cloud with headlong fall,
as if it meant to rise no more, dyeing all the air about it with
blood. Has Claude given this? And then you shall hear the
fainting tempest die in the hollow of the night, and you shall
see a green halo kindling on the summit of the eastern hills,
brighter—brighter yet, till the large white circle of the slow
moon is lifted up among the barred clouds, step by step, line
by line; star after star she quenches with her kindling light,
setting in their stead an army of pale, penetrable, fleecy
wreathes in the heaven, to give light upon the earth, which
move together, hand in hand, company by company, troop by
troop, so measured in their unity of motion, that the whole
heaven seems to roll with them, and the earth to reel under

them. Ask Claude, or his brethren, for that. And then wait yet for one hour, until the east again becomes purple, and the heaving mountains, rolling against it in darkness, like waves of a wild sea, are drowned one by one in the glory of its burning: watch the white glaciers blaze in their winding paths about the mountains, like mighty serpents with scales of fire: watch the columnar peaks of solitary snow, kindling downwards, chasm by chasm, each in itself a new morning; their long avalanches cast down in keen streams brighter than the lightning, sending each his tribute of driven snow; like altar-smoke, up to the heaven; the rose-light of their silent domes flushing that heaven about them and above them, piercing with purer light through its purple lines of lifted cloud, casting a new glory on every wreath as it passes by, until the whole heaven, one scarlet canopy, is interwoven with a roof of waving flame, and tossing, vault beyond vault, as with the drifted wings of many companies of angels: and then, when you can look no more for gladness, and when you are bowed down with fear and love of the Maker and Doer of this, tell me who has best delivered this his Message unto men! *John Ruskin.*

356. LANDSEER'S ART

IT was not by the study of Raphael that Landseer attained his eminent success, but by a healthy love of Scotch terriers.

John Ruskin.

357. NIGHT A-ZETTÈN IN

WHEN leäzers wi' ther laps o' earn
    Noo longer be a-stoopèn,
An' in the stubble, all varlarn,
    Noo poppies be a-droopèn;
When ðeos young harvest-moon da wiane,
    That now've his harns so ðin, O,
We'll leäve off wa'kèn in the liane,
    While night's a zettèn in, O.

When zummer doust is al a-laid
   Below our litty shoes, O;
When all the rain-chill'd flow'rs be dead.
   That now da drink the dews, O;
When beauty's neck, that's now a-show'd,
   'S a-muffled to the chin, O,
We'll leave off wa'kèn in the road,
   When night's a-zettèn in, O.

But now, while barley by the road
   Da hang upon the bough, O,
A-pull'd by branches off the luoad
   A-ridèn huome to mow, O;
While spiders roun' the flower-stā'ks
   Ha' cobwebs eet to spin, O,
We'll cool ourzuvs in out-door wā'ks,
   When night's a-zettèn in, O.

While down at vuord the brook so small,
   That liately wer so high, O,
Wi' little tinklèn sounds da vall
   In roun 'the stuones hafe dry, O;
While twilight ha' sich air in store,
   To cool our zunburnt skin, O,
We'll have a ramble out o' door,
   When night's a-zettèn in, O.
                    William Barnes.

358. I DO NOT SEEK, I FIND

   ... I found the poems in the fields,
      And only wrote them down....
                    John Clare.

359. TRANSCENDENTAL VIEWS

TRANSCENDENTAL views are merely those taken from pinnacles instead of flats, at all the shining eminences within a panorama, instead of the little objects and obscurities within a limited landscape: nor are the loftiest summits to which genuine transcendentalism mounts, though above common sight, more *en l'aire* than the peaks of Chimborazo or Chandrasichara are flying islands. Very true, clouds often gather on the mountain tops—but do mists never thicken on the plain? do not fogs love the lowest ground? Nay, do not all three, fogs, mists, and clouds, rise from the *sea-level* perpetually, while they rest on the pinnacles only by accident? We admit contemplative occupations liable to abuse: are worldly liable to none? If those sometimes take our wits a flight to the moon, do these never stoop them in the sludge of earth? Is the one extreme, an erratic mind, worse than the other, a grovelling; or is he more a madman who would feed his bodily person upon ether than he who would batten his immortal spirit upon ox-beef? There may be a sound as well as an unsound transcendentalism—an *English* as well as a *German*. Icarus who soared too high fell into the sea, but Dedalus, who imagined and wrought the wings, because he kept the middle air between earth and heaven, flew over. *George Darley.*

360. THE ASPIRATION FOR SUPERNAL BEAUTY

I HAVE endeavoured to convey to you my conception of the Poetic Principle. It has been my purpose to suggest that, while this Principle itself is, strictly and simply, the Human Aspiration for Supernal Beauty, the manifestation of the Principle is always found in *an elevating excitement of the Soul* —quite independent of that passion which is the intoxication of the Heart—or of that Truth which is the satisfaction of the Reason. For, in regard to Passion, alas! its tendency is to degrade, rather than to elevate the Soul. Love, on the contrary —Love —the true, the divine Eros—the Uranian, as distinguished from the Dionæan Venus—is unquestionably the purest and truest of all poetical themes. And in regard to Truth—if, to be sure, through the attainment of a truth, we are led to perceive a harmony where none was apparent before, we experience, at once, the true poetical effect—but this effect is referable to the harmony alone, and not in the least degree to the truth which merely served to render the harmony manifest.

We shall reach, however, more immediately a distinct conception of what the true Poetry is, by mere reference to a few of the simple elements which induce in the Poet himself the true poetical effect. He recognizes the ambrosia which nourishes his soul, in the bright orbs that shine in Heaven—in the volutes of the flower—in the clustering of low shrubberies—in the waving of the grain-fields—in the slanting of tall, Eastern trees—in the blue distance of mountains—in the grouping of clouds—in the twinkling of half-hidden brooks—in the gleaming of silver rivers—in the repose of sequestered lakes—in the star-mirroring depths of lonely wells. He perceives it in the songs of birds—in the harp of Æolus—in the sighing of the night-wind—in the repining voice of the forest—in the surf that complains to the shore—in the fresh breath of the woods—in the scent of the violet—in the voluptuous perfume of the hyacinth—in the suggestive odour that comes to him, at eventide, from far-distant, undiscovered islands, over dim oceans, illimitable and unexplored. He owns it in all noble thoughts—in all unworldly motives—in all holy impulses—in all chivalrous, generous, and self-sacrificing deeds. He feels it in the beauty of woman—in the grace of her step—in the lustre of her eye—in the melody of her voice—in her soft laughter—in her sigh—in the harmony of the rustling of her robes. He deeply feels it in her winning endearments—in her burning enthusiasms—in her gentle charities—in her meek and devotional endurances—but above all—ah, far above all—he kneels to it—he worships it in the faith, in the purity, in the strength, in the altogether divine majesty—of her *love*. *Edgar Allan Poe.*

361. THE EXILE

LOVE is the mainspring of existence. It
  Becomes a soul whereby I live to love.
On all I see that dearest name is writ;
  Falsehood is here—but truth has life above,
  Where every star that shines exists in love.

Skies vary in their clouds, the seasons vary
   From heat to cold, change cannot constant prove;
The south is bright—but smiles can act contrary;
My guide-star gilds the north, and shines with Mary.

My life hath been one love:—no, blot it out;
   My life hath been one chain of contradictions,
Madhouses, prisons, whoreshops—never doubt
   But that my life hath had some strong convictions,
   That such was wrong; religion makes restrictions
I would have followed—but life turned a bubble,
   And clomb the giant stile of maledictions;
They took me from my wife, and to save trouble
I wed again, and made the error double.

Yet absence claims them both, and keeps them too,
   And locks me in a shop, in spite of law,
Among a low-lived set and dirty crew:
   Here let the Muse oblivion's curtain draw,
   And let man think—for God hath often saw
Things here too dirty for the light of day;
   For in a madhouse there exists no law.
Now stagnant grows my too refined clay;
I envy birds their wings to fly away.

Absence in love is worse than any fate;
   Summer is winter's desert, and the spring
Is like a ruined city desolate;
   Joy dies and hope retires on feeble wing;
   Nature sinks heedless; birds unheeded sing.
'Tis solitude in city's crowds; all move
   Like living death, though all to life still cling.
The strongest, bitterest thing that life can prove
Is woman's undisguise of hate or love.

How beautiful this hill of fern swells on,
   So beautiful the chapel peeps between
The hornbeams, with its simple bell; alone
   I wander here, hid in a palace green.
   Mary is absent, but the forest queen,

Nature, is with me; morning, noon, and gloaming,
   I write my poems in these paths unseen;
And when among these brakes and beeches roaming,
   I sigh for truth and home and love and woman.

Here is the chapel yard enclosed with pales,
   And oak-trees nearly top its little bell;
Here is the little bridge with guiding rails
   That lead me on to many a pleasant dell;
   The fern-owl chitters like a startled knell
To nature, yet 'tis sweet at evening still;
   A pleasant road curves round the gentle swell,
Where nature seems to have her own sweet will,
Planting her beech and thorn about the sweet fern-hill.

I have had many loves, and seek no more;
   These solitudes my last delights shall be.
The leaf-hid forest and the lonely shore
   Seem to my mind like beings that are free.
   Yet would I had some eye to smile on me,
Some heart where I could make a happy home in,
   Sweet Susan that was wont my love to be,
And Bessy of the glen—for I've been roaming
With both at morn and noon and dusky gloaming.

Cares gather round; I snap their chains in two,
   And smile in agony and laugh in tears;
Like playing with a deadly serpent who
   Stings to the death, there is no room for fears,
   Where death would bring me happiness; his shears
Kills cares that hiss to poison many a vein;
   The thought to be extinct my fate endears;
Pale death, the grand physician, cures all pain,
The dead rest well who lived for joys in vain.

This twilight seems a veil of gauze and mist;
   Trees seem dark hills between the earth and sky;
Winds sob awake, and then a gusty hiss
   Fans through the wheat, like serpents gliding by.
   I love to stretch my length 'tween earth and sky,

And see the inky foliage o'er me wave.
   Though shades are still my prison where I lie,
Long use grows nature, which I easy brave,
And think how sweet cares rest within the grave.

Remind me not of other years, nor tell
   My broken hopes of joys they are to meet,
While thy own falsehood rings the loudest knell
   To one fond heart that aches, too cold to beat.
   Mary, how oft with fondness I repeat
That name alone to give my troubles rest;
   The very sound, though bitter, seemeth sweet;
In my love's home and thy own faithless breast,
Truth's bonds are broke and every nerve distressed.

Life is to me a dream that never wakes;
   Night finds me on this lengthening road alone;
Love is to me a thought that ever aches,
   A frost-bound thought that freezes life to stone.
   Mary, in truth and nature still my own,
That warms the winter of my aching breast,
   Thy name is joy, nor will I life bemoan;
Midnight, when sleep takes charge of nature's rest,
Finds me awake and friendless—not distressed.

Friend of the friendless, from a host of snares,
   From lying varlets and from friendly foes,
I sought thy quiet truth to ease my cares,
   And on the blight of reason found repose.
   But when the strife of nature ceased her throes,
And other hearts would beat for my return,
   I trusted fate to ease my world of woes,
Seeking love's harbour where I now sojourn;
But hell is heaven, could I cease to mourn.

For her, for one whose very name is yet
   My hell or heaven, and will ever be.
Falsehood is doubt—but I can ne'er forget
   Oath's virtuous falsehood volunteered to me,
   To make my soul the bonds, which God made free.

God's gift is love, and I do wrong the giver
   To plead affections wrong from God's decree?
No, when farewell upon my lips did quiver
And all seemed lost I loved her more than ever.

Now come the balm and breezes of the spring;
   Not with the pleasures of my early days,
When nature seemed one endless song to sing
   Of joyous melody and happy praise.
   Ah, would they come agen! But life betrays
Quicksands and gulfs and storms that howl and sting
   All quiet into madness and delays.
Care hides the sunshine with its raven wing,
And Hell glooms sadness o'er the songs of spring.

My mind is dark and fathomless, and wears
   The hues of hopeless agony and hell;
No plummet ever sounds the soul's affairs;
   There death eternal never sounds the knell;
   There love imprisoned sighs the long farewell,
And still may sigh, in thoughts no heart hath penned,
   Alone, in loneliness where sorrows dwell;
And hopeless hope hopes on and meets no end,
Wastes without springs and homes without a friend.

Yet love lives on in every kind of weather,
   In heats and colds, in sunshine and in gloom;
Winter may blight and stormy clouds may gather,
   Nature invigorates and love will bloom;
   It fears no sorrow in a life to come,
But lives within itself from year to year,
   As doth the wild flower in its own perfume;
As in the Lapland snows spring's blooms appear,
So true love blooms and blossoms everywhere.

The dew falls on the weed and on the flower,
   The rose and thistle bathe their heads in dew;
The lowliest heart may have its prospering hour,
   The saddest bosom meets its wishes true;
   E'en I may love and happiness renew,

Though not the sweets of my first early days,
   When one sweet face was all the loves I knew,
And my soul trembled on her eyes to gaze,
Whose very censure seemed intended praise.

Flow on, my verse, though barren thou mayst be
   Of thought; yet sing, and let thy fancies roll;
In early days thou swept a mighty sea,
   All calm in troublous deeps, and spurned control.
   Thou fire and iceberg to an aching soul,
And still an angel in my gloomy way,
   Far better opiate than the draining bowl,
Still sing, my nurse, to drive care's fiends away,
Nor heed what loitering listener hears the lay.

Her looks were like the spring, her very voice
   Was spring's own music, more than song to me;
Choice of my boyhood, nay, my soul's first choice,
   From her sweet thraldom I am never free.
   Yet here my prison is a spring to me,
Past memories bloom like flowers where'er I rove,
   My very bondage, though in snares, is free;
I love to stretch me in this shady grove
And muse upon the memories of love.

Hail, solitude, still peace, and lonely good,
   Thou spirit of all joys to be alone,
My best of friends, these glades and this green wood,
   Where nature is herself, and loves her own;
   The heart's hid anguish, here I make it known,
And tell my troubles to the gentle wind;
   Friends' cold neglects have froze my heart to stone,
And wrecked the voyage of a quiet mind,
With wives and friends and every hope disjoined;

Wrecked of all hopes save one, to be alone,
   Where solitude becomes my wedded mate;
Sweet forest! with rich beauties overgrown,
   Where solitude is queen and reigns in state;
   Hid in green trees, I hear the clapping gate

And voices calling to the rambling cows.
   I laugh at love and all its idle fate;
The present hour is all my lot allows;
An age of sorrows springs from lovers' vows.

Sweet is the song of birds, for that restores
   The soul to harmony, the mind to love;
'Tis nature's song of freedom out of doors,
   Forests beneath, free winds and clouds above;
   The thrush and nightingale and timid dove
Breathe music round me where the gypsies dwell;
   Pierced hearts left burning in the doubts of love,
Are desolate where crowds and cities dwell;
The splendid palace seems the gates of hell.

John Clare.

362. SWEET CASTLE HYDE

As I roved out on a summer's morning,
   Down by the banks of Blackwater side
To view the groves and meadows charming
   And pleasant gardens of Castle Hyde:
It is there you will hear the thrushes warbling,
   The dove and partridge I now describe,
The lambkins sporting each night and morning
   All to adorn sweet Castle Hyde.

If noble princes from foreign places
   Should chance to sail to this Irish shore,
It is in this valley they could be feasted
   As often heroes had done before.
The wholesome air of this habitation
   Would recreate your heart with pride,
There is no valley throughout this nation
   With beauty equal to Castle Hyde.

There's a church for service in this fine harbour,
   Where nobles often in their coaches ride
To view the streams and pleasant gardens
   That do adorn sweet Castle Hyde.

There is fine horses and stall-fed oxen
    And a den for foxes to play and hide,
Fine mares for breeding and foreign sheeping,
    And snowy fleeces in Castle Hyde.

The richest groves in this Irish nation
    In fine plantations you'll find them there
The rose, and tulip, and fine carnation,
    All vie with the lily fair.
The buck, the doe, the fox, the eagle,
    Do skip and play by the river-side,
The trout and salmon they play backgammon
    In those clear streams of Castle Hyde.

I rode from Blarney to Bally-Kenealy,
    To Thomastown and sweet Doneraile,
To sweet Kilshannock and gay Rathcormick,
    Besides Killarney and Abbey-fail.
The river Shannon and pleasant Boyne
    The flowing Barrow and rapid Bride,
But in all my ranging and serenading
    I saw no equal to Castle Hyde.

                                  Edward Kenealy.

363. HEEDLESS O' MY LOVE

OH! I vu'st knew o' my true love
    As the bright moon up above,
Though her brightness wer my pleasure
    She wer heedless o 'my love.
Tho' 'twer all gay to my eyes
Where her feäir feäce did arise,
She noo mwore thought upon my thoughts
    Than the high moon in the skies.

Oh! I vu'st heard her a-zingèn
    As a sweet bird on a tree,
Though her zingen wer my pleasure
    'Twer noo zong she zung to me.

Though her sweet vaïce that wer nigh
Meäde my wild heart to beat high,
She noo mwore thought upon my thoughts
   Than the birds on passers by.

Oh! I vu'st knew her a-weepen,
   As a rain-dimm'd mornen sky,
Though her teär-drops dimm'd her blushes
   They wer noo drops I could dry.
Ev'ry bright tear that did roll
Wer a keen pain to my soul,
But noo heart's pang she did then veel
   Wer vor my words to console.

But the wold times be a-vanish'd,
   An 'my true love is my bride,
An' her kind heart have a-meade her
   As an angel at my zide,
I've her best smiles that mid play,
I've her me'th when she is gaÿ,
When her tear-drops be a-rollèn
   I can now wipe em away.

William Barnes.

364. WRITTEN IN A THUNDERSTORM, 15 JULY 1841

The heavens are wroth; the thunder's rattling peal
   Rolls like a vast volcano in the sky;
Yet nothing starts the apathy I feel,
   Nor chills with fear eternal destiny.

My soul is apathy, a ruin vast;
   Time cannot clear the ruined mass away;
My life is hell, the hopeless die is cast,
   And manhood's prime is premature decay.

Roll on, ye wrath of thunders, peal on peal,
   Till worlds are ruins, and myself alone;
Melt heart and soul, cased in obdurate steel,
   Till I can feel that nature is my throne.

I live in love, sun of undying light,
　　And fathom my own heart for ways of good;
In its pure atmosphere, day without night
　　Smiles on the plains, the forest, and the flood.

Smile on, ye elements of earth and sky,
　　Or frown in thunders, as ye frown on me;
Bid earth and its delusions pass away,
　　But leave the mind, as its creator, free.
　　　　　　　　　　　　　　　John Clare.

365. FRAGMENT

As balmy as the breath of her you love
When deep between her breasts it comes to you.
　　　　　　　　　　　　　　　D. G. Rossetti.

366. FRAGMENT

The hedgerow hips to glossy scarlet turn,
Haws swarm so thick till bushes seem to burn,
And blackthorn sloes, some hung in misty dew,
True to the season, darken into blue.
　　　　　　　　　　　　　　　John Clare.

367. SUNSET WINGS

To-night this sunset spreads two golden wings
　　Cleaving the western sky;
Winged too with wind it is, and winnowings
Of birds; as if the day's last hour in rings
　　Of strenuous flight must die.

Sun-steeped in fire, the homeward pinions sway
　　Above the dovecote-tops;
And clouds of starlings, ere they rest with day,
Sink, clamorous like mill-waters, at wild play,
　　By turns in every copse:

Each tree heart-deep the wrangling rout receives,—
    Save for the whirr within,
You could not tell the starlings from the leaves;
Then one great puff of wings, and the swarm heaves
    Away with all its din.

Even thus Hope's hours, in ever-eddying flight,
    To many a refuge tend;
With the first light she laughed, and the last light
Glows round her still; who natheless in the night
    At length must make an end.

And now the mustering rooks innumerable
    Together sail and soar,
While for the day's death, like a tolling knell,
Unto the heart they seem to cry, Farewell,
    No more, farewell, no more!

Hope not plumed, as 'twere a fiery dart?
    And oh! thou dying day,
Even as thou goest must she too depart,
And Sorrow fold such pinions on the heart
    As will not fly away?
                            D. G. Rossetti.

368. THE WIND AT THE DOOR

As day did darken on the dewless grass,
There, still, wi' nwone a-come by me
To stay a-while at hwome by me
Within the house, all dumb by me,
I zot me sad as the eventide did pass.

An' there a win'blast shook the rattlen door,
An' seemed, as win' did mwoan without,
As if my Jeäne, alwone without,
A-stannèn on the stwone without,
Wer there a-come wi' happiness oonce mwore.

I went to door; an' out vrom trees above
My head, upon the blast by me,
Sweet blossoms wer a-cast by me,
As if my Love, a-past by me,
Did fling em down—a token ov her love.

"Sweet blossoms o' the tree where I do murn,"
I thought, "if you did blow vor her,
Vor apples that should grow vor her,
A-vallen down below vor her,
O then how happy I should zee you kern!"

But no. Too soon I voun my charm a-broke.
Noo comely soul in white like her—
Noo soul a-steppèn light like her—
An 'nwone o' comely height like her
Went by; but all my grief ageän awoke.
William Barnes.

369. DREAMS OF MY YOUTH

   . . . In those sweet days
When o'er me childhood shed its purple light,
The world seemed some vast garden faëry-bright,
Through which my spirit wander'd plucking flowers
Under fair skies and sunshine-laden hours;
And many a fancy garland then I twin'd
And many a rosy hope employed my mind
       In those sweet days.

    All the day long
In sunshine would I sit near some old tree,
Dreaming o'er Spenser's precious minstrelsy,
Of towers and silver lutes and ladyes gay,
Of tilt and tournament and knightly fray,
And songs—old songs, the music of the soul—
These thoughts across my busy brain would roll
       All the day long.

>   At other hours
> Beneath some ruin I was wont recline
> Profusely mantled o'er with ivy twine,
> Catching sweet pictur'd fancies from my books,
> While round me cawed the old monastic rooks,
> And dappled deer and silver-footed fawns
> Flitted like nymphs across the emerald lawns
>   At other hours.
>
>   At Evening's fall
> By the dark Ocean I would slowly pace,
> Watching the star-beams mirror'd on its face;
> Or stretched along the strand, sedgy and damp,
> Until the Moon lit up her crystal lamp,
> Gaze upward to the Heaven and pray that some
> Celestial shape thence to my side would come
>   At Evening's fall. . . .

Edward Kenealy.

370. MARY

It is the evening hour,
   How silent all doth lie:
The hornèd moon she shows her face
   In the river with the sky.
Prest by the path on which we pass,
The flaggy lake lies still as glass.

Spirit of her I love,
   Whispering to me
Stores of sweet visions as I rove,
Here stop, and crop with me
Sweet flowers that in the still hour grew—
We'll take them home, nor shake off the bright dew.

Mary, or sweet spirit of thee,
   As the bright sun shines to-morrow
Thy dark eyes these flowers shall see,
   Gathered by me in sorrow,
In the still hour when my mind was free
To walk alone—yet wish I walked with thee.

John Clare

371. THE DWARF DEATH

SHE stood in a long, dark, empty gallery; on her one side was father, and on the other my eldest sister, Amelia; then myself, and the rest of the family according to their ages. At the foot of the hall stood my younger sister, Alexes, and above her my sister Catherine—a creature, by the way, in person and mind more like an angel of heaven than an inhabitant of earth. We all stood silent and motionless. At last *It* entered—the unimagined *something* that, casting its grim shadow before, had enveloped all the trivialities of the preceding dream in the stifling atmosphere of terror. It entered, stealthily descending the three steps that led from the entrance down into the chamber of horror: and my mother *felt It was Death*. He was dwarfish, bent, and shrivelled. He carried on his shoulder a heavy axe; and had come, she thought, to destroy "all her little ones at one fell swoop." On the entrance of the shape my sister Alexes leapt out of the rank, interposing herself between him and my mother. He raised his axe and aimed a blow at Catherine: a blow, which, to her horror, my mother could not intercept; though she had snatched up a three-legged stool, the sole furniture of the apartment, for that purpose. She could not, she felt, fling the stool without destroying Alexes, who kept shooting out and in between her and the ghastly thing. She tried in vain to scream; she besought my father, in agony, to avert the impending stroke; but he did not hear, or did not heed her; and stood motionless, as in a trance. Down came the axe, and poor Catherine fell in her blood, cloven to "the white halse bane." Again the axe was lifted by the inexorable shadow, over the head of my brother, who stood next in the line. Alexes had somewhere disappeared behind the ghastly visitant; and, with a scream, my mother flung the footstool at his head. He vanished and she awoke. This dream left on my mother's mind a fearful apprehension of impending misfortune, "which would not pass away." It was *murder* she feared; and her suspicions were not allayed by the discovery that a man—some time before discarded by my father for bad conduct, and with whom she had, somehow, associated the *Death* of her dream—had been lurking about the place, and sleeping in an adjoining outhouse on the night it occurred, and for some nights previous and subsequent to it. Her terror increased; sleep forsook her; and every night, when the house was still, she arose and stole, sometimes with a candle, sometimes in the dark, from room to room, listening, in a sort of waking nightmare, for the breathing of the assassin, who she imagined was lurking in some one of them. This could not last. She reasoned with herself; but her terror became intolerable, and she related her dream to my father, who of course called her a fool for her pains—whatever might be his real opinion of the matter. Three months had elapsed, when we children were all of us seized with scarlet fever. My sister Catherine died almost immediately—sacrificed, as my mother in her misery thought, to her (my mother's) over-anxiety for Alexes, whose danger seemed more imminent. The dream-prophecy was in part fulfilled. I also was at death's door—given up by the doctors, but not by my mother: she was confident of my recovery; but for my brother, who was scarcely considered in danger at all, but on whose head *she had* seen the visionary axe impending, her fears were great; for she could not recollect whether the blow had, or had not, descended when the spectre vanished. My brother recovered, but relapsed, and barely escaped with life; but Alexes did not. For a year and ten months the poor child lingered; and almost every night I had to sing her asleep; often, I remember, through bitter tears, for I knew she was dying, and I loved her the more as she wasted away. I held her little hand as she died; I followed her to the grave—the last thing that I have *loved* on earth. And *the dream was fulfilled.*

J. Noel Paton.

372. THE ORCHARD-PIT

PILED deep below the screening apple-branch
   They lie with bitter apples in their hands:
And some are only ancient bones that blanch,
And some had ships that last year's wind did launch,
   And some were yesterday the lords of lands.

In the soft dell, among the apple trees,
   High up above the hidden pit she stands,
And there forever sings, who gave to these,
That lie below, her magic hour of ease,
   And those her apples holden in her hands.

This in my dreams is shown to me; and her hair
   Crosses my lips and draws my burning breath;
Her song spreads golden wings upon the air,
Life's eyes are gleaming from her forehead fair,
   And from her breasts the ravishing eyes of Death.

Men say to me that sleep hath many dreams,
   Yet I never knew but this dream alone:
There, from a dried-up channel, once the stream's,
The glen slopes up; even such in sleep it seems
   As to my waking sight the place well known.

*   *   *   *

My love I call her, and she loves me well:
   But I love her as in the maelstrom's cup
The whirled stone loves the leaf inseparable
That clings to it round all the circling swell
   And that the last same eddy swallows up.

D. G. Rossetti.

373. SPECTRAL ILLUSION

WHOEVER has seen Great Pond, in the east parish of Haverhill, has seen one of the very loveliest of the thousand lakes or ponds of New England. With its soft slopes of greenest verdure —its white and sparkling sand-rim—its southern hem of pine and maple, mirrored, with spray and leaf, in the glassy water— its graceful hill-sentinels round about, white with the orchard bloom of spring, or tasselled with the com of autumn—its long sweep of blue waters, broken here and there by picturesque headlands—it would seem a spot, of all others, where spirits of evil must shrink, rebuked and abashed, from the presence of the beautiful. Yet here, too, has the shadow of the supernatural fallen. A lady of my acquaintance, a staid, unimaginative church member, states that a few years ago, she was standing in the angle formed by two roads, one of which traverses the pond shore, the other leading over the hill, which rises abruptly from the water. It was a warm summer evening, just at sunset She was startled by the appearance of a horse and cart, of the kind used a century ago in New England, driving rapidly down the steep hill-side, and crossing the wall a few yards before her, without noise or displacing of a stone. The driver sat sternly erect, with a fierce countenance, grasping the reins tightly, and looking neither to the right nor the left. Behind the cart, and apparently lashed to it, was a woman of gigantic size, her countenance convulsed with a blended expression of rage and agony, writhing and struggling, like Laocoon in the folds of the serpent. Her head, neck, feet, and arms were naked; wild locks of grey hair streamed back from temples corrugated and darkened. The horrible cavalcade swept by across the street, and disappeared at the margin of the pond. *J. G. Whittier.*

374. TIDES OF THE SOUL

As the waifs cast up by the sea change with the changing season, so the tides of the soul throw up their changing drift on the sand, but the sea beyond is one for ever.

D. G. Rossetti.

375. THE DEAD-HOUSE

WHAT seemed the most remarkable about this venerable old church, and what seemed the most barbarous, and grated upon the veneration with which I regarded this time-hallowed structure, was the condition of the graveyard surrounding it. From its close vicinity to the haunts of the swarms of labourers about the docks, it is crossed and recrossed by thoroughfares in all directions; and the tombstones, not being erect, but horizontal (indeed, they form a complete flagging to the spot), multitudes are constantly walking over the dead; their heels erasing the death's-heads and cross-bones, the last mementoes of the departed. At noon, when the lumpers employed in loading and unloading the shipping retire for an hour to snatch a dinner, many of them resort to the graveyard; and seating themselves upon a tombstone, use the adjoining one for a table. Often, I saw men stretched out in a drunken sleep upon these slabs; and once, removing a fellow's arm, read the following inscription, which, in a manner, was true to the life, if not to the death: —

HERE LYETH THE BODY OF

TOBIAS DRINKER

... In the basement of the church is a Dead-house, like the Morgue in Paris, where the bodies of the drowned are exposed until claimed by their friends, or till buried at the public charge. From the multitudes employed about the shipping, this dead-house has always more or less occupants. Whenever I passed up Chapel Street, I used to see a crowd gazing through the grim iron grating of the door, upon the faces of the drowned within. And once, when the door was opened, I saw a sailor stretched out, stark and stiff, with the sleeve of his frock rolled up, and showing his name and date of birth tattooed upon his arm. It was a sight full of suggestions; he seemed his own head-stone.

I was told that a standing reward was offered for the recovery of persons falling into the docks; so much. if restored to life, and a less amount if irrecoverably drowned. Lured by this, several horrible old men and women are constantly prying about the docks searching for bodies. I observed them principally in the early morning, when they issued from their dens, on the same principle that the rag-rakers, and rubbish-pickers in the streets, sally out bright and early; for then, the night harvest has ripened.

There seems to be no calamity overtaking man, that cannot be rendered merchantable. Undertakers, sextons, tomb-makers and hearse-drivers, get their living from the dead; and in times of plague most thrive. And these miserable old men and women hunted after corpses to keep from going to the churchyard themselves; for they were the most wretched of starvelings. *Herman Melville.*

376. THE MOTHER'S DREAM

I'D a dream to-night
As I fell asleep,
Oh I the touching sight
Makes me still to weep:
Of my little lad,
Gone to leave me sad,
Aye, the child I had,
But was not to keep.

As in heaven high,
I my child did seek,
There, in train, came by
Children fair and meek,
Each in lily white,
With a lamp alight;
Each was clear to sight,
But they did not speak.

Then, a little sad,
Came my child in turn,
But the lamp he had,
Oh! it did not burn;
He, to clear my doubt,
Said, half turned about,
"Your tears put it out;
Mother, never mourn."

William. Barnes.

377. THE PRERAPHAELITE IN AUSTRALIA

Friday, December 24.—We started in good time this morning . . . came to Lock's Station near which we have camped for the night. It is a lovely place, a swamp and mountains before, with wattle, honeysuckle, and gum trees behind: the sun shines cleanly now and everything looks bright, fair and tranquil, but the day has been blurred with plentiful showers. A lovely place, filled with the noise and flight of strange birds: I saw one tree as thick with white cockatoos as the balls of bloom on the guelder-rose: the rosellas dart and flutter their rich hues thro' the air.

Saturday, December 25.—Christmas! . . . Mr. Graves went on his mare to examine the road to Blanket Creek and found it very good: I believe we start for that place to-morrow. Some of our fellows are cleaning the gold we got at Reid's Creek before we divide it. . . .

I am lying along the grass behind the dead honeysuckle's branches; it is near evening and the sun sends long shadows. . . .

If one thing in nature could send me suddenly mad it would be a clear and settled conviction that I should never see England again.

January 11th.—I expected a letter from Mrs. Orme and one from Wm. Rossetti—did not get them. It is raining hard this day: everything looks fresh and beautiful but wonderfully sad to me; looking from the window I see a fine pomegranate tree. It is a body of sparkling and deep green with such out-breakings of scarlet splendours that my soul feels sick for love of it, yet I am sad; it sprung from darkness, aspires through light, seemingly towards gloom again, this vainly beautiful pomegranate tree. *Thomas Woolner.*

378. LOVE OF NATURE

I LOVE thee, nature, with a boundless love,
   The calm of earth, the storm of roaring woods;
The winds breathe happiness where'er I rove,
   There's life's own music in the swelling floods.
My heart is in the thunder-melting clouds,
   The snow-capt mountain, and the rolling sea;
And hear ye not the voice where darkness shrouds
   The heavens? There lives happiness for me.

Death breathes its pleasures when it speaks of him;
   My pulse beats calmer while his lightnings play.
My eye, with earth's delusions waxing dim,
   Clears with the brightness of eternal day.
The elements crash round me: it is he!
   Calmly I hear his voice and never start.
From Eve's posterity I stand quite free,
   Nor feel her curses rankle round my heart.

Love is not here. Hope is, and at his voice—
   The rolling thunder and the roaring sea—
My pulses leap, and with the hills rejoice;
   The strife and turmoil are at end for me,
No matter where life's ocean leads me on;
   For nature is my mother, and I rest,
When tempests trouble and the sun is gone,
   Like to a weary child upon her breast.
                              John Clare.

379. THE NEW HOUSE A-GETTÈN WOLD

AH! when our wedded life begun,
   Theäse clean-wall'd house of ours wer new;
Wi 'thatch as yollor as the Zun
   Avore the cloudless sky o' blue:
The sky o' blue that then did bound
The blue-hill'd worold's flow'ry ground.

An' we've a-vound it weather-brown'd,
   As spring-tide blossoms, open'd white,
Or Fall did shed, on zunburnt ground,
   Red apples vrom their leafy height:
Their leafy height, that winter soon
Left leafless to the cool-feäced moon.

An' raïn-bred moss ha' staïn'd wi' green
   The smooth-feäced wall's white-morter'd streaks,
The while our childern zot between
   Our seats avore the fleäme's red peaks:

The fleäme's red peaks, till axan white
Did quench em vor the long-sleep'd night.

The bloom that woonce did overspread
　　Your rounded cheäk, as time went by,
A-shrinkèn to a patch o' red,
　　Did feäde so soft's the evenèn sky:
The evenèn sky, my faithful wife,
O' days as feäir's our happy life.
　　　　　　　　　　William Barnes.

380. LOVE LIVES BEYOND THE TOMB

　　Love lives beyond
The tomb, the earth, which fades like dew!
　　I love the fond,
The faithful, and the true.

　　Love lives in sleep,
The happiness of healthy dreams:
　　Eve's dews may weep,
But love delightful seems.

　　'Tis seen in flowers,
And in the morning's pearly dew;
　　In earth's green hours,
And in the heaven's eternal blue.

　　'Tis heard in spring
When light and sunbeams, warm and kind,
　　On angel's wing
Bring love and music to the mind.

　　And where is voice,
So young, so beautiful, and sweet
　　As nature's choice.
Where spring and lovers meet?

Love lives beyond
The tomb, the earth, the flowers, and dew.
I love the fond,
The faithful, young, and true.

John Clare.

381. LONDON RESTAURANT

THE floor was tesselated with snow-white, and russet-hued marbles; and echoed to the tread, as if all the Paris catacombs were underneath. I started with misgivings at that hollow, boding sound, which seemed sighing with a subterraneous despair, through all the magnificent spectacle around me; mocking it, where it most glared.

The walls were painted so as to deceive the eye with interminable colonnades, and groups of columns of the finest Scagliola work of variegated marbles—emerald-green and gold, St. Pons veined with silver, Sienna with porphyry—supported a resplendent fresco ceiling, arched like a bower and thickly clustering with mimic grapes. Through all the east of this foliage, you spied in a crimson dawn, Guido's ever youthful Apollo, driving forth the horses of the sun. From sculptured stalactites of vine-boughs, here and there pendent hung galaxies of gas lights, whose vivid glare was softened by pale, cream-coloured porcelain spheres, shedding over the place a serene, silver flood; as if every porcelain sphere was a moon; and this superb apartment was the moonlit garden of Portia of Belmont; and the gentle lovers, Lorenzo and Jessica, lurked somewhere among the vines.

At numerous Moorish-looking tables, supported by Caryatides of turbaned slaves, sat knots of gentlemanly men, with cut decanters and taper-waisted glasses, journals and cigars, before them.

To and fro ran obsequious waiters, with spotless napkins thrown over their arms, and making a profound salaam, and hemming deferentially whenever they uttered a word.

At the further end of this brilliant apartment, was a rich mahogany turret-like structure, partly built into the wall, and communicating with rooms in the rear. Behind was a very handsome florid man with snow-white hair and whiskers, and in a snow-white jacket—he looked like an almond tree in blossom—who seemed to be standing a polite sentry over the scene before him; and it was he, who mostly ordered about the waiters; and with a silent salute, received the silver of the guests. *Herman Melville.*

382. GOOD NIGHT

WHILE down the meads wound slow
    Water vor green-wheel'd mills,
Over the streams bright bow,
    Win 'blew vrom dark-back'd hills.
Birds on the wind shot along down steep
Slopes, wi' a swift-swung zweep.
Dim grew the red-streak'd west.
Lim'-weary souls "Good rest."

Up on the plough'd hill brow,
    Still wer the zull's wheel'd beam,
Still wer the red-wheel'd plough,
    Free o' the strong-limb'd team,
Still wer the shop that the smith meäde ring,
Dark where the sparks did spring;
Low, shot the zun's last beams.
Lim'-weary souls "Good dreams."

Where I vrom dark bank-sheädes
    Turn'd up the west hill road,
Where all the green grass bleädes
    Under the zunlight glow'd,
Startled I met, as the zunbeams plaÿ'd
light, wi' a zunsmote maïd,
Come vor my day's last zight.
Zun-brighten'd maid "Good night."
                    William Barnes.

383. COPYING NATURE

i

DEAR ROSSETTI,

If I were to find funds, would you be ready on Wednesday morning to take a run into Wales, and make me a sketch of some rocks in the bed of a stream, with trees above, mountain ashes, and so on, scarlet in autumn tints? If you are later than Wednesday, you will be too late; but if you can go on Wednesday, let me know by return of post, or by bearer. I will send funds. I want you to go to Pont-y-monach, near Aberystwith, and choose a subject thereabouts. I shall be very much obliged to you if you will do this for me.

Most truly yours,
J. RUSKIN.

ii

DEAR ROSSETTI,

I never should think of your sitting out to paint from Nature. Merely look at the place; make memoranda fast, work at home at the inn, and *walk* among the hills. . . . If you can do it, be ready at any rate by Thursday—a bit of paper fastened on a board is all you can possibly want. Send me word to-morrow if you go, and I will send funds for Thursday. . . .

J. RUSKIN.

iii

DEAR ROSSETTI,

You are a *very* odd creature, that's a fact. I said I would find funds for you to go into Wales to draw something I wanted. I never said I would for you to go to Paris, to disturb yourself and other people, and I won't. . . .

J. RUSKIN.

384. THE DEATHLY BOOKS

ARTHUR ELLIOTT was the only son of a wealthy landed proprietor, one of my nearest neighbours, and a brother magistrate. Arthur had a most amiable nature, and was tenderly loved, not only by his parents, but by all who knew him intimately.

His attainments were remarkable, as I can testify; for we read, much together. He was an excellent classical scholar, but his favourite study was that of metaphysics, from which he was led to the study of natural science. But religion was the poetry and passion of his life; and though of a different belief, it afforded me pleasure to hear him discourse on the grandeur and benevolence of God. Sometimes when we were together in a deep green wood on a sultry summer afternoon; or sometimes walking at night beneath the glorious star-lit sky; or sometimes, when reading the dialogues of Plato, some divine thought rose from the book like an immortal spirit from the grave, and passed into his soul, then the tears would stream from his eyes, and falling on his knees he would utter praises or prayers in words of surpassing eloquence, and with a voice of the sweetest melody. And often—how well I remember it now—often at such times his gestures grew wild and almost furious, his utterance was choked, and a strange bubbling sound came from his mouth. . . . .

One day he came to me in trouble. He had been reading the great work of Malthus—the Essay on Population—and said that it made him doubt the goodness of God. I replied with the usual commonplace remarks; he listened to me attentively, then sighed, shook his head, and went away. A little while afterwards he read The Origin of Species, which had just come out, and which proves that the Law of Population is the chief agent by which Evolution has been produced. From that time he began to show symptoms of insanity—which disease it is thought he inherited from one of his progenitors. He dressed always in black, and said that he was in mourning for mankind. The works of Malthus and Darwin, bound in sombre covers, were placed on a table in his room; the first was lettered outside, *The Book of Doubt*, and the second, *The Book of Despair*. . . .

. . . In the grey hour of the dawn they heard a struggle in the room, and a choked kind of cry. They pushed the door, but it had been secured from within by a small piece of wood wedged in underneath. They forced it open at last, and the body of the unfortunate young man was found hanging from the window bar. Life was extinct. *Winwood Reade.*

385. THE TUFT OF KELP

ALL dripping in tangles green
  Cast up by a lonely sea,
If purer for that, O Weed,
  Bitterer, too, are ye?

Herman Melville.

386. FATHER MAPPLE'S SERMON

". . . God came upon him in the whale, and swallowed him down to living gulfs of doom, and with swift slantings tore him along 'into the midst of the seas,' where the eddying depths sucked him ten thousand fathoms down, and 'the weeds were wrapped about his head,' and all the watery world of woe bowled over him. Yet even then beyond the reach of any plummet—'out of the belly of hell'—when the whale grounded upon the ocean's utmost bones, even then, God heard the engulphed, repenting prophet when he cried. Then God spake unto the fish; and from the shuddering cold and blackness of the sea, the whale came breeching up towards the warm and pleasant sun, and all the delights of air and earth; and 'vomited out Jonah upon the dry land'; when the word of the Lord came a second time; and Jonah, bruised and beaten—his ears, like two sea-shells, still multitudinously murmuring of the ocean—Jonah did the Almighty's bidding. And what was that, shipmates? To preach the Truth to the face of Falsehood! That was it!

"This, shipmates, this is that other lesson; and woe to that pilot of the living God who slights it. Woe to him whom this world charms from Gospel duty! Woe to him who seeks to pour oil upon the waters when God has brewed them into a gale! Woe to him who seeks to please rather than to appal! Woe to him whose good name is more to him than goodness! Woe to him who, in this world, courts not dishonour! Woe to him who would not be true, even though to be false were salvation! Yea, woe to him, who, as the great Pilot Paul has it, while preaching to others, is himself a castaway!"

He dropped and fell away from himself for a moment; then lifting his face to them again, showed a deep joy in his eyes as he cried out with a heavenly enthusiasm,—"But oh I shipmates! on the starboard hand of every woe, there is a sure delight; and higher the top of that delight, than the bottom of the woe is deep. Is not the main-truck higher than the kelson is low? Delight is to him—a far, far upward, and inward delight—who against the proud gods and commodores of this earth, ever stands forth his own inexorable self. Delight is to him whose strong arms yet support him, when the ship of this base treacherous world has gone down beneath him. Delight is to him who gives no quarter in the truth, and kills, burns, and destroys all sin though he pluck it out from under the robes of Senators and Judges. Delight,—top-gallant delight is to him, who acknowledges no law or lord, but the Lord his God, and is only a patriot to heaven. Delight is to him, whom all the waves of the billows of the seas of the boisterous mob can never shake from this sure Keel of the Ages. And eternal delight and deliciousness will be his, who coming to lay him down, can say with his final breath—O Father!—chiefly known to me by Thy rod—mortal or immortal, here I die. I have striven to be Thine, more than to be this world's, or mine own. Yet this is nothing; I leave eternity to Thee; for what is man that he should live out the lifetime of his God?"

He said no more, but slowly waving a benediction, covered his face with his hands, and so remained kneeling, till all the people had departed, and he was left alone in the place.

Herman Melville.

387. I LOST THE LOVE OF HEAVEN

I LOST the love of heaven above,
   I spurned the lust of earth below,
I felt the sweets of fancied love,
   And hell itself my only foe.

I lost earth's joys, but felt the glow
    Of heaven's flame abound in me,
Till loveliness and I did grow
    The bard of immortality.

I loved, but woman fell away;
    I hid me from her faded flame.
I snatched the sun's eternal ray
    And wrote till earth was but a name.

In every language upon earth,
    On every shore, o'er every sea,
I gave my name immortal birth
    And kept my spirit with the free.

John Clare.

NOTES

1. The second part of "A Pastoral Ballad."
2. WILLIAM STUKELEY (1687-1765). Part of a letter to Samuel Gale, 1726/7, in "Family Memoirs of the Rev. William Stukeley." Surtees Society,1882.
3. Heliotrope, *i.e.* a plant which turns to the sun, and here rather the sunflower than our heliotrope. It would be worth tracking out the uses of this image from the account of heliotropism in Hales's "Vegetable Staticks" in 1727, to Blake, and so on. From "Reflections on a Flower Garden" in "Meditations and Contemplations," 1746-7. A book read eighty years later by Samuel Palmer.
4. From "The Adventures of Ferdinand Count Fathom" (1755). For the Æolian Harp, read the note on
5. No. i. comes from William Stukeley's "Abury: A Temple of the British Druids," published in 1743. No. ii. comes from an earlier letter (1730) to Roger Gale (see Note 2). Stukeley was friendly with scientists such as Halley and Newton and Stephen Hales, the plant physiologist; but he also read the Cambridge Platonists and sought after the One. Archaeologists complain because he twisted archaeology to his beliefs. He did, and seems to have invented one of two avenues at Avebury, to make Avebury into the symbol of the Snake and Circle. But Stukeley lived when he did; had he been less interested in neo-platonism and less convinced about Druids, he might have been a less good archaeologist. Modern archaeologists cannot have it both ways.
6. From "Agrippina: A Fragment of a Tragedy."
7. From Stukeley's Commonplace Book, in "Family Memoirs." See Notes 2 and 5.
8. From "An Account of the Glacieres or Ice Alps of Savoy, in two Letters "(1744), reprinted in G. R. de Beers'" Early Travellers in the Alps."
9. See Note 3. Also from "Reflections on a Flower Garden."
10. Part of a letter to Samuel Gale, 1728, in "Family Memoirs." See Notes 2 and 5. The private Stonehenge was in his garden at Grantham; and "Ivo Talbois, King of the Girvii," is Stukeley's friend, Maurice Johnson, the Lincolnshire antiquary.
11. See Note 9.
13. See Notes 2 and 5. Also from "Family Memoirs," from a letter to Samuel Gale, 1727. What set off the fact of things in Milton was actually the moon, not the sun.
14. Part of "Ode to the Evening Star."
15. WILLIAM LAW. Law (1686-1761) was one of the prime enthusiasts

and disciples of Jakob Boehme. This is from a letter to Thomas Yate written in 1756 and quoted in Walton's "Notes and Materials For an Adequate Biography of William Law" (1854) on p. 572.
16. From "The Natural History of Norway, translated from the Danish Original of the Right Revd. Erich Pontoppidan, Bishop of Bergen in Norway and Member of the Royal Academy of Sciences at Copenhagen." London, 1755. A storehouse for romantic imagery and subject.
17. See Note 15. Also from Walton's "Notes and Materials," p. 55.
19. From "Conjectures on Original Composition" (1759). The Conjectures were in the form of a letter to Samuel Richardson, who ought also to be represented in an anthology such as this; "Clarissa" was Fuseli's favourite book. But long diffuse novels are not so well summarized in an extract.
20. DON SALTERO'S COFFEE-HOUSE OF RARITIES. This was the Charlie Brown's of the eighteenth century. It was in Chelsea, a sight for all visitors, and a museum from which the directors of the V. & A. and the B.M. might learn. For more about it, see the "Dictionary of National Biography," under James Salter, Chambers's "Book of Days," and the "Tatler," No. 34; and compare the contents of William Stukeley's head.
21. GOLDSMITH'S ROME. "All this is taken, you see, from Nature," said Goldsmith. Black champagne is stout. The game of goose was like snakes and ladders, and "The Seasons" and "King Charles's Twelve Good Rules" were the normal things for the wall. King Charles's Rules: Rudyard Kipling's "If" in poker-work on a three-ply panel.
22. "From the Icelandic," 1761.
23. SOLOMON GESSNER (1730-1788), the "Swiss Theocritus." Everyone read "The Death of Abel," from which this comes. It had the bad luck to be translated by Mary Collyer, who turned simple German into pseudo-genteel English. The translation came out in 1761. The "Quarterly Review" said, in 1814, that no foreign book had ever been so popular: "It has been repeatedly printed at country presses, with worn types and on coarse paper; and it is found at country fairs, and in the little shops of remote towns almost as certainly as the" Pilgrim's Progress" and "Robinson Crusoe."The "Quarterly" compares it with Ossian, and with Hervey's" Meditations and Contemplations,"from which sententious, but underrated, book I have taken Nos. 3, 9, and 11. See Bertha Reed's "Influence of Gessner Upon English Literature" (Philadelphia, 1905); but though he was read by Wordsworth and Coleridge and Byron, I should think he had as much effect on English painters. His "New Idyls. With a Letter to M. Fuslin on Landscape Painting," translated by W. Hooper in 1776, was a book which

delighted Constable, who certainly must have enjoyed Gessner's charming and delicately honest illustrations.
24. From Ossian's, or Macpherson's, "Carthon."
25. A degree of superstition, melancholy and enthusiasm might have thickened and livened up John Langhorne's poetry. See No. 46. His dates are 1735 to 1779; and he was rector of Blagdon in Somerset. This is from "Letters on Religious Retirement, Melancholy and Enthusiasm," 1762.
26. From "Berrathon."
27. Why is there no edition of Christopher Smart? When his large and odd reality is made visible by an editor, many of the pale eighteenth-century shadows cried up by university pedants will look paler still.
28. Part of Mickle's "Ode on Vicissitude."
29. The first three stanzas only. "Hymns," 1755.
30. Part of "Pollio: An Elegy. Written in the Wood near Roslin Castle," 1762.
31. A stanza from "A Noon Piece, or, The Mowers at Dinner."
32. The closing piece of "Carthon."
33. From "Temora."
34. The best, I think, from "A Translation of the Psalms of David," 1765.
35. For the whole of this poem see "Poems Chiefly Pastoral," 1766. "A Landscape" is like a vast oil on a dining-room wall in an eighteenth-century mansion—the kind that goes with the house because it is too big for the auctioneer to sell.
36. From "Syr Martyn," Canto 11, first published in 1767 as "The Concubyne."
37. Part of "New Year, Hymn 1" in "Hymns and Spiritual Songs for the Feasts and Festivals of the Church of England"; printed with the Psalms of David, 1765. Mr. Edmund Blunden has edited rather too short a selection from these hymns.
38. Out of a letter to George Montagu.
39. Three of eight stanzas from "All Saints, Hymn XXVIII." See No. 37.
40. Hymn XXXIII. See Note 37.
41. Part of a letter to William Cole, March 9, 1765. One of the early samples of acknowledged writing from a dream. See Nos. 305 and 299, for instance, on "Eugene Aram" and "Frankenstein."
42. A stanza from Canto I of "Syr Martyn." See Note 36.
43. Part of "Circumcision, Hymn 11." See Note 37.
44. I have put this a bit before its time. It comes from Walpole's essay "On Modern Gardening" of 1785. Milton is the great goldfield, the Klondike of the Romantic Miners. Samuel Palmer is one of the last in this gold rush.
45. From "Syr Martyn," Canto 11. See Note 36.
46. Number VII of "The Fables of Flora," less twelve of the more sententious verses. "That swells the golden breast of May"

is worth much of the orthodox inane we are expected to admire according to Professors X and Y. For Langhorne, read Note 25. "The Fables" were popular, three editions in the first year.
47. See Notes 46 and 25.
48. Part of "Hymn XIV; The Ascension of Our Lord Jesus Christ." See Note 37.
49. REJOICE IN THE LAMB, edited by W. Force Stead (Cape,1939). The great find, "Jubilate Agno," written in Smart's madness, was copied from the original manuscript by Mr. Stead, and was first printed and published as "Rejoice in the Lamb" by Jonathan Cape. Mr. Stead puts Smart in the line of enthusiasts, who draw, like Blake, from Paracelsus, Boehme, the Cabalists, and Neo-platonism. The musk which Jeoffrey leaps up to catch, Mr. Stead explains as a musk ball, swung by Smart; or else as the plant.
50. Out of "Contemplation: A Night Piece": Poems, "Chiefly Pastoral," 1766.
51. From "Jubilate Agno." See Note 49.
52. This is from "A Letter on Landscape Painting," already mentioned in the note on Gessner, No. 23.
53. Journal, October 3rd, 1769. Volume iii. of Tovey's edition of "Gray's Letters."
54. From "Jubilate Agno" (Note 49).
55. "Observations on Modern Gardening Illustrated by Descriptions," 1770.
56. "Jubilate Agno" again (Note 49).
57. Part of "Heccar and Gaira."
58. When I first read this, quoted without name and source by De Quincey (p. 301, Vol. xi., Works, 1862), I wondered—see for instance No. 60—if it was by Christopher Smart. Then suddenly I saw it, or thought I saw it, in Wordsworth: but Wordsworth's "Song for the Wandering Jew" reads to me like this poem rewritten and ruined, with 1765 smoothed out into his own idiom. Compare the two versions of the Chamois and the Seahorse lines. So I kept the poem here, where I put it first of all.
59. "Natural History of Selborne": from Letter v.
60. Part of "Hymn XIII: St. Philip and St. James." See Note 37.
61. J. C. LAVATER (1741-1801). No. i. is from "Secret Journal of a Self-Observer: or Confessions and Familiar Letters of the Rev. J. C. Lavater," translated by the Rev. Peter Will, 1795, and quoted by A. M. Kelty in" Solace of a Solitaire," 1869. Miss Kelty was one of the last Beamenists of the authentic tradition. Nos. ii. and iii. are from Lavater's "Aphorisms on Man," translated by Fuseli (1788). Blake's comment on these two aphorisms was" Most Excellent! ", and he wrote in his copy of the book" The name Lavater is the amulet of those who purify the heart of man."

62. From "The Fool of Quality," 1766-1770. Brooke, too, was a Behmenist.
63. Six lines from "The Death of Nicou."
64. Journal, October 13th, 1769. Tovey's edition of "Gray's Letters," Vol. iii.
65. From Fuseli's "Lectures on Painting."
66. Part of "Elegy to the Memory of Mr. Thomas Philips of Fairford."
67. SIR WILLIAM JONES (1746-1794): one of the great men of the eighteenth century, F.R.S., Judge of the High Court at Calcutta, explorer of Sanskrit, and a founder of the scientific study of language. The pre-Kipling Age of Empire.
68. One of Fuseli's aphorisms in Vol. iii. of the life of Fuseli by Knowles.
70. First reprinted and assigned to Chatterton by Mr. E. H. W. Meyerstein in his "Life of Thomas Chatterton," 1930.
71. See Note 55.
72. Part of "The Mynstrelles Songe" in "Ælla." "Blake" means naked; "levynne," lightning; "lemes," lights or rays; "steynced" is unexplained, but my guess is "stained," for which Chatterton elsewhere has "stente." Stained seems the right autumnal meaning.
73. The opening lines of "The Country Walk."
74. Part of "Hymn VI: The Presentation of Christ in the Temple." See Note 37. An eighteenth-century altar-cloth in the chancel of Cliffe Pypard church in Wiltshire always makes me remember the eye and force behind the fourth stanza.
75. Part of "Elegy."
76. HAFOD. Hafod is still there, the hills above the Ystwyth speckled with the white stumps of trees which have been felled, the gardens decaying, and the turf beyond the ha-ha slashed by tractors and timber-waggons. The dome over the gutted library is in danger through the rotting of the timbers. Up above, the church has been restored after a fire, but the burnt arms and legs and heads of Chantrey's memorial to Colonel Johnes's daughter are heaped about still inside the railing. But the Hafod valley is still the sublimest illustration of the modern gardening which Walpole said was invented by Milton (see No. 44). These descriptions are from "An Attempt to Describe Hafod, An Ancient Seat Belonging to Thomas Johnes, Esq." (1796), by Blake's friend, George Cumberland. Near Hafod is the Devil's Bridge, visited, among others, in the romantic noon, by Wordsworth and Coleridge and Cotman (who drew it) and Edward Irving. When Napoleon was threatening England with invasion, the romantic Johnes made a speech which delighted Coleridge: "Houses plundered, then burnt, sons conscribed, wives and daughters ravished, etc., etc.,—*but as*

for *you, you luxurious Aldermen! with your fat will he grease the wheels of his triumphal chariot!"*
77. Rutty's "Spiritual Diary," 1776, is a strange story of the struggle this Quaker doctor had between the spirit and flesh, divine discipline and the delights of botany and good meals. *"January 25, 1729: Read Law, to great illumination and improvement in love. A luxurious dinner on apple-pie."*

"From 1740 to 1745, engaged in the Natural History of the County of Dublin, and was led a long dance on birds, fishes, and fossils, and in compotations for information, and was greatly hurt in my spirituals by this means, preferring nature to grace...." No. 77 comes from the "Natural History."
78. Part of "Narva and Mored."
79. From White's "Naturalist's Journal" in "Life and Letters of Gilbert White, "edited by R. Holt White.
80. See Note 66.
81. See Note 55.
82. See Note 68.
83. From the preface to the second edition, "Of the Origin and Progress of Language," 1774.
84. See Note 83; from Chapter v., Book 11.
86. "Natural History of Selborne": Letter XIII.
87. From "A Letter on Landscape Painting." See Note 23.
88. Part of an undated letter to William Jackson of Exeter, now in the Royal Academy Library. The letter is printed in W. T. Whitley's "Thomas Gainsborough." Barak Norman was probably the first Englishman to make cellos. He died in 1740. Jaye, another musical instrument maker.
89. See Note 68.
90. Quoted by Constable's biographer, Leslie, in his "Handbook for Young Painters" (1854). The Raphaelite view, in opposition to the Preraphaelite.
92. From "Italy; With Sketches of Spain and Portugal," published in 1834, but as a revision of "Dreams, Waking Thoughts, and Incidents; in a Series of Letters, from Various Parts of Europe," published in 1783, and then suppressed by Beckford.
95. Burns's Commonplace Book of 1783-1785.
96. "Natural History of Selborne": Letter XXVII.
97. "The Task," VI, 11.76-82 (1785).
98. From the Commonplace Book See Note 95.
99. "The Task," III, ll. 108-133, 191-220.
100. Part of "The Little Black Boy."
101. "The Task," III, ll. 243-251.
102. THE GLORY. "Memoirs of the Literary and Philosophical Society of Manchester," Vol. iii., 1790. One of the favourite light phenomena of the period; and this is the place from which Coleridge seems first to have known of the Glory.

The classical locality for it is on the Brocken (where Mr. F. S. Smythe has photographed it). Coleridge experienced the Glory; and he writes of it in "Constancy to An Ideal Object," and, figuratively, in "Aids to Reflection." Those, he says, in "Aids to Reflection," who are not delighted by Genius, "are disturbed, perplexed, irritated. The beholder either recognizes it as a projected form of his own Being, that moves before him with a Glory round its head, or recoils from it as a Spectre." That is Coleridge's total use of the Romantic sparkle of nature.

James Hogg uses the Glory at a critical point in his grim and brilliant "Private Memoirs and Confessions of a Justified Sinner" (1824), George Colwan sees his own Glory on the cloud; and then the terrific shadow of the Sinner coining to murder him. For the ill-understood mechanism of the Glory, see M. Minnaert: "Light and Colour in the Open Air." Bell, 1940

103. From "A Letter on Landscape Painting." See Note 23.
104. "The Task," vi, ll. 149-176.
105. See Note 68.
106. From "Biographical Memoirs of Extraordinary Painters," first published in 1780.
107. From "An Island in The Moon," about 1787.
108. ERASMUS DARWIN (1731-1802). Those who anthologize the worst poems take plenty from Erasmus Darwin. But read his prose, for all that. Try "Zoonomia" (his chief speculative book); and "Phytologia; or the Philosophy of Agriculture and Gardening" (1800); and the notes to all his poems. He was one of the minds who livened Coleridge and Shelley (see Mary Shelley on the birth of Frankenstein, No. 299), to say nothing of livening up science and founding a great dynasty.
He and the terrific John Hunter, who set himself to dissect all creation, are two of the eighteenth-century Englishmen to read about; and Sir Joseph Banks is another. Imagine two lines, two straight lines, one running through Isaac Newton, Hunter, Monboddo, and Darwin, the other through William Law and the mystics. Between them the wavy line of romantic sensibility and speculation. The three lines intersect in a few great men uch as Coleridge and Goethe. In England, Sir William Jones, the poet (see No. 67), explored Sanskrit, doing for philology what John Hunter did for anatomy; and George Stubbs, the painter and friend of Hunter, died regretting he had not finished his comparative anatomy of man, tiger and hen; in Germany the romantic writer Chamisso discovered how generations alternate in the curious breeding of the mollusc *salpa*.
This description of Fuseh's picture comes from Canto 111 of the poem on plant reproduction, "The Loveo of the Plants," 1789.

THE ROMANTICS

109. From Samuel Henley's English version of "Vathek" (1786), which Beckford wrote in French and published in Lausanne in 1787. Paul Elmer More in "The Drift of Romanticism" boils everything down to this one symbol of the flaming heart.
111. "The Task," v, ll. 379-397.
112. Part of a letter to Samuel Barker, April 17, 1786. "Life and Letters of Gilbert White," edited by R. Holt White.
113. "Loves of the Plants": a note to Canto I. See Note 108.
115. From a letter, 13th May 1662, in Lady Morgan's "Life and Times of Salvator Rosa." The favourite painter of English connoisseurs of the picturesque and the sublime, above Claude and the two Poussins.
116. See No. 92.
117. "Cod": a pillow. "Sark": a shirt.
118. From "A Provincial Glossary, with a collection of Local Proverbs and Popular Superstitions," 1787.
119. Two lines from the song "Open the Door to Me, Oh!" Lines much admired by Yeats.
120. From "The Romance of the Forest," 1791.
121. Note in Canto 11, "The Loves of the Plants." See Note 108.
122. Part of "The Vision": Burns's Native Muse speaking. There is a nicely put note in the Oxford edition that Burns had "the good taste" to "keep some of the stanzas in this poem in MS."
123. From "The Marriage of Heaven and Hell."
125. CONSTANTIN FRANÇOIS CHASSEBŒUF DE VOLNEY (1757-1820). From the invocation prefixed to "Les Ruines, ou Meditation sur les Revolutions des Empires," 1791. The English translation (? 1795) was in its fifth edition in 1811. A book read by Shelley.
127. From the "Essay on the Picturesque," 1794. The copy I have of this belonged to John Constable. In his second lecture at the Royal Institution in 1856, Constable talked of Claude's "calm sunshine of the heart" (Leslie's "Constable," chapter 18); a reminiscence, obviously of Uvedale Price's "mild and equal sunshine of the soul."
128. Part of "An Evening Walk," 1787-89.
129. See Note 127.
130. From "The Marriage of Heaven and Hell."
131. From "Europe."
135. See Note 92.
136. From "The Marriage of Heaven and Hell."
137. From "The Ruins." See Note 125.
138. From "America."
142. From "The Vision of the Daughters of Albion."
143. THE UPAS TREE. appeared an account of the Upas Tree in the "London Magazine" for 1783—mainly a spoof heightening

of previous accounts of a real poisonous tree in Java. "Upas" is the Malay for poison all right. George Steevens, the Shakespeare scholar and practical joker, may have been the magnifying-glass. But the story was just right. Darwin brought it into verse, knowing that though it mightn't exist, it would certainly root in the imagination. The Upas Tree grew well. Southey uses it in "Thalaba," Byron in "Childe Harold," Danby exhibited a picture of the Upas Tree in 1820, George Colman built a play round it in 1822, and Emerson in "Mithridates" (1847) brought vampyres to roost in its branches. Sir Henry Yule (1829-1889), writing about the Upas Tree in "Hobson-Jobson," recalls seeing a diorama of the tree when he was a boy.

For poets the Upas Tree wore out. But eventually what poets have used—like the discoveries of science—sinks down into the consciousness of politicians, and the Upas Tree became a metaphor for platforms. The O.E.D. quotes it from speeches by Gladstone (1868), Lord Edmond Fitzmaurice (1873), Joe Chamberlain (1873), Lord Crichton (1880). I fancy its present lodging is in the mind of Mr. Garvin; leader-writers in "The Times" bring it out now and then, all shrivelled and dry and incapable of poisoning an earwig.

Yule thinks the Anaconda—the monstrous snake of Ceylon, which seizes tygers, and winds round them till, one by one, the tyger's ribs crack, the tyger howling at every "loud crash of its bones"—was invented by the same mind. The Anaconda appears first in the "Scots Magazine" for 1768, but it has never had quite the success of the Upas. It never fitted so well. But I see the Anaconda in Coleridge's "Religious Musings" (1794):

> ... where by night
> Fast by each precious fountain on green herbs
> The lion couches: or hyaena dips
> Deep in the lucid stream his bloody jaws
> Or serpent rolls his vast moon-glittering bulk
> Caught in whose monstrous twine Behemoth yells
> His bones loud-crashing!

Coleridge says that Behemoth here "designates any large Quadruped."

This Darwin entry for the Upas Tree is a note to "The Loves of the Plants" (1789). See Note 108.

144. See Note 118.
145. From "Vala, or the Four Zoas."
146. i. Part of Additional Note iv. ii. Part of Additional Note II. "The Economy of Vegetation," 1791. See Note 108.
147. From his annotation to Sir Joshua Reynolds's "Discourses."
148. "Prelude," 11, ll. 105-144.

149. "Minor Poems of Schiller," translated by J. H. Merivale, 1844.
150. From "Milton."
151. See Note 149.
152. From "A Vision of the Last Judgement": Rossetti MS.
153. i. From "Jerusalem."
    ii. From "Religious Musings." Coleridge adds, "This paragraph is intelligible to those who, like the Author, believe and feel the sublime system of Berkley; and the doctrine of the final happiness of all men."
154. From "The Everlasting Gospel."
155. THE ÆOLIAN HARP —is really the prime romantic image. The Farmer's Boy, Robert Bloomfield, made Æolian harps for a living and compiled a short Æolian harp anthology called "Nature's Music," published in 1808, but most easily come by in his "Remains," Vol. i., 1824. It was invented by the Jesuit Athanasius Kircher (1601-1680), who also invented the Magic Lantern, was lowered into the crater of Vesuvius, tried to construct a world language, and studied Egyptian hieroglyphics. The English story is that the harp was invented by James Oswald, who died (see Grove's "Dictionary of Music and Musicians") in 1769. He acted on a hint in the Greek commentary of Eustathius which Pope found while translating Homer: the hint was that wind on strings could be made to produce harmonious sounds. He experimented, failed, and tried again when told that an ordinary harp, on a Thames houseboat, had sounded in the wind. Finally, he devised a "harp of Æolus" —the God of the Winds—to fit into the window. This was before 1748. The harp became popular. Thomson writes about it in "The Castle of Indolence" (1748). Smollett's smart adventurer, Ferdinand Fathom (see entry No. 4) uses it to seduce a country girl. "Ferdinand Count Fathom" came out in 1753, and Smollett suggests that country people knew nothing of this new instrument. The harp now begins to romp through literature. It is in Gray's letters. In "Jubilate Agno" Smart insists it was the biblical shawm. There are poems about it by Mason, who made his own harp, Dibdin and Mrs. Opie. Gilbert White mentions it in 1775 in a letter. Sir John Hawkins gives an account of it in his "History of Music" (1776), and William Jones in his "Physiological Disquisitions" (1781). Bishop Young deals with it in his "Enquiry into the Principal Phenomena of Sounds and Musical Strings (1784). James Montgomery bought one from Bloomfield. What was an Æolian harp badly disguised, James Macpherson rather incautiously allowed into Ossian, in "Berrathon" and "Temora" and "Dar-Thula." Erasmus Darwin used it in his "Economy of Vegetation" (1791). And the harp is still sounding away in Edgar Allan Poe in

"The Poetic Principle" (see No. 360), and in De Quincey (see No. 287). French critics compared Constable's painting to Æolian harp music (see Note 210). But the *locus classicus* for the harp is this poem by Coleridge, who used it seriously, as he used the Glory (Note 102) and so many other things he experienced. At the time of this poem he and Sara Fricker had just been married, and the harp was clamped into their cottage window at Clevedon. Coleridge took his Æolian harp off to the Lakes with him, and Charles Lamb saw it lying in his study in Greta Hall, where he no doubt allowed it to play in the wind off Skiddaw. Æolian images are used by Wordsworth, Keats, Shelley, Darley, Allingham, and Tennyson. Berlioz liked the Æolian harp, and his friend Kastner had one fixed into a small tower in his garden at Versailles. Herman Melville published an Æolian harp poem as late as 1888.

I wanted to hear an Æolian harp before writing this note, but the commercial manufacture of the harp seems to have gone out some years ago. A London harp and spinet maker tells me that the Æolian harp is an "elusive instrument and often refuses to speak for no apparent reason." William Jones says: "If we consider the quality of its harmony, it very much resembles that of a chorus of voices at a distance; with all the expressions of the *forte*, the *piano*, and the *swell*; in a word, its harmony is more like to what we might imagine the aerial sounds of magic and enchantment to be, than to artificial music—we may call it, without a metaphor, the music of inspiration" (1781). Coleridge's "long sequaceous notes" sound a brilliant and lovely description.

Will the Æolian harp work without being clamped into a window? By the way, for the stringing of it, and for photographs, see Grove's "Dictionary."

156. AFTER-IMAES. Coleridge on light again; but what he saw had nothing to do with electricity. It was an after-image; look at the sun, turn away, or shut your eyes, and you see little suns. Erasmus Darwin investigated after-images: "I covered a paper about four inches square with yellow, and with a pen filled with a blue colour wrote upon the middle of it the word BANKS in capitals; and sitting with my back to the sun, fixed my eyes for a minute exactly on the centre of the letter N in the word. After shutting my eyes, and shading them somewhat with my hand, the word was distinctly seen in the spectrum, in yellow colours on a blue ground; and then on opening my eyes on a yellowish wall at twenty feet distance, the magnified name of BANKS appeared on the wall written in golden characters" ("Zoonomia, or the Laws of Organic Life," 1794-6). There is plenty about after-images in Professor Minnaert's "Light and Colour in the Open Air" (Bell, 1940). Linnæus's daughter Elisabeth saw the "light" from

the flower of *Tropæolwn majus*, which is the yellow nasturtium, not monk's-hood. Charles Darwin saw it from a South African lily. Goethe saw after-images from peonies, crocuses, marigolds, and poppies. His "Farbenlehre" or "Theory of Colours" (1840) is the book to read: "One night as I entered the room of an inn, a fine girl came towards me. Her face was of a dazzling whiteness, her hair black, and she was wearing a scarlet bodice. I looked at her intently in the dim twilight while she was standing some distance away from me. When after a moment she left me, I saw on the white wall opposite me a black face, surrounded by a bright glow, and the dress of the very well defined figure was a beautiful sea-green." Minnaert says that after-images are best seen in the evening, when the eyes aren't too strained and the lighted West contrasts with the darkened East.

157. "Memoirs of the Life of Sir Humphry Davy," by John Davy, 1839: from one of Davy's early notebooks.
158. From the extracts from her journals, in the memoir prefixed to "Gaston de Blondeville," published in 1826, three years after her death.
159. From "Public Address: Chaucer's Canterbury Pilgrims."
160. From "Journals of Dorothy Wordsworth," 1897: The Alfoxden Journal, 1798.
161. From "Omniana" (1812), Vol.i.
162. The horror-height in Lewis's play, "The Castle Spectre," published in 1798, and six times reprinted before the end of the year.
163. John Leyden (1775-1811): from the note introducing his poem, "The Cout of Keilder."
164. Scott's note to "The Eve of St. John" (1800).
166. Glittering ice. Coleridge and light. From "Christmas Out of Doors "in" The Friend," Vol. ii. The year: 1798.
167. "The Farmer's Boy" (1798), 11.142-147.
168. The last nine lines left out.
169. Out of Book Seven of "Gebir" (1798).
170. From the Gutch Memorandum Book in the British Museum, 1795-1798.
172. Part of "Gebir."
173. "Omniana" (1812), Vol.i.
174. See Note 170.
175. Part of "Frost at Midnight."
176. "Prelude," XI, ll.395-395.
177. "Omniana" (1812), Vol. ii.
179. All from "Anima Poetae," edited by E. H. Coleridge, 1895.
180. Part of "France: An Ode."
181. From "The Birds" in "Aristophanes: A Metrical Version of the Acharnians, the Knights, and the Birds," 1840.

182. See Note 158.
183. From "Journals of Dorothy Wordsworth," 1897; The Grasmere Journal, 1800.
184. "Prelude," iv, ll. 231-255.
185. See Note 185.
186. From "Anima Poetae."
187. From his letter to Wordsworth, 30th January 1801.
188. From part of a journal contributed by the Rev. G. B. H. Coleridge to "Wordsworth and Coleridge: Studies in Honour of George McLean Harper." Edited by E. L. Griggs. Princeton University Press, 1939.
190. From "Journals of Dorothy Wordsworth," 1897; The Grasmere Journal, 1802.
191. Leslie's "Life of Constable," edited by Hon. Andrew Shirley, 1937. Part of a letter to John Dunthorne, senior, 29th May, 1802.
192. Out of Canon Jackson's "Wiltshire MSS. Collections," belonging to the Society of Antiquaries.
193. See Note 190.
194. Nine lines left out.
196. Blake on this poem: "This is all in the highest degree Imaginative and equal to any Poet, but not Superior. I cannot think that Real Poets have any competition. None are greatest in the Kingdom of Heaven; it is so in Poetry."
197. From Annotations to Wordsworth's "Poems."
199. Part of "Resolution and Independence."
200. OPIUM AND POETS. Crabbe started to take opium for stomach trouble in 1790. Of his two opium ejaculations, "The World of Dreams," out of which these four stanzas come, was first published after his death. The other (see No. 202) was "Sir Eustace Grey," published by Crabbe in 1807, but Crabbe put his own dreams into the wicked baronet in the mad-house. Both Crabbe and De Quincey (see No. 278) were fixed on high places—Crabbe, the clergyman, on church spires and above rooks' nests; De Quincey, the dreamer, at the summit of pagodas. Both, and Coleridge too, experienced the horrible infinite of space and time. There is a good pamphlet on the opium-eating of Crabbe, Coleridge, De Quincey and Francis Thompson—"The Milk of Paradise," by Meyer H. Abrams, Cambridge, Mass., 1934.
201. From the Gutch Memorandum Book, 1795-1798. See the last note.
202. Part of "Sir Eustace Grey." Crabbe's text for the poem, from Seneca's "Hercules Furens," is "Veris miscens falsa." See Note 200.
203. "Travel in Various Countries of Europe, Asia, Africa," by Edward Daniel Clarke (1769-1822).

THE ROMANTICS 346

204. From "Anima Poetae."
205. See Note 157.
206. Out of "Public Address": the Rossetti Manuscript.
207. Out of "Remorse," Act iv, Scene iii.
208. From "The Pentameron," 1837.
209. Part of "Letter XXIII: Prisons," in "The Borough."
210. The sparkle and dewy freshness of Constable, his dislike for the autumnal tints and preference for spring. Constable was a Romantic trying to catch the glitter like everyone else. He liked the "Ancient Mariner" best of modern poems, seeing in it "the rich preludes in musick, and the full harmonies of the Eolian Lyre" which the French critics saw in his own pictures and found meaningless. "Is not some of this *blame*, the highest *praise*?" Letter to John Fisher, December 17th, 1824.

    No. 210 is from Solomon Hart's "Reminiscences," 1882.

211. From "Daylight: a Recent Discovery in the Art of Painting, with Hints on the Philosophy of the Fine Arts and on that of the Human Mind as first dissected by Emmanuel Kant. Though Richter (a friend of Blake's) drew Stothard-like illustrations for the booksellers, he concerned himself with painting under direct sunlight. He painted his" Christ Giving Sight to the Blind"—where is it now?—in a blaze of sun on top of his house in Newman Street; and his text for this pamphlet is:

> "Night's tapers are burnt out, and jocund day
> Stands tiptoe on the misty mountain's top."

A man to be explored.

212. From W. P. Frith's "Further Reminiscences," 1888.
213. Part of "Letter XXII: Peter Grimes" in "The Borough."
214. From Leslie's "Life of Constable."
216. Out of Scene the Eleventh: "Antony and Octavius."
217. Prelude, XIV, 11.11-69.
218. From "TheDirector," No. 19, 1807; "Works of Sir Humphry Davy," Vol 8, 1840.
219. Sparkle and light. No. i. is from Davy's own paper "On some new phenomena of chemical changes produced by electricity, particularly the decomposition of the fixed alkalis, and the exhibition of the new substances which constitute their bases; and on the general nature of Alkaline bodies." Read to the Royal Society, November 19th, 1807. "Works" (1840), Vol. 5.

    No. ii. is from John Davy's "Memoirs of Sir Humphry Davy," 1839.

    Coleridge went to Davy's lectures "to increase his stock of metaphors."

NOTES

220. Part of "Dejection: An Ode."
221. From "Anima Poetae."
222. "Prelude," VII, ll. 18-42.
223. "Prelude," XIV, ll. 168-192.
224. "Lectures and Notes on Shakespeare," 1883.
225. From "The Pentameron": Boccaccio speaking.
226. Part of a poem written in 1844; the second stanza of seven.
227. "Prelude," iv, ll. 379-459.
228. From "Imaginary Conversations": "Southey and Porson" (Southey speaking).
229. Part of "Letter III:: The Vicar—The Curate, etc.", in "The Borough."
231. From "Anima Poetae."
232. From Leslie's "Life of Constable": part of a letter to John Fisher, October 23rd, 1821.
233. Part of Scene the Twelfth: "Antony and Octavius."
235. From "Literary Remains." The image of the fire-screen has to do with the use of cobalt salts as invisible or "sympathetic" inks. "The solution of the oxide of cobalt in muriatic acid forms one of the most beautiful of the sympathetic inks. This solution when concentrated is pale rose-coloured in the cold, but becomes blue-green when heated; letters or figures traced by it upon paper are invisible in the cold, but become blue-green when held before the fire." Sir Humphry Davy, "Elements of Chemical Philosophy, 1812."
    Nitrate of cobalt turns blue with oxalic acid, iodine or potassium ferrocyanide.
236. From "The Pentameron"; Petrarch speaking.
237. CHARLES ABRAHAM ELTON. Sir Charles Abraham Elton (1778-1853) of Clevedon. He knew Coleridge, and Southey, and John Clare. He wrote an honest, pleasant poem to Clare, whom he called "my man of men," mentioning

> "The thoughtful eyes that steady shine,
> The temples of Shakespearian line,
>   the quiet smile;
> The sense and shrewdness which are thine,
>   withouten guile."

Elton shows how the Wordsworth-Coleridge style could be picked Up and used for the simple needs of rather a simple, best is:

> "Oh thou fair river! Flowing calm and full
> Midst thy green islets, while the poised swan broods
> O'er his clear shadow in thy crystal depth. . . ."

Or—using the image of the moon in the blue sky (which can

be found in Burns, Wordsworth, Coleridge, Humphry Davy's notebooks, etc. See Nos. 114, 128, 205)—

> ". . . Shine, my bed's mute visitant,
> Thou moon! whose orb, like an ensanguin'd shield,
> Leans on heaven's reddening verge, till slow it climbs,
> And lessens as it climbs, and soaring high,
> On the blue calm of ether, sheds abroad
> A snowy splendour. . . ."

No. 237 comes from "The Brothers," in "The Brothers: A Monody, and Other Poems," 1820.

238. From Leslie's "Life of Constable." A note found among Constable's papers.
239. From "A Descriptive Catalogue of Pictures painted by James Ward, Esq., R.A., now exhibiting at No. 6 Newman Street," 1822.
240. From "Reminiscences," 1822. See also No. 356.
241. From Leslie's "Life of Constable." Part of a letter to Leslie, January 1832.
242. From "Aids to Reflection." De Quincey talks of an edition of Boehme elaborately annotated all through the margins by Coleridge. These unpublished annotations still exist and were transcribed by E. H. Coleridge.
244. From "Letters of John Constable, R.A., to C. R. Leslie, R.A.," edited by Peter Leslie (Constable, 1931). From a letter of 1835.
246. From "Anima Poetae."
247. Part of the preface to "Alastor."
248. "Childe Harold's Pilgrimage," Canto iv, 121 and 122.
249. Note to "The Lord of the Isles."
250. Last two stanzas of "When the Lamp is Shattered."
253. The Spanish original is in the collection "Cancionero de Romances," published in Antwerp in 1555.
254. Part of a letter of April 1817.
255. Part of a letter to Bailey, November 1817.
256. From Haydon's "Autobiography."
257. i. From "Life of George Petrie," by William Stokes (1868). Francis Danby is a painter who has "disappeared." His pictures were admired by Lawrence, Beckford, Linnell, Samuel Palmer, Smetham, Ford Madox Brown, and many others. A few, like the famous "Opening of the Sixth Seal," were apocalyptic. But he is better expressed by the title of a picture of 1823: "The Enchanted Island." He had a row —sex was involved—with the Royal Academy and went into exile in Switzerland for many years. His reputation did not recover, some of his pictures have darkened, most are inaccessible, or have vanished. I like this by Thomas Seddon, the Preraphaelite, of a picture by Danby in the Academy of 1853:

"Danby has a beautiful coast scene—a rock-bound shore, with the gaunt ribs of an ancient wreck lying before the setting sun, skeleton-fashion, among the breakers, and little gulls deliriously tripping on the wet sands in the sun's gleam."

The setting that needs renewing in this extract from an undated letter of Danby's, is the mind's setting of fresh natural scenery.

ii. "History of the Peace," Vol. 4, p. 417 (1877 edition).

258. "Diary of John William Polidori," ed. W. M. Rossetti, 1911. Polidori prefaced his tale "The Vampyre" with this, more vaguely told. There is a woman whose breasts can see, in this way, in a drawing or painting, I think, by Hieronymus Bosch. Sir Walter Raleigh reported a race of people in South America with eyes in their breasts. D. G. Rossetti's fatal woman in the prose and verse of "The Orchard-Pit" (No. 372) has life's eyes—

". . . gleaming from her forehead fair,
And from her breasts the ravishing eyes of Death."

Rossetti's mother was Polidori's sister, so Polidori's memory must have concerned him. But they never met. Polidori committed suicide with prussic acid seven years before Rossetti was born.

260. T. G. WAINEWRIGHT (1794-1852), the poisoner, artist, and connoisseur, who was transported to Van Diemen's Land. He knew John Linnell, and Blake, Lamb, Clare, etc., and, like Linnell and Palmer, admired the engraver Bonasoni. Fuseli, in his old age, was looked to by the younger men for his difference, energy, and unexpectedness.

This comes from an article in the "London Magazine," for April 1820, reprinted in "Essays and Criticisms of Thomas Griffiths Wainewright," edited by W. Carew Hazlitt.

261. From Haydon's "Autobiography and Memoirs."
262. Part of letter, November 1317.
263. "Childe Harold's Pilgrimage," 111, 113 and 114.
264. Part of a letter, 1819.
265. From "Melmoth the Wanderer," 1819.
266. Part of a letter, October 1818. "What page the sorcerer John Keats tore from the shut book" (Wyndham Lewis).
267. "Endymion," 11, 11.640-649.
269. From "Narrative of the Operations and Recent Discoveries within the Pyramids, Temples, Tombs, and Excavations, in Egypt and Nubia," 1820.
270. Song quoted by Keats in a letter to J. H. Reynolds, January 1818.
271. From W. C. Dendy's "Philosophy of Mystery," 1841. Dendy was a psychologist and a doctor; he analysed the Romantic rainbow, or tried to, and found himself digging as hard as

anyone after its gold. He became a British Museum character (B. M. characters in our day are shoddy in mind as well as in cliffs and collars: they read "Sunday at Home" for 1859); and driven to the islands of the mind, he wrote two books, "The Beautiful Islets of Britaine" and "Islets of the Channel," which are very pretty, are illustrated by himself, and are good reading.

275. Written by a woman? Perhaps I ought to know who the author is. I took the poem from a Regency picture, framed with seaweed.

Crabbe's seaweed descriptions in "The Borough" (No. 209) are on the path that winds into the taste for the accessible miniature paradise of the rock-pool full of anemones and coral; look at the books by G. H. Lewes—-the husband of George Eliot—Charles Kingsley and Philip Gosse. Also the books on seaweeds, actually illustrated by the seaweeds themselves, dried and mounted, and bound in silk.

276. Find two more lovely and romantic lines than:

"The gookoo auver white-wiav'd seas
Da come to zing in thy green trees."

"Rig" is to climb or play in wantonness; "parrick" is small enclosed field; "gil'cup" a gilt cup, *i.e.* buttercup The sense of "mid" is may or might. "Alassen" is lest.

278. From "The Confessions of an English Opium Eater," 1821 See Note 200.
280. From "The English Mail Coach," 1849.
282. From "Autobiographic Sketches," 1849. Sarsar is the icy wind of death, first used by Beckford in "Vathek," according to the O. E. D.
283. Part of a letter, 1819.
286. Part of "The Two Spirits: An Allegory."
287. From "Autobiographic Sketches."
288. i. Part of a letter, February 27, 1818. ii. Part of a letter, October 27 of the same year.
290. Part of "Lines written in the Highlands after a Visit to Burns's Country."
292. Part of a letter, 1819.
293. Part of a letter, May 1817.
294. The close of "Prometheus Unbound."
295. Out of a letter to Fanny Brawne, July 25, 1819.
297. From the journal, in "Autobiography and Memoirs."
298. Part of "The Sensitive Plant."
299. From the introduction to the new edition of "Frankenstein, or the Modern Prometheus," published in 1839.
300. Out of the verse letter written in 1825 to B. W. Procter.
301. From "The Second Brother."
303. Part of "A Preface."

304. From "Wanderings in South America, in the Years 1812, 1816, 1820, and 1824."
305. Part of the preface to "The Dream of Eugene Aram."
307. First stanza of the poem.
308. See Note 304.
309. From Samuel Calvert's "Memoir of Edward Galvert." Calvert hid from the nineteenth century, remembered Blake and the Fowey Valley of his youth, and set up an altar to Pan in his garden.
310. From an MS. letter written by Palmer's son, the late A. H. Palmer. The date of the poem is 1825, or thereabouts.
311. Part of a letter to John Linnell, from Shoreham, December 21, 1828, in the "Life and Letters of Samuel Palmer," by A.H. Palmer.
313. Quoted by Hartley Coleridge as the text of one of his poems.
314. Part of an imprinted letter from Samuel Palmer to George Richmond, written from Shoreham when Palmer was twenty-two, on November 14, 1827.
316. The first three lines left out.
317. Part of "Letter to Mr. . . ." from West Point, 1831.
318. Out of "Pastoral Poesy."
319. Part only of a folk-song worked over by Clare.
320. Part of a letter to George Richmond from Shoreham, October 16, 1834.
322. Part of "Harvest Home."
325. Part of "The Lover's Invitation."
326. The second half of "A Dream Within a Dream."
327. Out of an MS. letter to George Richmond, written from Naples in 1838.
328. From "Samuel Palmer: A Memoir," by A. H. Palmer, 1882.
329. All from "On the Poetry of the Chinese," by John Francis Davis, F.R.S., President for the East India Company in China. Printed at Macao, 1834.
330. "Gil'cup" is g iltcup, i.e. buttercup; "drong-way," a hedged track. The last stanza omitted.
331. One stanza left out.
332. See Note 328.
334 and 335. Both part of "Nepenthe."
338. Part of "The Flitting."
341. Part of a fragment.
345. See Note 271. Catherine Crowe has one of these in the "Night Side of Nature." "On the 16th of August, 1769, Frederick II of Prussia is said to have dreamt that a star fell from heaven, and occasioned such an extraordinary glare that he could with great difficulty find his way through it. He mentioned the dream to his attendants, and it was afterwards observed that it was on that day Napoleon was born."

344. In "Blackwood's Magazine," September 1841, and also in "Literary Works of James Smetham," 1893. Smetham was a painter and etcher of imagination and skill, much admired by Rossetti. His painting survives, mostly in the Smetham family, and must some day be better known. He went mad. Where is his painting in scarlet and green of a sleeping beauty, before a long Chirico arcade?
345. From "Two Years Before the Mast" (1840).
346. Part of "It is not Beauty I demand."
347. Very much shortened.
352. From "Memorials of Thomas Hood" in "Complete Works," Vol.x.
353. From his diary, May 1, 1844. Works (1903), Vol. iii., p. xxv.
354. "Piavier," a paving stone; "Robin hood," red campion or ragged robin. Last two stanzas left out.
355. "Modern Painters," Part 11, Section ii., Chapter 4.
356. See also No. 240. Quoted in "Neo-Classicism; Platonism and Romanticism," "by Paul Goodman." Journal of Philosophy," Vol. xxxi. (1934), p. 161.
357. "Leazers" are gleaners; "litty" means "of light and easy bodily motion."
358. Part of "Sighing for Retirement."
359. From an article in "The Athenaeum," 1839, quoted by C. C. Abbott in his "Life and Letters of George Darley."
360. From "The Poetic Principle."
362. EDWARD KENEALY —a man who did not come to terms with the century. Irish, a lawyer, one of the defenders of the murderer William Palmer, and later counsel for the Tichborne Claimant. "I saw two Judges sit to try this man, who in the eyes of the law was innocent, with the spirit of the old and worst times, when Judges came to execute and not to hear." For his conduct in the case he was disbarred and disbenched. "There is a great deal of cant," he says in his autobiography ". . . about the purity of the Bench. . . . I have seen such old rogues in Scarlet and Ermine as it would be difficult to match even in Norfolk Island."

This poem is in his early book, "Brallaghan or the Deipnosophists," 1845.
363. "Mid" means may. "Me'th" means mirth.
368. "Kern" means set to fruit.
369. See Note 362. Also from "Brallaghan."
371. From Sir Noel Paton's letter written to Catherine Crowe in 1847, and published by her in "The Night Side of Nature" (1848).
372. See Note 258.
373. From J. G. Whittier's "Supernaturalism in New England," quoted by Catherine Crowe in "The Night Side of Nature" (1848).
374. Fragment in "Collected Works," Vol. i., p. 512, 1886.

375. The church is in Liverpool. From "Redburn" (1849).
377. From "Thomas Woolner, R. A., Sculptor and Poet: His Life in Letters," by Amy Woolner, 1917.
379. "Peaks" are points; "axen" are ashes; "or" is before.
381. From "Redburn" (1849).
382. A "plough" in Vale of Blackmore dialect was a waggon; "zull" was a plough.
383. From "Ruskin-Rossetti-Preraphae'litism," edited by W. M. Rossetti, 1899. A sample of the conflict between the fag-ends of Romance and Nature. Mystery did not wish to go out twig-counting in awkward Welsh valleys. Millais, who wanted to paint a reed-warbler's nest in the minutest detail, also complained how difficult it was to get Rossetti out to draw from Nature. Millais drew too much from Nature,—the Nature of old boots and water-soaked ladies and sex,—Rossetti too little.

Moreover, the art-patron with ideas always likes the artist he approves of, patronizes, and establishes, to bend his way in twigs and subject. Woolner wrote to Tennyson's wife about Ruskin's impatient egoism: "I should like Ruskin to know what he never knew—the want of money for a year or two; then he might come to doubt his infallibility and give an artist working on the right road the benefit of any little doubt that might arise. The little despot imagines himself the Pope of Art and would wear 3 crowns as a right, only they would make him look funny in London." (1856.)

Ruskin was not the last of the rich Popes of Art.
384. From Winwood Reade's last book "The Outcast," 1875.
386. Part of Father Mapple's Sermon in the Whalemen's Chapel, in New Bedford. "Moby Dick," Chapter ix.
387. Americans, madmen, and Catholics, and Dorset clergymen resist the bullying and nagging of the nineteenth century. "He had his favourite window corner in the common sitting-room, commanding a view of Northampton and the valley of the Nene, and books and writing material were provided for him. Unless the Editor's memory is at fault, he was always addressed as ' Mr. Clare,' both by the officers of the Asylum and the towns-people; and when Her Majesty passed through Northampton, in 1844, in her progress to Burleigh, a seat was specially reserved for the poet near one of the triumphal arches. He was classified in the Asylum among the" harmless, "and for several years was allowed to walk in the fields or go into the town at his own pleasure. His favourite resting-place at Northampton was a niche under the roof of the spacious portico of All Saints' Church, and here he would sit, sometimes fo hours, musing, watching the children at play, or jotting down passing thoughts in his pocket-book. In the course of time it was found expedient not to allow him to wander beyond the

Asylum grounds. He . . . appears never to have been visited by either relatives or friends. . . . At length he had to be wheeled about the Asylum grounds in a Bath chair. As he felt his end approaching he would frequently say, 'I have lived too long,' or 'I want to go home.' Until within three days of his death he managed to reach his favourite seat in the window, but was then seized with paralysis. . . ."

Clare died on May 20, 1864. He wrote this poem and many more of his best (No. 380, No. 378 and No. 370, for example) in the Northampton Asylum. And Barnes wrote his poems in the asylum of a Dorset rectory. As for Herman Melville's room in New York—the asylum of his defeat—"It looked bleakly North. The great mahogany desk, heavily bearing up four shelves of dull gilt and leather books; the high dim bookcase, topped by strange plaster heads . . . the small black iron bed, covered with dark cretonne; the narrow iron grate; the wide table in the alcove piled with papers."

CLARE'S SKETCH FOR HIS OWN GRAVESTONE

LIST OF AUTHORS

(Item numbers, not page numbers, are given)

Akenside, 14, 18
Anon., 58, 273, 313, 339, 375

Barnes, 276, 323, 324, 330, 354, 357, 363, 368, 376, 379, 382
Beckford, 92, 106, 109, 116, 135
Beddoes, text to Part Four (before 298), 300, 301, 336, 341, 349
Belzoni, 269
Blake, 69, 85, 95, 100, 107, 123, 124, 126, 130, 131, 156, 158, 140, 142, 145, 147, 150, 152, 153 (i), 154, 159, 197, 206
Bloomfield, 167
Boehme, text to Part One
Bowles, 192
Brooke, 62
Burns, 91, 94, 95, 98, 110, 114, 117, 119, 122, 132, 134, 135, 139, 141
Byron, 248, 259, 263

Calvert, 309
Callanan, 251
Campbell, 165
Cary, 272, 274
Chatterton, 57, 63, 66, 70, 72, 75, 78, 80
Clare, 252, 275, 281, 307, 312, 515, 318, 319, 325, 328, 358, 358, 361, 364, 366, 370, 378, 380, 387
Clarke, 203
Coleridge, 153 (ii), 155, 156, 166, 170, 174, 175, 178, 179, 180, 186, 188, 201, 204, 207, 215, 220, 221, 224, 231, 235, 242, 243, 245, 246
Coleridge (Hartley), 351
Constable, 191, 210, 212, 214, 232, 238, 241, 244
Cowper, 97, 99, 101, 104, 111
Crabbe, 200, 202, 209, 213, 229
Crowe, Note to Nos. 343 and 371
Cumberland, 76

Cunningham, 35, 50
Curran, 31, 289

Dana, 345
Danby, 257 (i)
Darley, 322, 331, 333, 334, 335, 346, 348, 350, 359
Darwin, 108, 113, 121, 145, 146
Davis, 329
Davy, 157, 205, 218, 219
Dendy, 271, 343
De Quincey, 278, 280, 282, 287
Doddridge, 29
Dyer, 73

Elton, 237

Foster, R., text to Part Three (before 247)
Frere, 181
Fuseli, 65, 68, 82, 89, 105, 108, 260

Gainsborough, 88
Gessner, 23, 52, 87, 105
Goldsmith, 21
Gray, 6, 22, 53, 64
Grose, 118, 144

Hart, 210, 240
Haydon, 256, 261, 297
Haygarth, 102
Hervey, 3, 9, 11
Hood, 284, 302, 305, 306, 316, 337, 347, 352
Hunt, 291

Jones, 67

Keats, 254, 255, 262, 264, 266, 267, 270, 271, 285, 288, 290, 292, 295, 295, 297
Kenealy, 362, 369

Lamb, 187
Landor, text to Part Two (before

148), 169, 172, 189, 195, 208, 216, 225, 228, 230, 233, 234, 236
Landseer, 240, 356
Langhorne, 25, 46, 47
Lavater, 61, 90
Law, 15, 17
Lewis, 162
Leyden, 165
Lockhart, 253

Macpherson, 24, 26, 32, 33
Martineau, 257 (ii)
Maturin, 265
Melville, 375, 381, 385, 386
Mickle, 28, 30, 36, 42, 45
Monboddo, 83, 84
Moore, 192

New Monthly Magazine, 313
Nicholson, 257 (ii)

Palmer, 310, 311, 314, 320, 321, 327, 328, 332
Paton, 371
Polidori, 258
Pontoppidan, 16
Poe, 317, 321, 326, 340, 342, 360
Praed, 303
Price, 127, 129

Radcliffe, 120, 158, 182
Reade, 384
Richter, 211
Rossetti, 365, 367, 372, 374

Ruskin, 355, 355, 356, 383
Rutty, 77

Saltero, 20
Salvator Rosa, 115
Schiller, 149, 151
Scott, 164, 249
Shelley, 247, 250, 268, 277, 279, 285, 286, 294, 296, 298
Shelley, Mary, 299
Shenstone, 1, 12
Smart, 27, 31, 34, 39, 40, 45, 48, 49, 51, 54, 56, 60, 74
Smetham, 344
Smollett, 4
Southey, 161, 173, 177
Stukeley, 2, 5, 7, 10, 13

Volney, 125, 137

Wainewright, 260
Walpole, 38, 41, 44
Ward, 239
Waterton, 304, 308
Whately, 55, 71, 81
White, 59, 79, 86, 96, 112
Whittier, 373
Windham, 8
Woolner, 377
Wordsworth, 58 (?), 128, 148, 168, 171, 176, 184, 194, 196, 198, 199, 217, 222, 225, 226, 227
Wordsworth, Dorothy, 160, 183, 185, 190, 193

Young, 19